Hintergrund 56

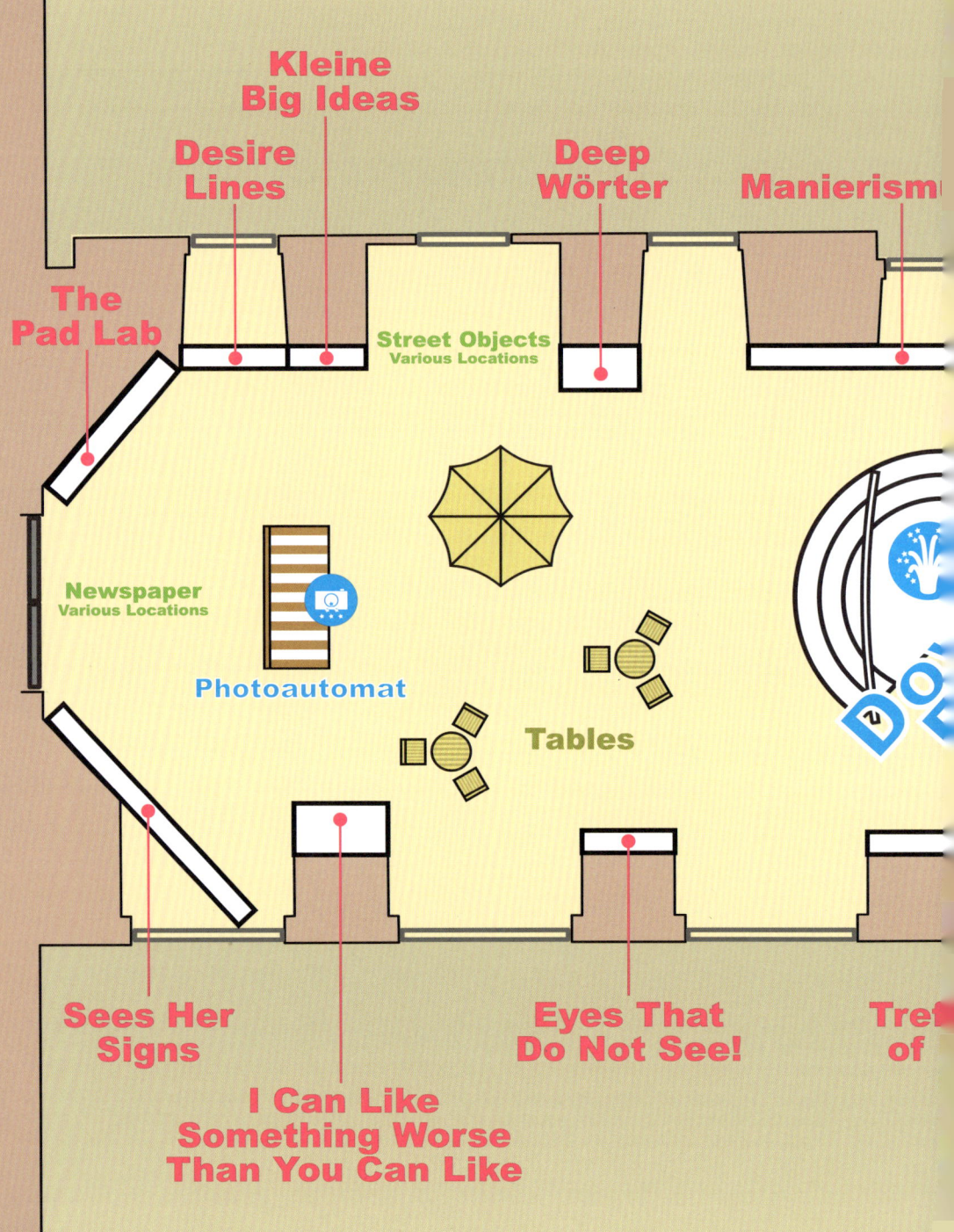

Scott Brown
NOVEMBER 22, 2018 TO MARCH 18, 2019

DSB

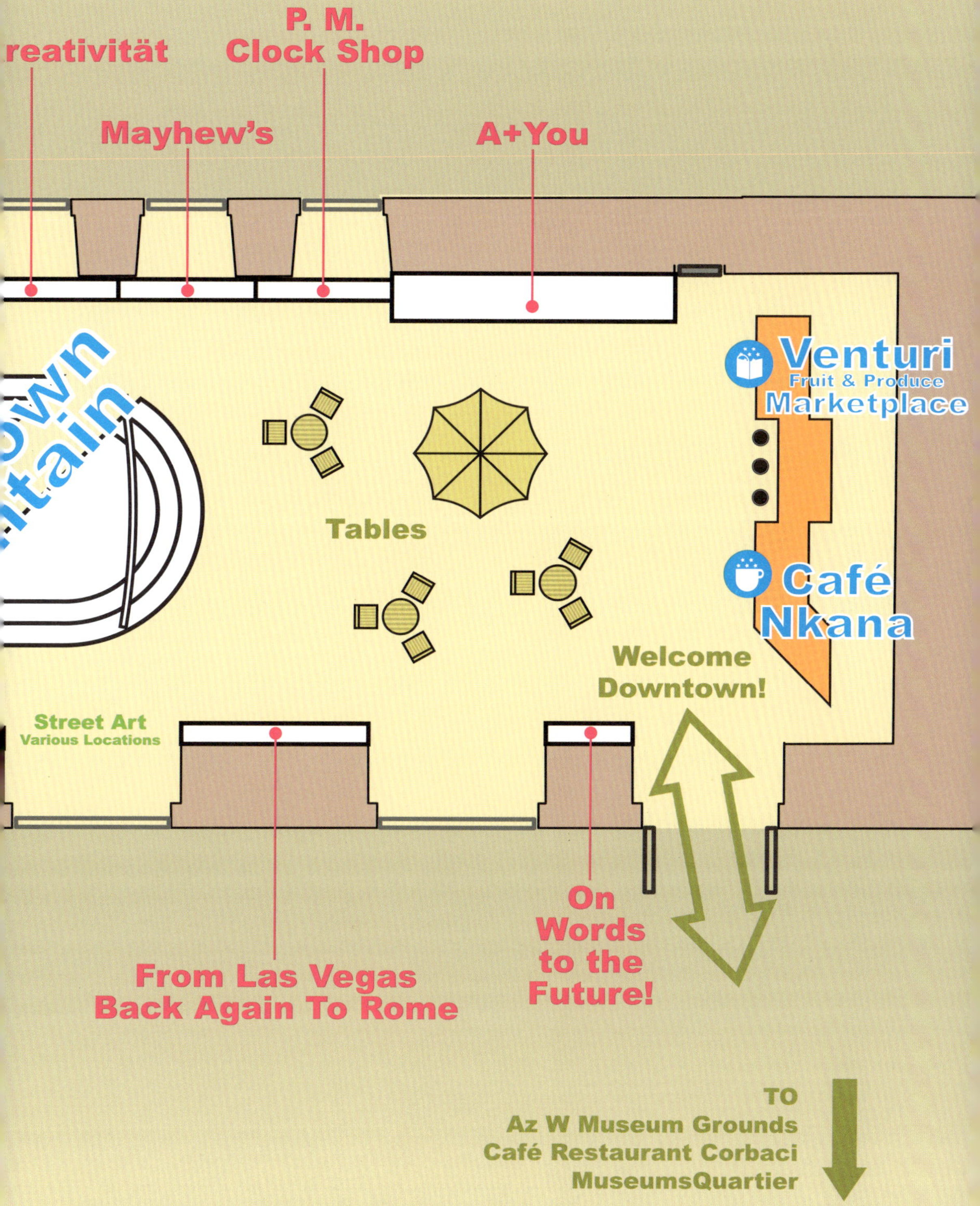

iii

– reativität
– Mayhew's
– P. M. Clock Shop
– A+You
– Venturi Fruit & Produce Marketplace
– Café Nkana
– own ntain
– Tables
– Welcome Downtown!
– Street Art Various Locations
– From Las Vegas Back Again To Rome
– On Words to the Future!

TO
Az W Museum Grounds
Café Restaurant Corbaci
MuseumsQuartier

iv

1. Las Vegas, 1965

Your Guide to DOWNTOWN DENISE SCOTT BROWN

By
Jeremy Eric Tenenbaum

with
Denise Scott Brown

Edited by
Angelika Fitz and Katharina Ritter
Architekturzentrum Wien

PARK BOOK

Imprint

Author and Designer: Jeremy Eric Tenenbaum
Contributing Author: Denise Scott Brown
Contributing Authors and Editors: Angelika Fitz and Katharina Ritter, Architekturzentrum Wien
Translator and Proofreader: Brian Dorsey
Cover Photography: Denise Scott Brown and Robert Venturi
Cover Design: Jeremy Eric Tenenbaum
Printer: Medienfabrik Graz

This book was published on the occasion of the exhibition
Downtown Denise Scott Brown
Architekturzentrum Wien   22 November 2018 to 18 March 2019

Designers: Jeremy Eric Tenenbaum with Denise Scott Brown, Angelika Fitz, and Katharina Ritter
Curators: Angelika Fitz and Katharina Ritter, Architekturzentrum Wien

Grateful thanks to Denise Scott Brown for guidance, inspiration, and trust
Grateful acknowledgements to the:
  Chamber of Labour Vienna
  Federal Ministry Republic of Austria, Transport, Innovation and Technology
  Federal Ministry Republic of Austria, Digital and Economic Affairs
  United States of America Embassy

Park Books is being supported by the Federal Office of Culture
with a general subsidy for the years 2016–2020

ISBN 978-3-03860-127-2

© 2018 Architekturzentrum Wien and Park Books, Zurich

Architekturzentrum Wien, Museumsplatz 1, 1070 Wien
t +43 1 522 31 15   f +43 1 522 31 17   office@azw.at   www.azw.at

Park Books, Niederdorfstrasse 54, CH-8001 Zürich
www.scheidegger-spiess.ch

2. Mohave Desert, 1960s

| MAP | ii |

YOUR QUICK GUIDE — 1

Getting Around	3
Top Sights	4
Itineraries & Interests	7
For the Kids	9

WELCOME DOWNTOWN — 10

The Meet Point: Denise Scott Brown	13
Downtown History	21
Behind the Scenes	31
Angelika Fitz: "Entangled Places"	32
Katharina Ritter: "The Universe of Denise Scott Brown"	36
Jeremy Eric Tenenbaum: "Storytelling"	38

UP AND DOWN DOWNTOWN — 44

Downtown Fountain and the Photoautomat	47
Shopping	49
Food and Drink: Café Nkana	117
The Marketplace: Venturi Fruit and Produce	123
Street Lounge	128
Street Art	130
Street Life	133

DSB A TO Z — 140

Learning from Who's Who	143
Learning from Where's Where	147
Learning from the Lingo	150

BEYOND DOWNTOWN — 156

| About the Az W | 162 |
| Team Az W | 163 |

| CREDITS AND CITATIONS | 166 |
| AFTERWORD DEDICATION | 168 |

3. Traveling with Robert Scott Brown, mid- to late-1950s, meets planning for the University of Michigan, 2002

Your Quick Guide

2

Your Quick Guide

4. Denise in New York City

Getting Around

Downtown Denise Scott Brown is the world's most comprehensive solo exhibition dedicated to American architect **Denise Scott Brown**. The show runs November 21, 2018 to March 18, 2019 in the exhibition space of the **Architekturzentrum Wien** in the MuseumsQuartier, Vienna.

Denise Scott Brown is an architectural monument. Since the 1960s, Scott Brown – together with partner and husband **Robert Venturi** – has inspired generations of designers and thinkers worldwide. She has rewritten the rules of architectural design, urbanism and urban design, social consciousness, pedagogy and studio process, photography, and innumerable other disciplines within architectural, academic, artistic, and social fields. Despite this tremendous impact, Denise remains misunderstood and marginalized. *Downtown Denise Scott Brown* is designed to fix that.

"Downtown" -- a *place* as well as an exhibition -- is a new temporary urban plaza nestled within the Architekturzentrum Wien's exhibition space. Under its vaulted brick sky, Downtown creates a fantasy fountain square – a piazza or platz – surrounded by shops, cafés, markets, and signs celebrating the wide universe of Scott Brown's life and work, both alone and with Bob Venturi. Look into each shop window to discover Denise's stories, projects, photos, decorative objects, books, and secrets. You'll learn about everything from her African childhood to the groundbreaking *Learning from Las Vegas* to what she's working on right now.

And at the center of this dreamland? The magnificent mountain of **Downtown Fountain**. While one side shows a projection of Denise, the other side – through Photoautomagic – shows *you!*

Downtown is intensely site-specific: the fountain, storefronts, café, market, and streetscape are carefully crafted to celebrate the space and to build on urban patterns through the space. More broadly, Downtown is inspired by **Vienna** – both its historic grandeur and its vibrantly modern commercial and social life.

Downtown Denise Scott Brown is  Vienna's new downtown!

Downtown Denise Scott Brown is designed by **Jeremy Eric Tenenbaum** (your personal tour guide and author of this book!) with contributions by Denise Scott Brown and the Architekturzentrum Wien's director **Angelika Fitz** and curator **Katharina Ritter**.

Top Sights

5. Robert Venturi Sketch, c. 1971

Downtown Fountain and the Photoautomat

PAGE 47

"I AM A MONUMENT" and you are too! You haven't been Downtown until you've seen yourself projected atop **Downtown Fountain** at the heart of the plaza. One side shows Denise's smiling face, then digital water, then other scenes from Denise's life. The other side though? Discover by using the nearby **Photoautomat**. And that's just one of the fountain's secrets. While honoring Denise, the fountain also serves as an anti-heroic civic respite. Have a seat on the low tiers. Stand on it, climb on it! Let your kids crawl and play while you relax with a cappuccino and watch Downtown go by. And be sure to look around carefully. Local lore says that there's a **hidden passage** at the heart of the fountain – with a secret message from Denise herself!

Shopping

PAGE 49

Wander away the afternoon meandering among Downtown's **shops and boutiques**, all packed with things to see. While there's something to discover in every corner of the plaza, these stores are where you'll find the most diverse variety of information on Denise. Why, it seems like every window has a display dedicated to her life, philosophy, or work!

It makes sense that Downtown's shops are celebrating this way: Denise and Bob are known for embracing the commercial and vernacular. Still, like their exploration of Las Vegas, their love of commercial life is complex and strained. Bob has asked, "Is not Main Street almost alright?" While many critics focus on "alright," maybe we should stress "almost"?

6. South Street, Philadelphia

Top Sights

Food and Drink: Café Nkana `PAGE 117`

Like all geniuses, Denise loves coffee. **Café Nkana** will serve you a *Denisuccino* made just the way she likes. Hang around to check out their photos and stories about Denise's childhood. Café Nkana is named after Denise's African hometown in Rhodesia (now Zambia). Africa is the ancestral nucleus of Denise's perspective, a foundation for her thoughts on urbanism, aesthetics, and design. The café also represents the importance of social gathering spaces in Denise's work. In academic buildings, from campus centers to labs, Denise and Bob place cafés and lounges at the intersection of circulation routes, places where people from different disciplines can meet and talk. What exciting possibilities might arise from these incidental meetings? Denise asks, "Where will the next Nobel Prize be won – at the lab bench or the coffee lounge?"

7. High Point Cafe, Philadelphia, c. 2017

8. South Street, Philadelphia

The Marketplace: Venturi Fruit and Produce `PAGE 123`

Bob Venturi's father, Robert Venturi, Sr., operated a fruit and vegetable shop on **Philadelphia's South Street** until his death in 1959. (A decade later, Denise helped defeat plans for a crosstown expressway that would have destroyed the street.) For a short time while teaching at the University of Pennsylvania and before opening his first practice, Bob took over the family business. Downtown's **Venturi Fruit and Produce Marketplace** is a loving homage to Bob's working class family background as well as Denise's advocacy planning. It's more than just a gift shop: each object at the market is emblazoned with Denise and Bob's thoughts about **humanism** – information you can't see or read anywhere else around here. Low prices encourage you to take home your own piece of Downtown!

Top Sights

I Can Like Something Worse Than You Can Like

PAGE 70

Let's play a game: I can name something uglier than you can. That drain pipe? That Bankomat? That absurdly kitschy deer antler hat rack! Just look around Downtown: there's a lot of beautiful design, sure, but what about the *ugly* stuff? The things you're not supposed to notice? The structural, functional, accidental, ridiculous? Look *behind* the storefronts! What's the "stone" fountain really made of? What are Downtown's meta-physical secrets? Quick, photograph them! And upload them to your Instagram with the hashtag **#uglyinstagram_azw**. Then head to the **I Can Like Something Worse Than You Can Like** store to see them displayed on vintage televisions.

Now ask yourself: what's "ugly" really? Why call these things ugly? Because they're "ordinary" or meant to be hidden? Who finds these things "beautiful"? Are these differences in perception based on class, education, culture? Le Corbusier lamented "eyes that do not see" – preconceptions blinding us to everyday forms, forces, and functions. To reveal and shake apart these biases, Denise and Bob played "I Can Like Something Worse Than You Can Like" as they traveled around America. They embraced the "ordinary and ugly" vernacular and formed a deeply humanistic sensibility. When you leave Downtown, keep playing the game. Keep examining your prejudices – your sense of "beautiful" and "ugly." Look at the backs of stores, the awkward extension cords, the functional systems that pervade our environments. Are they beautiful? Aren't they?

9. 1965

Itineraries & Interests

10. Venice, 1955

Downtown has a lot to see! We think there's no better way to experience Downtown than to set aside the afternoon and wander. Sit on the fountain tiers, stroll the shops. Each store has a huge amount of information to absorb. Don't worry about seeing everything or traveling in the right order: indulge in your curiosity and wander accordingly.

After a while all that exploration can wear you down, so perk back up with an espresso from Café Nkana and hang out at one of the tables scattered about. While you're there, check out the Venturi Fruit and Produce Marketplace and take home part of the show. Then it's back to sightseeing – be sure to play the Ugly Instagram Game and snap a few pics at the Photoautomat. The longer you stay, the more fun you'll have discovering all of Downtown's secrets.

But maybe you're on a tight schedule and could use some advice? You're in luck! Here are a few itineraries to help you tailor your visit according to your time and interest.

How Much Time Do You Have?

We think you should spend your whole day Downtown, but here are three tours to suit your busy schedules.

LITTLE TIME (30 Minutes or Less)
1. Shops
2. Fountain / Photoautomat
3. Venturi Marketplace

MEDIUM TIME (About an Hour?)
1. Shops
2. Café Nkana
3. Fountain / Photoautomat
4. Venturi Marketplace

WHOLE LOT OF TIME (Over an Hour!)
1. Shops
2. Ugly Instagram Game
3. Café Nkana
4. Newspaper
5. Fountain / Photoautomat
6. Venturi Marketplace

Are You a Major or Minor?

Whether you've written your dissertation on Denise or you're in the intro class, Downtown has something great for you.

FIRST YEAR STUDENTS

This itinerary is packed with information but isn't too overwhelming. It's just enough to leave you hungry for more.
1. Shops
2. Café Nkana
3. Fountain / Photoautomat
4. Venturi Marketplace

Your Quick Guide

Itineraries & Interests

Your Quick Guide

ART MAJORS

Want the artsy side of Downtown? Here are Denise's photos and decorative arts! Snap some pics at the Photoautomat! Play the Ugly Instagram Game!
1. The Pad Lab
2. From Las Vegas Back Again To Rome
3. Street Art
4. Ugly Instagram Game
5. Fountain / Photoautomat
6. Venturi Marketplace

GRADUATE STUDENTS

So you think you know Denise? Well, here's the advanced class. (But even experts deserve a treat, so you should still hit up the Photoautomat and Marketplace.)
1. Eyes That Do Not See!
2. Kleine Big Ideas
3. Newspaper
4. Ugly Instagram Game
5. Fountain / Photoautomat
6. Venturi Marketplace

Do You Like Things in Order?

Downtown stores are arranged according to a complex city-logic. While each storefront is dedicated to a specific topic, the storefronts aren't set in a thematic or chronological order. But perhaps you like to follow a story in a clear chronological line from start to end? Then this is the tour for you!
1. Café Nkana
2. From Las Vegas Back Again To Rome
3. Eyes That Do Not See!
4. Newspaper
5. Sees Her Signs
6. Ugly Instagram Game
7. Jointkreativität
8. Deep Wörter
9. Kleine Big Ideas
10. Manierismuseum
11. P. M. Clock Shop
12. Desire Lines
13. Treffpunkt of Minds
14. A+You
15. Mayhew's
16. The Pad Lab
17. On Words to the Future!
18. Venturi Marketplace

11. The circus comes to Downtown

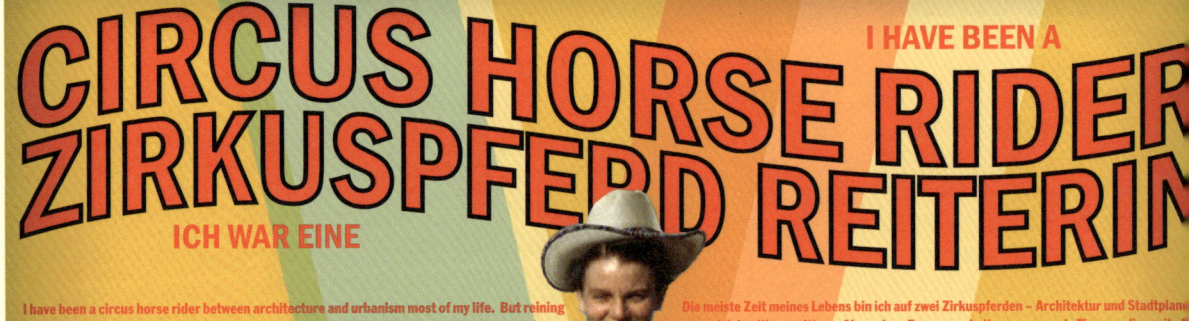

For the Kids

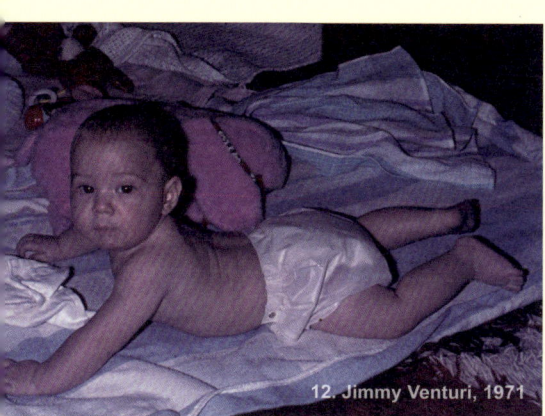

12. Jimmy Venturi, 1971

Downtown is made for children! Children of all ages will love to play on **Downtown Fountain**, climbing and hiding and making up games. You won't be able to tear them away from the **Photoautomat** as they project themselves endlessly. They'll also be hooked on the Ugly Instagram Game at the **I Can Like Something Worse Than You Can Like** storefront. Reward them for their self-control with treats from **Café Nkana** and the **Venturi Fruit and Produce Marketplace**.

But Downtown also has some adventures specifically designed for your youngest little architects and urbanists:

Find the Duck

There are **15 little yellow ducks** (like the one below -- though they may be disguised) hidden in the storefronts. Can you find them all?

Duck Duck Shed

Children sit along the fountain edge. You walk past them, gently tapping each on the head and saying "duck." Randomly, tap a child and shout "shed!" Then they have to chase you once around the fountain and try to catch you before you can sit back in their seat.

Hide and Beak

Children take turns hiding (*everyone* hides inside the fountain) while you seek them. Any child who is discovered has to quack loudly like a duck. It's silly, but the kids seem to like it.

13. Find the Duck

14. Las Vegas, late 1960s, meets South Africa

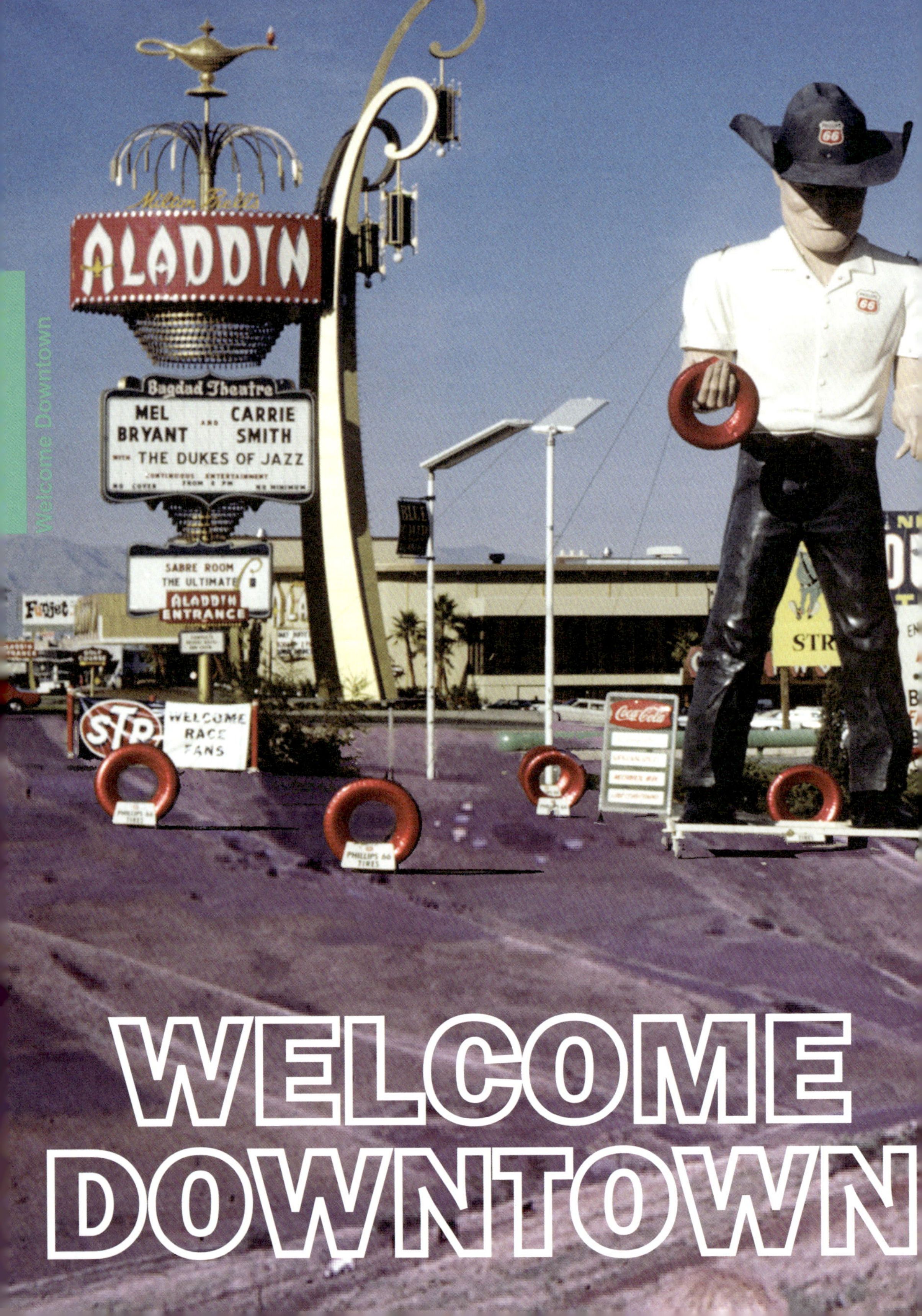

WELCOME DOWNTOWN

15. Las Vegas selfie, 1968

The Meet Point: Denise Scott Brown

"I use my life as a quarry. This is a trick I learned while teaching: students understand better and can take possession of knowledge and skills more easily if you share with them your experiences in acquiring them. So the accounts of my life are not autobiography but parable."

Having Words

Come on then, you and I. Let's go meet Denise.

At twilight, we cross the courtyard of the Architekturzentrum Wien. A sundown yellow glows across the windows. We slip between silhouetted trees and enter Downtown Denise Scott Brown.

A soft sound of water, golden lights winking above, the café hum. Ahead of us, high up on the far wall – a woman's face, grand but half-hidden. We turn to the murmuring fountain and there she is again, projected across the monument's summit, smiling wryly down on us – then flowing away into digital sparkle, transformed into her other faces, old then young, leaves from her tree. Along its curving façade, the fountain declares: "I AM A MONUMENT."

This woman is a famous architect and urbanist. Together with her partner and husband, she redirected the course of 20th century design. She's a teacher and writer whose ideas have guided lifetimes. Now some at last celebrate her and others discover her for the first time. Denise Scott Brown *is* a monument, famous if half-hidden, center of our story.

A Counterclockwise Life

Denise Scott Brown and Robert Venturi led a movement against sterile, doctrinaire late Modernism. Working at the crossroads of architecture and urbanism, Denise and Bob freed architects to embrace history, context, communication, social concern, symbolism, Pop Art, multicultural and pluralistic perspectives, and the "messy vitality" of the vernacular. "High art" and "low art" were brought eye-to-eye and purity of expression was challenged by lively impurity.

16. With Jimmy, 1972

Denise's counterclockwise life arcs from South Africa to England, Philadelphia to California, back to Philadelphia. Denise Lakofski was born October 3, 1931 in the mining town **Nkana**, Rhodesia (now Zambia). At the **University of the Witwatersrand** in **Johannesburg**, she studied liberal arts and architecture. She met **Robert Scott Brown** and they were married in London, where she attended the **Architectural Association**. They traveled through Europe, photographing extensively, then emigrated to America to study urban planning and architecture at the **University of Pennsylvania**. Robert was killed in a car accident; Denise rebuilt her soul through study and work. In 1960 while teaching at Penn, Denise met a fellow architecture teacher who finally *got her*. Denise and **Robert Venturi** joined together in teaching, then marriage, then design.

While teaching in California, Denise discovered Las Vegas, crass paragon, and "corrupted" Bob by bringing him there. Like Nabokov, Denise saw America with an outsider's incisive, aghast love. A serious architect would no sooner study Las Vegas than a doctor learn anatomy from a bathroom wall. But Denise and Bob allowed themselves to be taught by Las Vegas. When you're clever, everything teaches. ***Learning from Las Vegas*** by Denise, Bob, and **Steven Izenour** made the Las Vegas Strip a sandbox for the exploration of symbolism, scale, the auto city, social impacts – the 20th century. Their study and book transformed architectural pedagogy and studio education while blowing apart conventions. Denise went on to publish, *inter alia*, *Urban Concepts*, *Architecture as Signs and Systems for a Mannerist Time* (with Bob), and *Having Words* – forty years of essays including the clarion "Room at the Top?: Sexism and the Star System in Architecture."

Buoyed by Bob's *Complexity and Contradiction in Architecture* and the quietly outrageous house he made for his mother, the young firm got good at making both buildings and waves. Happy controversy followed: the historically riotous Guild House, Pop fire stations, decorated sheds, houses both expressionistic and deeply contextual, Mannerist collisions of old and new out of which arose alien new beauties. The conservative ethos of college campuses wouldn't restrain their invention: their Princeton labs played with pattern and ornament as if newly invented; Harvard's campus center was historically delicate with one hand while colorfully, digitally outrageous with the other. Denise and Bob were famous. They were ready for the *big projects*.

> **Denise had traveled to Las Vegas four times before she invited Bob Venturi to join her on a trip there in November 1966.**

17. At home in Philadelphia

Let's pause: which of these projects is "Denise's"? Why, nearly *all* the firm's work is "hers"! It's a strange question to ask when you consider that the ideas permeating each project were developed via collaboration, Denise plus Bob (plus a vast array of architects and clients). The ambiguity of joint creativity becomes even more confusing and wonderful when the collaborators are married theoreticians. How would you parse Denise and Bob's collaboration? And why would you want to? So many of her ideas are his and his hers. (But to the sexist eye, her ideas are credited as all his.)

Still, some projects are particularly Denise's – in fact, those *big projects* we just mentioned: the **Sainsbury Wing** of London's National Gallery – a **provincial capitol** building in Toulouse, France – the **Mielparque Nikko Kirifuri hotel and spa** in Japan – campus planning and a life sciences complex at the **University of Michigan** – **campus plans** for prestigious colleges and universities, including **Tsinghua University** in Beijing.

Acclaim for the firm followed: they garnered more than 140 major design awards, including nine National Honor Awards from the American Institute of Architects (AIA) and the AIA's highest corporate honor, the Architectural Firm Award.

Denise's own renown, however, remained in constant contention – as a controversial architect, as a female practitioner, as the wife of an architectural *guru*. At times, Denise has been well recognized: among other awards, she has received the United States National Medal of Arts, the Association of Collegiate Schools of Architecture's AIA Topaz Medallion, and the Jane Drew Prize for Women in Architecture. But she has also been well slighted: she has suffered decades of marginalization and eclipse, culminating symbolically in being denied equal share in the **Pritzker Prize** when it was handed to Bob alone. (The award involved considerable money, which their young firm needed. She and Bob decided he should accept the prize, but she would protest by skipping the ceremony.) But old wrongs have begun to be righted: in 2016, Denise and Bob became the first joint winners of the American Institute of Architects's **Gold Medal** – and Denise became the first living woman to receive that prize.

> The ambiguity of joint creativity becomes even more confusing and wonderful when the collaborators are married theoreticians.

> And what was their heroic champion in this war?:
>
> The *ordinary*.

So Why Are Denise and Bob – and *Particularly* Denise – So Loved and So Hated?

Odi et amo says poet Catullus: I hate and I love. For sixty years that has been the architectural world's sonnet on Denise and Bob. Passions soar on both sides; the same person may embrace *and* dissent. Why such love and such hate?

Denise and Bob gently bombed apart the constrictions of late Modernism. Ostracized concepts were welcomed: history, the vernacular, impurity. (Remember that these ideas weren't merely unstylish but incorrect: the late Modern architect who dabbled in historic appropriations was a poor architect.) Amidst this *glasnost*, Bob and Denise didn't propose a new orthodoxy and didn't lead the usual kind of artistic revolution. These omissions were unforgivable. A political party is happily supplanted by its opposite party, but the person who shows how to live well without political parties is loathed by both sides for being an anarchist. To supporters, though, that person is a liberator.

Denise and Bob proposed an evolutionary update inspired by neither "vision" nor "manifesto" – or a self-conscious "gentle" manifesto. In fact, their evolutionary push was a return to early Modernism, a restoration of its youthful vitality now reborn seachanged, richer, stranger, a mature Modernism made sensitive to the pressures and needs (and neuroses) of the mid-century. The comforts of a former orthodoxy, any orthodoxy, might palliate but never cure our unease.

And what was their heroic champion in this war?: *the ordinary*, a secret weapon in plain sight hidden to "eyes that do not see." The world that *is* is valid. Main Street might almost be alright. These are dangerous ideas! "How vulgar!" Meaning: how common. But why this disdain for the common? If the ordinary is outrageous, who do architects serve? In fact, embracing the existing world is always more provocative than disdaining it one way or another. Denise and Bob didn't *create* Las Vegas or suburbia – they didn't even *advocate* for these places – but they recognized their existence and legitimacy. At the same time, they loudly failed to condemn the "high" architecture of Michelangelo, Louis Kahn, Frank Lloyd Wright, Le Corbusier. Architecture wasn't an "either / or" proposition – but a "both / and" ethic.

Oh, that's not how their fiercest critics framed the *odi et amo* issue, naturally. They called Denise and Bob's work ugly or, at best, insincere. The historical references weren't pure enough and the contemporary elements not slick enough. Playfulness, gentility alongside monumentality, irony: these are tricks of the amateur, not serious professionals! Their work lacked the proper obeisance to "ghastly good taste," but it also resisted libertine camp and kitsch. Critics called their architecture an arch joke; supporters counter that everyone is invited to enjoy the joke – and it's a serious, sometimes even painful joke, a trench laughter at such difficult choices. It *used* irony but was not, overall, ironic; it respected those that lived and worked there, as well as those not yet born who would one day inherit it, and the community beyond.

Odi or not, the work was too important to ignore, too useful and too liberating. In fact, its widespread influence and popularity would contribute to its criticism. Ideas that Denise and Bob developed are now thoroughly integrated into the world. ("Context? *Everyone* does context!") Already these ideas are viewed in the rear-view mirror. ("Iconography was twenty years ago!") And some ideas they first explored were developed and popularized by others. (By *everyone*.) Most of all, their evolutionary push was a threat. Some saw their cloistered, late Modern worlds eroding; cultures that had been marginalized were rising and the generation in power was frightened angry. How like the '60s; how like today.

And who bore and continues to bear the brunt of this anger? Denise Scott Brown. Bob can be dismissed as an unruly genius, but who does this *woman* think she is?

Denise has the temerity to be a female, and a female architect, and a female architect married to an architectural *guru*. Many aren't willing to believe she's a famous architect. ("She's not famous if I haven't heard of her!") Many aren't willing to believe she's an architect at all. ("Taking credit for Venturi's work!") So the popular perception of Denise's role – her architecture, her theory, her pervasive influence – has been neglected at best, suppressed at worst. But *Downtown Denise Scott Brown* doesn't retaliate: it celebrates. Look around the plaza and discover buildings, books, decades, continents – and real people! Real lives that have been changed through these ideas. Come on, let's go explore it! Let's go – you and I and Denise.

> **And who bore and continues to bear the brunt of this anger?**
>
> **Denise Scott Brown.**
>
> **Bob can be dismissed as an unruly genius, but who does this *woman* think she is?**

Welcome Downtown

c. 1933
18. Circa two years old

Downtown History

Downtown Denise Scott Brown spans eighty-seven years and three continents: from Africa to Europe to North America. Within the United States, our story leaps from East Coast to West Coast and back again.

Here's a brief history of the projects, publications, battles, and adventures you'll meet along the way.

South Africa

October 3, 1931	Denise Lakofski is born in Nkana, a mining town in Rhodesia (now Zambia). She has two sisters, a brother, and a lively extended family.
1933	Contracts what may or may not be malaria. For her health, family moves to Johannesburg, South Africa.
1933	"I became a Modernist at two years old." Her mother hires architects Hanson Tomkin & Finkelstein to design an International Style family house.
1935	Family briefly travels to London because Denise's sister might have polio.
1936 - 1937	"I went to a Victorian Kindergarten run by Mrs. Fraser, American I think, who taught by the Froebel method that Frank Lloyd Wright's mother used for him."
1938 - 1947	Attends Kingsmead College, a private girls elementary and high school in Johannesburg. After kindergarten, Denise skipped ahead to study with students 1-2 years older.
1948 - 1952	Attends University of the Witwatersrand in Johannesburg. Meets Robert Scott Brown.

England and Europe

1952	After graduation, travels to London where she works for Ernö Goldfinger ("a Dickensian experience").
1952 - c. 1953	Works in London for Frederick Gibberd.
1953	Passes entrance exam for the Architectural Association (AA) and decides to attend.
1955	Completes AA degree.
July 21, 1955	Marries Robert Scott Brown in London.
1955 - 1958	Travels with Robert Scott Brown through Europe.
September 1956	Attends CIAM Summer School in Venice with Robert Scott Brown.
1956	Denise and Robert Scott Brown work for Giuseppe Vaccaro in Rome.

USA: East Coast

1958	On advice from Peter Smithson, Denise and Robert go to the University of Pennsylvania in Philadelphia to learn from Lou Kahn – but find he doesn't teach in the planning school.
1959	Robert Scott Brown dies in an automobile accident in Philadelphia.
1960	Completes master's degree in city planning at the University of Pennsylvania.
1960	Begins teaching as an instructor in Penn's School of Fine Arts.
1960	Meets Robert Venturi at a Penn faculty meeting.
1961 - 1964	Serves as assistant professor and soon begins teaching collaboration with Bob.
1961	Bob begins revising design for Vanna Venturi House in the Chestnut Hill neighborhood of Philadelphia
1964	Venturi and Rauch, Architects and Planners is founded in Philadelphia.
1965	Completes master's degree in architecture at Penn.

...niversity of the Witwatersrand. 11th April 1950

1955
Marrying Robert Scott Brown, London

1955
21. CIAM in Venice

1955
22. Working in Rome

1950s
23. Denise and Robert Scott Brown, South Africa

Welcome Downtown

USA: West Coast

1965	Leaves Penn to teach at the University of California Berkeley as a visiting professor in the School of Environmental Design.
1965	"The Meaningful City" published in the Journal of the American Institute of Architects.
1965	Begins teaching as associate professor in the University of California Los Angeles's School of Architecture and Urban Planning. Named co-chair of urban design program.
1965 - 1967	Travels and photographs throughout Southwest USA, including Las Vegas.
November 1966	Invites Bob to visit Las Vegas with her.
July 23, 1967	Marries Bob in Santa Monica, California.

USA: East Coast Again

1967	Returns to Philadelphia to join Venturi and Rauch.
1967 - 1971	Teaches as visiting professor in urban design at Yale University.
1968	Completes "Learning from Las Vegas" studio with Bob, Steven Izenour, and students from the Yale School of Architecture and Planning.
1969	Becomes principal with Venturi and Rauch.
1970	Completes planning for Philadelphia's South Street Crosstown Community.
1970	Completes "Learning from Levittown" studio with Yale School of Architecture and Planning.
May 15, 1971	Denise and Bob's child, James Venturi, is born.
1972	*Learning from Las Vegas* published, with Bob and Steven Izenour.
1976	Completes Allen Memorial Art Museum at Oberlin College.
1976	Completes Franklin Court for the National Park Service in Philadelphia.
1976	*Signs of Life* exhibition opens at the Smithsonian Institution, Washington, DC, in time for the American Bicentennial.

1966
24. Santa Monica

1967
25. Santa Monica

1977	*Learning from Las Vegas* Second Edition designed and published, with Bob and Steve.
January 31, 1980	Firm moves from downtown Philadelphia to Manayunk, a post-industrial mill neighborhood on the edge of the city.
1978	Completes the Washington Avenue Revitalization Plan for Miami Beach.
1979	Completes Historic District Planning Study for Jim Thorpe, Pennsylvania.
1980	Firm renamed Venturi, Rauch and Scott Brown.
1981	Completes Hennepin Avenue Transit / Entertainment Study in Minneapolis, Minnesota.
1984	*A View from the Campidoglio: Selected Essays, 1953-1984* published, with Bob.
1985	AIA Firm Award, to Venturi, Rauch and Scott Brown.
1987	Completes Center City Development Plan in Memphis, Tennessee.
1988	Completes campus planning at the University of Pennsylvania.
1989	Firm renamed Venturi, Scott Brown and Associates.
1990	*Urban Concepts* published.
1991	Completes Seattle Art Museum.
1991	Completes Sainsbury Wing of London's National Gallery.
1991	*Architecture and Decorative Arts, Two Naifs in Japan* published, with Bob.
1991	Pritzker Architecture Prize for joint work awarded to Bob alone. They need the award money, but Denise protests by staying home from the ceremony.
1992	Awarded National Medal of Arts, United States Presidential Award, with Bob.
1995	Completes Denver Civic Center Plan.
1996	Awarded Topaz Medallion by the American Institute of Architects.

1972
26. Cover photo for *Learning from Las Vegas*

1971
27. With baby Jimmy

1985
28. John Rauch, Denise, Bob, Manayunk office

1991
29. Seattle Art Museum

1991
30. National Gallery

1997	Completes Mielparque Nikko Kirifuri Resort near Nikko National Forest, Japan.
1999	Completes Provincial Capitol Building in Toulouse, France.
2000	Completes Perelman Quadrangle at the University of Pennsylvania.
2003	Visiting lecturer with Bob at Harvard University. Lectures form the basis for *Architecture as Signs and Systems for a Mannerist Time*.
2004	Completes campus planning at Tsinghua University in Beijing, China.
2004	*Architecture as Signs and Systems for a Mannerist Time* published, with Bob.
2005	Completes Palmer Drive Life Sciences complex at the University of Michigan.
2007	Awarded Vilcek Prize in Architecture by The Vilcek Foundation.
2009	*Having Words* published.
2012	Retirement with Bob from firm.
2013	Women In Design organize Change.org petition for Pritzker to recognize Denise. Over 20,000 people sign, but Pritzker fails to correct the record.
2016	Venice Biennale's *Wayward Eye* photography exhibition.
2016	Awarded the American Institute of Architects's Gold Medal with Bob – first awarded jointly and first awarded to a living woman.
2017	Awarded Jane Drew Prize.
2018	Awarded Soane Medal by Sir John Soane's Museum in London.

1997
31. Nikko Kirifuri Hotel and Spa, Nikko, Japan

1997
32. Bob and Denise in Japan

1999
33. Provincial Capitol, Toulouse, France

2016
34. Bob and Denise receive the first joint AIA Gold Medal

35. Provincial Capitol, Toulouse, France, 1999

Behind the Scenes

You may have noticed by now this isn't a typical exhibition catalog? Well, *Downtown Denise Scott Brown* isn't a typical exhibition.

Downtown is a *real place* – a temporary one, admittedly, but in the broader view which places are permanent? Like all places, Downtown contains information both explicit and incidental. Some systems are sculpted to particular purposes, some are loose and ill-defined to allow for change and chance. The plaza encompasses smaller spaces inside and connects to vast systems outside. Downtown is urbanistic in space and semantical in time.

These are qualities that all exhibitions, as well as places, share. Downtown's atypical nature reflects the degree to which its design has been pushed from a typical exhibition's representation toward an urban location's functionality. In other words, Downtown is *real*; it represents a function and functions accordingly. It's a toy car that actually drives. At the same time and in contrast, Downtown subverts the real with overt theatricality and Photoshoppery. The tension is (meant to be) exhilarating. It's a Mannerist thrill.

Compare Downtown with other exhibitions. Downtown steps back from typical didactic rigor. It lacks critical commentary; its textual content is almost entirely Denise's own unchallenged words. The exhibition isn't an academic reassessment of Denise (we use her first name; we're all friends here) but a device to bring her into contact with you. There is no linear circuit through. Information appears in attic-order: you open a box, read old papers, open another box, look at photographs. Information appears in fragments or repeats. (I emphasize these same points in my essay below.) Downtown democratizes the exhibition – or at least meets visitors halfway: now to lead with information, now to recede – always offering the freedom, richness, uncertainty, and love of a city for its people.

(The difference raises even grammatical concerns: as an <u>exhibition</u>, *Downtown Denise Scott Brown* should be italicized; as a <u>place</u>, capitalization would do.)

Now that we've peeled back the scenery a bit, let's take a moment to see how Downtown came to be: the ideas that instigated its creation, the people that shaped it, and the philosophies that animate its *genius loci* – the spirit of its place.

> (The difference raises even grammatical concerns: as an <u>exhibition</u>, *Downtown Denise Scott Brown* should be italicized; as a <u>place</u>, capitalization would probably do.)

Welcome Downtown

Angelika Fitz
Entangled Places:
Denise Scott Brown and the Az W

Angelika Fitz is Director of the Architekturzentrum Wien. Downtown Denise Scott Brown began as she envisioned the long overdue presentation of Denise's complete oeuvre. She wrote to Denise, "In times when the close and necessary link of social and aesthetic questions in architecture and urban planning as well responses to the history of architecture are seeing a comeback within the younger generation, we consider your work of crucial importance."

What is *Downtown Denise Scott Brown* doing in the Architekturzentrum Wien, the Austrian museum of architecture? I would like to start the story with a Skype conversation between Vienna and Philadelphia in March 2018. Together with my co-curator Katharina Ritter, I'm sitting in my office with a view of historic Vienna, waiting until a connection is established to the **"Peaceable Kingdom."** That's what Denise Scott Brown calls the house where she lives together with Robert Venturi, and where she has been researching, writing, and sharing space with international visitors since retiring from practice. It's wholly a "studio" – that specific space for collaborative production that inseparably belongs to architecture for Denise. And then the picture of Denise and her longtime colleague Jeremy Tenenbaum, co-author and designer of *Downtown Denise Scott Brown*, appears on the screen. In the background, a section of the "peaceable" cosmos: a painting with a coastal landscape on richly ornamented wallpaper, traditional chairs, and a Chinese vase, which will soon gain a special meaning. **Mannerism**, with which her work is often associated, is a fascinating creative process, according to Denise, by which a collection of things that do not fit together can join together and be beautiful. This directs the conversation to the Viennese architect **Josef Frank**. With his combination of modernity and coziness, which leaves room for life and chance, Frank irritated his fellow architects at the beginning of the 20th century much like Denise later did as one of the most influential critics of a dogmatic Modernism. And that's where the vase comes in. Years ago, when Denise and Bob visited Villa Beer (Josef Frank and Oskar Wlach, 1931) during a trip to Vienna, a Chinese vase stood there. Upon their return, they bought a similar vase in an American Chinatown as a reminder of this elective affinity. Did Denise purposely place it there for our Skype conversation, or was it just coincidence, as it plays out in life? [Editor's Note: She very purposefully placed it there.]

But the story goes on. The vase is definitely not an antique but mass-produced, bought for $160, as Denise recounts. A connection to her most famous work is suggested. In 1966, Denise – at that time a professor at UCLA – drove with her studio to Las Vegas to conduct research and invited Bob Venturi along. Together with Steven Izenour, they published *Learning from Las Vegas* (1972), which triggered a paradigm shift in the history of architecture by offering an unobstructed view of

36. Denise and Jeremy meet Katharina and Angelika via Skype, 2017

the ordinary. Since then, generations of architects and students, especially in Europe, have learned from their methods. And until today, the edges of the city, the intermediate city, and the urban sprawl must be re-viewed and re-understood. Only then can urgently needed new planning concepts be developed.

Whereby: Denise's photographic method, viewed hastily, could serve as a pretext to leave what was found as it is, to even declare it as a fetish. "Don't think, just shoot!" she advises the "eyes that do not see." Together with Bob, she invented a game titled "I Can Like Something Worse Than You Can Like" (which visitors can also play in *Downtown Denise Scott Brown)*. But photography is more than just inventory-taking for Denise; it's part of a transformative agenda. With her "City Physics" approach, she investigates the "gravity" of public spaces. Where and how do people meet? In numerous urban planning projects she designed spaces, paths, and their so-called "crossings" that promote movement and lingering, tranquility and communication in equal measure. With her "Outdoor Functionalism," which extends from the house to the region, she brought the urban dimension back into architecture. For example, the Provincial Capitol Building in Toulouse, France (VSBA, 1999), which one encounters in *Downtown Denise Scott Brown*, is a prime example of a "house as path and place" (Josef Frank). With a chuckle, she tells us that the central passage that runs through the complex of buildings corresponds exactly to a lost medieval route connection – which is something she first learned after winning the competition.

Her agenda for the "right to the city" (Henri Lefebvre) is also reflected in her activist projects. Having grown up in South Africa during the apartheid regime, she was astonished and outraged by the prevailing racism in the United States when she came there in the 1950s. A mixture of technocracy, social ignorance, and racism shaped city planning, for instance, when Philadelphia's South Street was to be destroyed for a new urban highway. Denise worked on participatory planning processes to rescue the threatened neighborhood. At the same time, she had to experience how difficult it was to bridge the gap between activism and planning. And to this day, when looking at urban development around the world, she asks: "Did we really take Jane Jacobs seriously?"

In the Az W's exhibition, she stages a public square together with Jeremy Tenenbaum. In *Downtown Denise Scott Brown* one can go on a journey of discovery or simply hang out, watch people, put oneself in the limelight, meet for a chat, or just stroll around quietly. So you don't miss anything, we've created this travel guide! It's also a souvenir and an echo for those who could not come in person. *Downtown Denise Scott Brown* not only brings a new attraction to the museum, but to the entire city, because Vienna only has a few squares – amazing for a European city. Do we therefore need to import urbanity from the US, mediated by a South African Jewish woman with Eastern European roots, socialized in Britain, who has lived the majority of her life in the US and worked on three continents? Such imports or re-imports were needed earlier. Victor Gruen, an architect who was expelled from Vienna in 1938, invented the shopping mall in the USA, originally intended as a pedestrian-friendly communicative center in the American sprawl. When he visited Vienna in the late 1960s, he was appalled by how the ideology of the car-friendly city was destroying the historic center. Gruen's ideas and interventions – "Cars do not buy anything" – were instrumental in the construction of Vienna's first pedestrian zone in the early 1970s.

I don't know if Denise really is a fan of pedestrian areas. [Editor's Note: She loves them!] What's certain is that her *Downtown Denise Scott Brown*, created together with Jeremy, is a congenial combination of global ideas with the local urban context in Vienna. If one goes on a journey through the complex universe of this architectural *grand dame* – easily accessible with its references to popular culture yet suffused with intellectual and linguistic complexity – it's nice to be able to tie into the familiar. In this sense, *Downtown Denise Scott Brown* is an entanglement, similar to quantum physics, a "mutual state" from faraway places, namely from the life and work of a citizen of the world, the historic walls of the Architekturzentrum Wien, and the exhibition venue of Vienna with its urban façades, from the traditional shop portal to iconic architectural references, right up to the junk shops. With this entanglement, *Down-*

town Denise Scott Brown not only outs a new exhibition format to test, but also opens a new series at the Architekturzentrum Wien – which we don't want to make too much fuss about, because it'll soon become a matter of course. When I became the director of the Az W almost two years ago, one of my goals was to increase the presence of women architects. I don't think it takes much explanation at this juncture about how urgent this is in a discipline that is even more dominated by male stars than art. A group exhibition of "Women in Architecture" didn't seem to be an appropriate response in the 21st century. Therefore, the Architekturzentrum Wien will show a set of solo exhibitions with outstanding female architects in the next few years – as far as I know, the first architecture museum in the world to do so. It was obvious to start this series with Denise Scott Brown, an architect who became a feminist icon despite her work being chronically underrepresented.

Denise published her essay "Room at the Top? Sexism and the Star System in Architecture" in 1989. That didn't change the fact that Bob Venturi was awarded the Pritzker Prize in 1991 alone, instead of the duo who had worked together for decades. In 2013, Women in Design launched a well-respected petition for the subsequent awarding of the prize to both office partners; this again drew more attention to the person than the work. And to this day, as Denise explains in a conversation with Jeremy, "No architect is prepared to conceive

Downtown Denise Scott Brown is an entanglement, similar to quantum physics, a "mutual state" from faraway places...

I'm an architect. They say, I'm a preservationist, I'm a planner, I'm part of the women's movement, I run the office – anything they don't care about at all. Don't let anyone think I'm a designer. It's hopeless."

But it's not hopeless, as *Downtown Denise Scott Brown* proves. This project is not driven by a kind of revanchism but by the trust in a joint creativity. Bob Venturi is present in many places in the exhibition and book, and Denise never tires of describing the success of this working and civil partnership in all its facets. How joint creativity can succeed, with Bob or with coworkers or with students, is a lifelong topic for Denise and it's also the key to this exhibition: "Earlier Jeremy worked with me; now I work with him," as Denise describes the joint effort on *Downtown Denise Scott Brown*. Sometimes her persistent modesty – "I am not a historian, I take the minutes" – leads me to contradiction. But then I think that precisely this post-heroic attitude creates the basis for shared creativity.

Most of all, I'm happy that we can show the world's first monographic exhibition on the complete works of Denise Scott Brown at the Architekturzentrum Wien. My thanks go to the entire Az W team and especially to my co-curator Katharina Ritter and my managing colleague Karin Lux. Ultimately, however, it's thanks to the generosity of Denise and Jeremy's playfulness that *Downtown Denise Scott Brown* was built in Vienna.

Katharina Ritter
The Universe of Denise Scott Brown

Katharina Ritter is Curator at the Architekturzentrum Wien. She led the planning and assembly of Downtown Denise Scott Brown *as well as oversaw the creation of this tour guide. In her essay, Katharina focuses on both the impact Denise and Bob have had on generations of architects and the uniquely urbanistic approach the designers have explored through this exhibition.*

In 2016, when researching for the Az W exhibition *In the End: Architecture*, I looked more closely at the life work of Denise Scott Brown and Robert Venturi. I was amazed at how incredibly up-to-date and entertaining their writings were, how refreshing the then-rebellious reading was, and how the architectural and urban planning work consequently developed. As a vehement critic of post-war functionalism which persistently ignored context and history, Scott Brown and her work seemed to have been dismissed for a long time as **postmodern**, and thus history itself. But saving the existing city and dealing with everyday forms are burning issues of architectural discourse – now as well as back then. While Denise did not address an ideal state of the city with the publication of *Learning from Las Vegas* at the beginning of the 1970s, she acknowledged its current condition, thereby setting a resounding signal in architectural debate for the existing fabric, an increasing resistance against the large-scale demolition of entire districts, and against undemocratic urban planning formed in Vienna. The movement called for a departure from the modernist *tabula rasa* and a revitalization of the old Viennese building stock.

Now that a younger generation of architects is attracting attention, one that appears to have no fear of historic design vocabulary and for whom cultural continuity is not something that has to be overcome, it is clearly time to rediscover and reassess the work of Denise Scott Brown. This generation faces up to the past, builds it further, and works with citations and ornaments. The contextual aspect is always the basis, and the goal is to create something trusted that can serve the user as a familiar, un-agitating background. Through the intensive dialog with the grown environment, they integrate something new into the existing structures. The architecture steps into the background and does not classify between everyday and prestigious projects. And they themselves refer to Denise, Bob, and Steven Izenour again and again.

But back then in 2016, I could not have guessed that only a year or so later we would write a letter to Denise asking for an exhibition on her work. The decision to start a series of monographs on female architects instead of the often requested exhibition about "Women in Architecture" was made in the first program sessions with our new director Angelika Fitz. From there it was more of a logical consequence to begin this series with that icon of architecture who was denied the **Pritzker Prize** for the joint creativity of an architectural office.

Since Denise is currently committed fully to writing, she called on her longtime colleague Jeremy Tenenbaum, virtually a foster son of VSBA. What a stroke of

37. At home, 2018

luck! Jeremy immediately fell in love with this idea and set to work with incredible drive and inventiveness. Together, we plunged into the universe of Denise Scott Brown, the teacher, the theorist, the city planner, and the architect – and the possibilities of presentation that resulted. In the autumn of 2017, Jeremy came to Vienna and together we explored the city, which this exhibition wanted to talk about and with Denise. The everyday structures of the city and the Viennese shop portals in particular became sources of inspiration, so the fictional urban "Downtown" setting, closely coordinated with Denise, was born as the giver of diverse, thought-provoking impulses which, together with documents from the eventful life of Denise Scott Brown and her partnership with Robert Venturi, are made available to the general public.

The fact that the exhibition design must pursue an urbanistic approach appeared compelling in relation to Denise's work. The absence of places offering a real staying quality in Vienna resulted in the next approach. *Downtown Denise Scott Brown* thus developed in the middle of the **MuseumsQuartier**, one of the few actually functioning plazas in Vienna, at the same time only a semi-public place, which, like the exhibition itself, is framed by cultural contents. The scenographically designed square at the Architekturzentrum Wien uses Viennese shop portals filled with the ideas and life of Denise Scott Brown. It shouts for attention itself with its carefully decorated shop windows but also offers visitors the unique opportunity to become "the monument," the center of the exhibition for a short time. The site itself becomes part of the exhibition's content. The mix of seemingly contradictory elements, the allusions and the playful, at times over-charged execution reflects Denise's love of diversity, mixing, and tradition. This was staged by Jeremy Tenenbaum, to whom we are grateful for his tireless efforts to bring us closer to Denise Scott Brown's universe in this indeed one-of-a-kind way!

Jeremy Eric Tenenbaum: "Storytelling"

Jeremy Eric Tenenbaum is Downtown's lead designer (and co-author of this book!). He has worked closely with Denise for 18 years, first as an assistant with Venturi, Scott Brown and Associates, then as writer and designer with their successor firm, VSBA Architects & Planners, and finally as her collaborator for publications and exhibitions. Jeremy writes about his relationship with Denise and how the design evolved.

Telling Her Story

Denise Scott Brown's life is told and retold. She writes her architecture and urbanism through the medium of her own history. She teaches person by person, book by interview. Her pedagogy is humanism: real people and the ideas that subtend their lives. Her classroom is three continents wide, at least.

Tonight Denise meets with an interviewer in her dining room, her home office and conference room. The table is laid with plates, books, computers, a printer. We can enter the conversation at any point – here she's narrating her photography – but soon the talk will take us to her African Modern babyhood, 1960s California, modern China, all the way to her unretiring retirement. These are neither digressions nor separate stories but one grand unified body of life and work and thought.

Denise speaks with a trim South African tone radiating cleverness, kindness, something lovingly wicked. She speaks beautifully but without embroidered oratory (like mine). She speaks with more matter and less art. Her lexicon, though, is formidable: "gormless," "Morganatic," "subtend." Her voice is soft but durable; you wouldn't imagine interrupting or speaking over her. (You get the idea that, when it was younger, her voice could and did soar.) Publicly, Bob would often shyly mumble; to both of their satisfaction, Denise owned conversations. At meetings, Denise sat at the head of the table and Bob sat to her right, doodling.

(I remember a story: One interviewer credited Denise and Bob as "the Venturis." She corrected him: "Venturi and Scott Brown." He protested: "I just said that!" The interviewer couldn't spare those two extra words. Also, he was proud of himself for including Denise in his article: "I'm on your side!")

Denise speaks in story. You won't coax her into pat didactic statements. (Bob Venturi is the aphorist, an editor's dream of unending succinct quotes.) Ask Denise her thoughts on functionalism in architecture. Eschewing portentous dicta, she'll tell you a story that winds around **Le Corbusier**, her first studio class, factories of the 1950s, **mittens**, and Lou Kahn. Her lesson on photography may begin with Cartier-Bresson but will end with Chicago urbanism. **Sad Old White Men** will malign this autobiographical and parabolic approach as "feminine," forgetting Fitzgerald, Joyce, Kerouac, and Christ. And every author, on or just below the surface.

38. Denise and Andrés Ramírez, 2018

But Denise says "don't navel-gaze!" and she takes her own advice. Her stories show herself as an active and central character, but she relates them for instruction not vanity. She tells stories to make theory personal and concrete, to show origins and connections and possibilities.

In fact, Denise communicates often enough via questions: What will happen if this happens? How can these people connect with those? How can we keep this building while creating that one? Her method is rooted in question but isn't Socratic; she doesn't lead toward pre-conceived ideas but the opposite: she focuses us on the conflicts and hard choices ahead. Her urbanism is a humane ordering of intersecting stories. She doesn't pore over the tea leaves of economic and land use formulae but instead learns from the real motivations, histories, needs, and passions of the messy human world – complex and contradictory, to coin a phrase. Her students, visitors, and audiences listen happily. (Yes, a one-hour lecture has been known to last three. Everyone remains seated and happy.)

Denise and I have talked for eighteen years. I've been her assistant, designer, and collaborator. The stories she shares with the interviewer have floated by me before but never quite in this combination, and here are details and side alleys I've never heard. Her interviews become family dinners, favorite anecdotes told and retold, grand theory alongside the secret histories and office politics. And with time comes intimacy: Denise talks about a young South African girl she helped and tears enter her voice. "Funny things are moving."

(Denise's life seems to tangent among famous people. She collaborates and collides with a Mannerist constellation of the century's stars – Tom Wolfe, Prince Charles, Ed Ruscha, Gay Talese. Does she think this is curious? "I think you'll find most people encounter just as many famous people, maybe not knowing it.")

Denise and the interviewer have been conversing for hours. She gathers strength through talking but has limits; she's human, I remind us. The interviewer seems overwhelmed and grateful – but also do I detect some hint of inexpressible un-fulfillment? We've heard so much of Denise's story, from childhood to this dining room, but what about the *real Denise*? I'm sure the interviewer quivers to ask, "But what do you think about Instagram? What's in your Netflix queue?" We want the ephemera as proof of "the real Denise." (Curiously Bob is *all* ephemera – the *petit éphémère* of ketchup and Britcoms and the *éphémère grand* of Michelangelo and Gershwin, all these bits brought together and synthesized.) But we *are* getting the real and personal Denise. Her work and life braid together. Her life is the story of her life.

Denise's force is bound up with her view and voice. "Mine is an African view of Las Vegas." She writes *A View from the Campidoglio* and *Having Words* and "A Worm's-Eye View" and *Wayward Eye*. She wears her eye on her sleeve, proudly subjective and personal. Turning away from ideology drained of time and context, postmodernism re-embraced history – even personal history. Still, Denise doesn't need an autobiography: she tells her story person by person, street by street.

But now at 87, Denise fears "I'm losing all my words." (Her memory remains encyclopedic. She knows the name of the professor's daughter she met once forty years ago. She has forgotten more than we'll ever know.) Cataracts now muddle her eye. Seemingly no amount of aging dares to alter her view and voice.

Telling the Story

So, obviously, the exhibition *Downtown Denise Scott Brown* at the Architekturzentrum Wien would be written in Denise's own **voice**. The words would be found in her books, lectures, and conversations. I wouldn't design the show as a critical examination or anaerobic academic exercise; I would make an immersion and celebration. (Besides, I'm not an architectural scholar and I'm too close to Denise to pretend objectivity.) I would create a show that puts us with Denise, looking over each other's shoulders.

So *Downtown* had to be designed **urbanistically**. To Denise, all systems – from cities to vegetable gardens – are urbanistic. This can serve as a metaphor or heuristic: "In the garden, where is City Hall? Where is the highway?" But more concretely, both garden and exhibition contain an innate urbanism: where is the street through the exhibition, and how does it tie to the institution, and how does that tie to the city beyond? I would be irresponsible and unethical not to design the show with an urbanistic eye.

So, like stories that interconnect and loop around, *Downtown* had to reflect the **"messy vitality"** of the world. It would be a crowded attic where you pry open each box, stochastically pull out stacks of photos or old newspapers or diary pages. Navigation wouldn't be direct but circuitous; information wouldn't be sequential but non-linear, arranged by city-logic. At the same time, the exhibition had to be structured and practical.

So the show would be a *place* filled with Denise's *voice* – It would be a platz, square, a piazza – and as *real* as we can make it!

Once the foundation of the game was established – that we would imagine the Architekturzentrum Wien's exhibition space to be an outdoor urban plaza – a play-pretend fidelity guided all our design choices and suggested the satellite elements. A piazza may be ringed by storefronts, there's always a café, tables accompany it, there are banners and signs and fanfare and postboxes.

But where would we put *the content?* Everywhere, everywhere! Imagine we take Denise (all of her history, all of her words) and place her in the center of the piazza and blow her up! Wherever little bits of Denise splatter, that's where we'll put the content.

But this raises the question: what's at the center of our exhibition space? Does any central element serve as a majestic, dominant force? Well, what else would crown a piazza but a fountain?

We would honor Denise in a Denisian way. We would create a fountain as a triumphant yet subversive urban gesture. As the space's geographical crossroads, **Downtown Fountain** would be both a culmination of forces and a centrifugal influence on its surroundings. It would divide and accentuate the scale of the space, large in size but larger still in scale. We would use the fountain as a canvas to display images of Denise, akin

> Viva stories inside stories! – and is there a more succinct definition of a city?

to the statue mounted atop a traditional civic monument. At the same time, we would playfully (and literally) cut down its heroic symbolism. While celebrating Denise, we would direct the fountain towards the social life of the exhibition – displaying visitors themselves! Downtown Fountain wouldn't be precious but accessible, permeable, with tiers that visitors can walk along and sit on. In a final *coup de grâce* for both populism and urbanism, we would carve a channel through the fountain – "the street to and through the building" – albeit a semi-secret street. And inside that channel, we would deliver a little message from Denise: her private message within this private exhibition mimicking a public space within a private institution surrounded by magical city.

Telling Stories

These layers delight me. Viva stories inside stories! – and is there a more succinct definition of a city?

Downtown Denise Scott Brown is a riot of realities: a play of indoor and outdoor, "two dimensional" and "three-dimensional," functional and flatly fake. An exhibition is always a costume party of authenticity and this is the Grand Ball.

These nested representations culminate in Downtown Fountain: a Pop Art artifice designed as representation of a fountain – white with black lines, fresh from and hardly off the drafting board, barely broken from Illustrator. It isn't *trompe l'oeil* reflective like the storefronts and other urban furniture; it's a wholly original construction designed to look "fake." But Denise and Bob might have designed just such a Pop Art interpolation, so to this perspective the overtly "fake" fountain becomes the realest object in the room. Meanwhile, while these semiotic perspectives wrestle, the fountain faithfully serves the urbanistic and social roles of a real fountain: a celebratory prominence, a gathering orbit, a rushing respite.

Or maybe these nested stories and plays of representation culminate in this book? – **your guide** to an unreal place where real people work and discover.

Or, better by far, I hope these stories culminate in a better life for everyone who hears and shares them. What Denise and Bob teach isn't architecture (only) but humanism. They teach the validity of play, personal experience, serious fun, heartbreaking irony – that vast existing world we love to hate. Learn from all of it, including the things you don't want to learn, but ultimately trust your loves. Here's a bad idea that might lead to a good idea. Here's a Mannerism that applies to all arts, engineering, cooking, law, wherever systems exist and conflict. A poet very well understands systems that clash and cannot all be followed. To better the world, and our own lives, we should learn when and how to bend rules and in the process bring together the seemingly incompatible.

> Sit on the fountain edge, surrounded by beautiful fakery, and fall in real love.

I am not an architect. (This allows me to design anything I like.) I'm a writer, a flâneur, a café habitué, an overactive observer. I just like telling stories. I explained this at the Az W when we first discussed the design. We were a mix of creative people from different backgrounds -- the museum's leadership, their fabricators, an English major from Philadelphia.

I said to the workshop staff, "I'll need to rely on your expertise."

They said, "We've never made a film set before."

So that's what it is! The exhibition is a film set: an unreal place woven throughout by real information, an imaginary bedroom filled with real diaries. A film set where you visitors act.

And I hope that *Downtown Denise Scott Brown*, like Pinocchio, is so good that it becomes real. Perhaps one evening, after closing, true night outside beyond the film set dusk windows, two staff members might sit on the fountain edge, surrounded by beautiful fakery, and fall in real love.

39. First office, Pine Street, Philadelphia

40. Venice, 1956, meets West Philadelphia, 1970s

Up and Down Downtown

UP AND DOWN DOWNTOWN

45

Up and Down Downtown

41. Robert Venturi Sketch, c. 1971

Downtown Fountain & the Photoautomat

Downtown Fountain is the center of the scene! Here's our meet point, Downtown's downtown, where everyone comes together to play and rest while twilight becomes night. The fountain proclaims "I AM A MONUMENT" and needs no further proof: rising into the ceiling-clouds, the imposing structure both divides and unites the plaza. Seen from either end, the fountain appears to be a rising cylinder. In plan, though, the fountain is shaped like a stadium: two separated circles connected by a length, suggesting a Pop Art extrusion, a two-dimensional figure come to life.

At the summit of either side, an arced screen receives a projection. On the entry side, Denise smiles down on us. Soon the image bubbles away into a rush of water then shimmers back to other scenes of Denise, old and young. On the opposite side, the screen often shows Denise as well, but sometimes instead it reveals...?

Try this: See that nearby **Photoautomat**? Step inside. Follow the instructions to have your photo taken (it's free) then step back out and *look up* to discover – y*ou are the monument!* So now? Take your selfie of course! Your double-selfie, Little You and Big You. Then why not post your pic to Instagram?:

#denisescottbrown_azw.

But Downtown Fountain is filled with secrets. As you walk around it you'll soon find an opening in the structure – a channel, a street to and through the fountain cleaving it into halves. It's graffiti-lined (it's so hard to keep clean). And at the center of the center, the holy of holies, a video monitor offers a secret message from Denise Scott Brown.

Downtown Fountain is urbanistic and democratic, linking both halves of the plaza and allowing visitors to permeate what would otherwise be a blockade. The passage transforms the dedicated devotional space at the core of an urban environment into a public thoroughfare and throughway.

Downtown Fountain is both art and life: a sketch come to life, an aberrant non-illusion among Downtown's *trompe l'oeils*. It's both duck and decorated shed. It's a stone dropped in a lake, rippling tiers.

Downtown Fountain is subversive, or at least naughty. Visitors crawl all over it. Its celebratory subject shares space with any guest. The singular masculine form is tugged apart like a cell's first division. The fountain is heroic and anti-heroic, contradictory and Mannerist.

Or it might just be...*cool?*

42. South Street, Philadelphia

Shopping

Downtown Denise Scott Brown is a shopper's Shangri-La! From the latest fashions to rediscovered classics, from books to games to electronics, you'll find it here. Downtown isn't big in size but it packs a lot in. Each shop is dedicated to a specific subject: urban theory, photography, Mannerism, women in architecture, and so on. Together they encompass the **universe of Denise Scott Brown**.

Downtown was conceived as a juxtaposition between Denise and the complex texture of Vienna's commercial life. The city's forms, fonts, and rhythms are represented faithfully but drained of their texts, replaced by Denise's own words.

The semantic meanings of this gambit are fun to explore: Does Downtown compare Denise's views to commodities? Does Downtown invite visitors to "window shop" only and therefore, perversely, go home empty-handed? Maybe! Or maybe, most insidiously, Downtown offers a pleasant stroll, a twilight diversion, and conversation with a new friend?

If you've read "Storytelling" ("Welcome Downtown," page 38), you know that Denise often communicates her concepts about architecture and urbanism through personal stories. For this guidebook, we sat down with Denise in June 2018 and talked for hours, alighting on each of the topics found Downtown. We didn't ask her to explain her ideas or work; so much has been written already, by Denise and countless others. Instead we asked her to reminisce, to recall her childhood, to walk with us through the landscape of her thought. Here's what she said, in the intimate cadence of her own spoken voice.

Here's what Denise Scott Brown says, in the intimate cadence of her own spoken voice.

Up and Down Downtown

On Words to the Future!

Who's Who?

From here to the end of "Up and Down Downtown," Denise's text to the right is in black.

There's no better place to start than the end! As you enter Downtown and not far from Café Nkana, you'll find this elegant storefront on your left. You've just started your journey, but why not pause a moment to reflect on where you're going?

We asked Denise: what pursuits in architecture are important now and into the future? For young designers, what's the critical work that lies ahead? To what should they devote their passions? Here's what she told us:

The issue of **social concern** in architecture in a very broad span is important. The part I've been talking about so much is: yes, you heard Jan Jacobs and what you did about it was *nothing*. From then on, the urbanism that comes out of architects is mostly destructive, today as then. Though I have no right to say that, because I don't keep up.

When we were in Shanghai, we looked across at Pudong, the new suburb on the island across the river, and it looks like Fairyland: with tall buildings and the lights and color and all of that. It just looks exquisite. And you go there and you come out of one of the buildings and you hit utter hell. There's no order for you as a pedestrian to find a way from a bus stop to a building, no order to deal with a service system. And that was also my impression on the ETH campus in Zurich, which I think was a translation of **Ville Radieuse**. There has to be some better understanding of the interrelation of urban patterns. That would also be a good place to start.

Also, you really want to have a much better idea of the needs of **housing** and different kinds of housing. For example, the housing that we saw in Mexico City, the housing that I learned about in Pakistan, it's not the house but the *infrastructure* that is supplied. Levittown is rather like that.

Also, employment for one building may involve thousands of people, from banks to bricklayers and all people in between – and architects are the shock troops of that. We set the schedules. But really we don't: the construction loan probably does, and that's why we have to wreck the lives of our young architects, to follow the schedules set by construction loans. Well, understanding all of this and where you fit and how housing comes about would be another great social asset.

On Words to the Future!

You Will Be Setting Out

as I did, sixty years ago – not to stay, and your routes will traverse another world... But I'm betting some things will stay the same... You will also, I hope, have learned to

Ihr werdet euch so wie ich vor sechzig Jahren auf den Weg machen – nicht stehen bleiben, eure Wege werden euch durch eine andere Welt führen ... Ich traue mich jedoch zu wetten, dass einige Dinge gleich bleiben ... Ihr werdet hoffentlich auch erkennen, dass ihr von eurer unmittelbaren Umgebung lernen müsst.'

Learn From What's Around You.

But one warning: Don't Navel-Gaze!

„Aber eine Warnung: gebt euch nicht mit dem Nabelschau."'

There are inspirations in many places but I would still turn early to everyday architecture...'

Obwohl viele Orte inspirierend sind, würde ich mich bald an der Alltagsarchitektur orientieren ...

My eye, still wayfaring, wondering, wondering, wayfinding, and wavering, also wavers.

Seeing becomes part memory...

If you have cataracts, you are in a yellow parchment world – a rosy fall in one eye and a cold blue-white light in the other – left eye Las Vegas, right eye North Pole.'

Mein Auge, noch immer wandernd, sich wundernd, Wege findend und wirr gibt heute manchmal wo.

Ich beziehe einen Teil meiner Sehkraft aus der Erinnerung ...

Wenn man grauen Star hat, lebt man in einer gelben Pergamentwelt ... – ein rosafarbener Wasserfall in einem Auge und ein kaltes blau-weißes Licht im anderen – das linke Auge Las Vegas, das rechte der Nordpol.'

Architecture's Grandmother

And no one has remembered the 1970s.'

A guardian of [architecture's] institutional memory

Who knows the schools and where the banks are buried.'

One of my roles, is to help us impartialize and form associations knitting architects who share our ideas.

Another role is 'writing the minutes.' I'm not an historian, but I take good notes.'

Eine Bewahrerin der institutionellen Erinnerung [der Architektur],

die die Hochschulen kennt und weiß, wo die Leichen vergraben sind.'

Eine meiner Aufgaben ist es, auf vergleichbare Weise ein- und verbindungen zwischen Architekten*innen zu schaffen, die unsere Ideen teilen ...

Eine andere Aufgabe ist es, „Protokoll zu führen". Ich bin keine Historikerin, aber ich mache gute Notizen.'

Up and Down Downtown

From Las Vegas Back Again To Rome

> **No architect is prepared to conceive I'm an architect.**
>
> But now I have a thin edge of a wedge -- and that's photography.

This travel agency is known for its gorgeous storefront windows bursting with photos of the world. Here's a fun idea: let's take photos of the photos!

Between the mid-1950s and early 1970s, Denise took thousands of photos – first while traveling in Europe with first husband Robert Scott Brown, later as an exploration of vernacular architecture while she lived in Southern California and discovered Las Vegas. Denise's photography is an important tool for understanding, teaching, and designing.

No architect is prepared to conceive I'm an architect. They say, I'm a preservationist, I'm a planner, I'm part of the women's movement, I run the office – anything they don't care about at all. Don't let anyone think I'm a designer. It's hopeless. But now I have a thin edge of a wedge – and that's **photography**.

> **"Do I hate it or love it?"**
>
> "Don't ask," said my inner voice.

If you look at most urban maps and USGS maps, you can see how a town grew up – when they brought the expressway in, how this little area developed. It's a very good translation between force and form. I show my aerial photos of Zulu kraals beside Philadelphia's transportation map: here's a subsistence economy, here's an advanced capitalistic mercantile economy. The form of one is very different from the form of the other, largely because of how they trade and how they travel.

My [forthcoming] photography book, **Wayward Eye**, opens eyes and shows some things very beautifully. I can start something with this. I could write something that would take people in steps, but my photography book is not the first step; my analysis of **Cartier-Bresson**'s photography is the first step, and showing that his photography says something about a society and its spans. That's the way I would have to go for architects because it has to stay physical.

Up and Down Downtown

43. West Philadelphia, 1964

Africa
44. Late 1950s to 1970

Up and Down Downtown

Las Vegas
45. 1966-1968

FREE ASPIRIN
ASK US ANYTHING

Up and Down Downtown

Up and Down Downtown

US West Coast
46. 1965 to 1967

Up and Down Downtown

US East Coast
47. 1958 to 1965+

Treffpunkt of Minds

Architectural Knitting

That's what I call an encounter with the palimpsest: how you encounter the patterns underneath.

This hardware store might look simple and plain, but you could spend hours here. It's filled with everything you need to build something wonderful. Also check out the street sign just beside the shop; it offers a bit of helpful guidance.

Working urbanistically – weaving together patterns of activity along with circulation, traffic, and urban systems – helps bridge connections and bring together different groups. At the University of Michigan, for example, Denise links the medical and main campuses to create a "meeting place of the minds." Her capitol building in Toulouse, France, is shaped around a main urban route that Denise devised – before learning she had uncovered an historic path. And while the Vanna Venturi House is entirely Bob's design, she and he met just as it was evolving dramatically toward its final form and reflecting their emerging joint ideas about circulation and urbanism.

A big scheme with several buildings almost always has urban components. I will start by understanding these **urban connections**, seeing where they are. Early in a project, Bob will say, "I'm still learning the system of this building"; very important to a system is its structure, but also its connections, its roadways, how it must accommodate these. This has been true for most of the campuses on which I've been a planner and an architect.

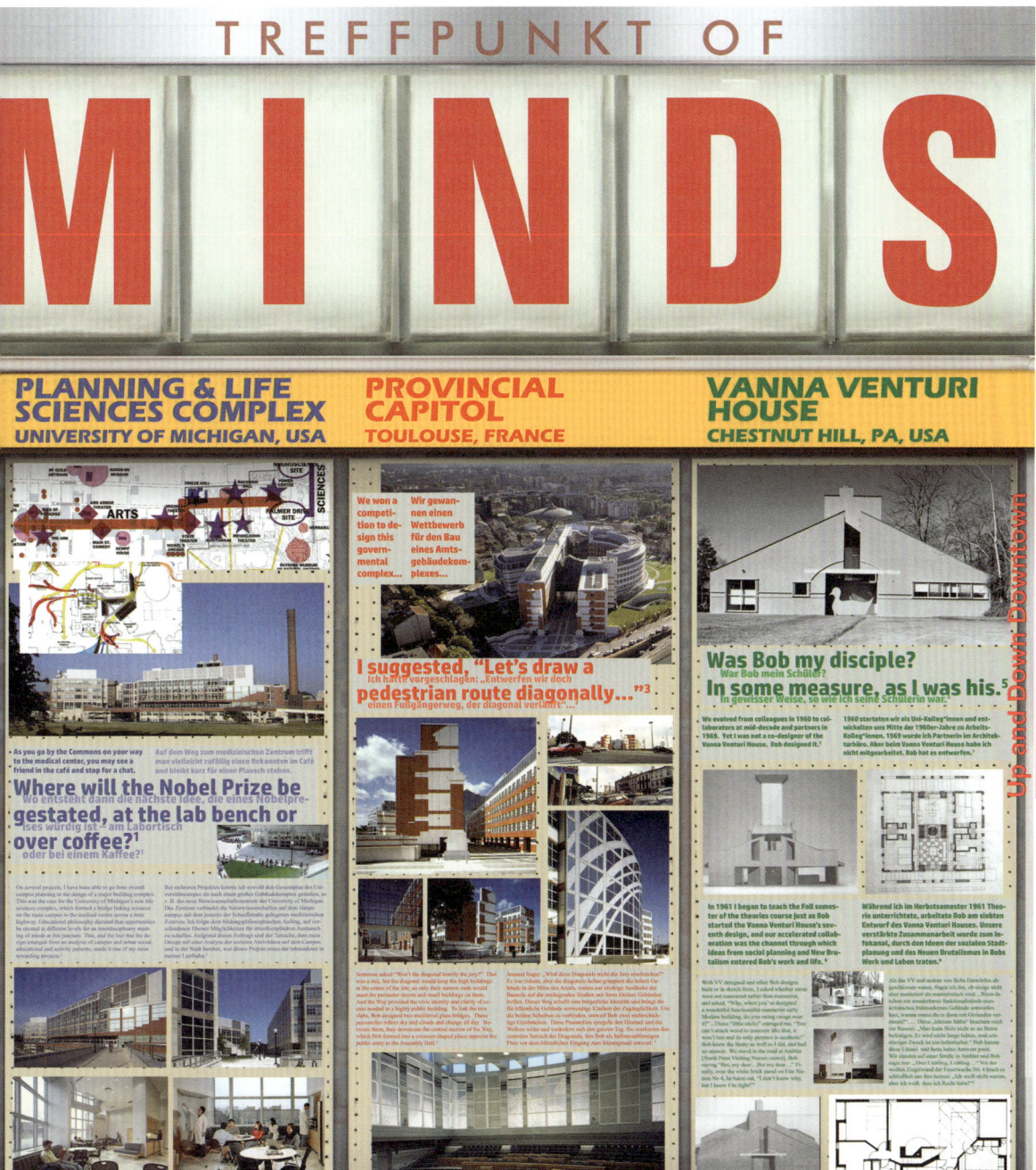

University of Michigan

48. Ann Arbor, Michigan   Campus Master Planning (2002)   Palmer Drive Life Sciences Complex (2007)

Up and Down Downtown

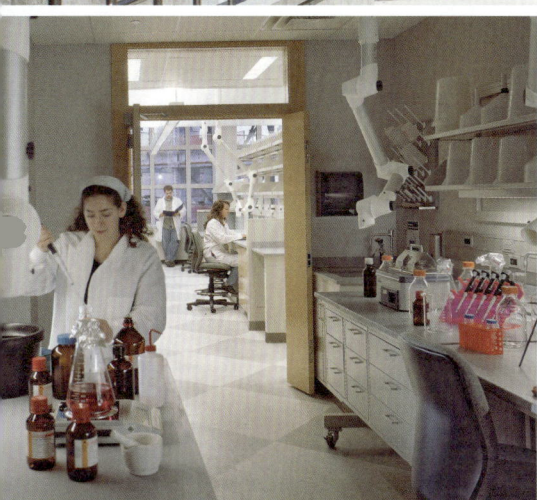

I'm very proud of the **University of Michigan** photos that show people sitting where I hoped they would sit. It really makes my intended public space real public space.

Provincial Capitol
49. Toulouse, France (1999)

Up and Down Downtown

In **Toulouse**, we had this wonderful discovery: a road that we suggested across the cleared site had previously existed in the same location. We were merely reconnecting two things that had previously been connected for maybe 500 years – reconnecting exactly where they should be! That's what I call an *encounter with the palimpsest*: how you encounter the patterns underneath.

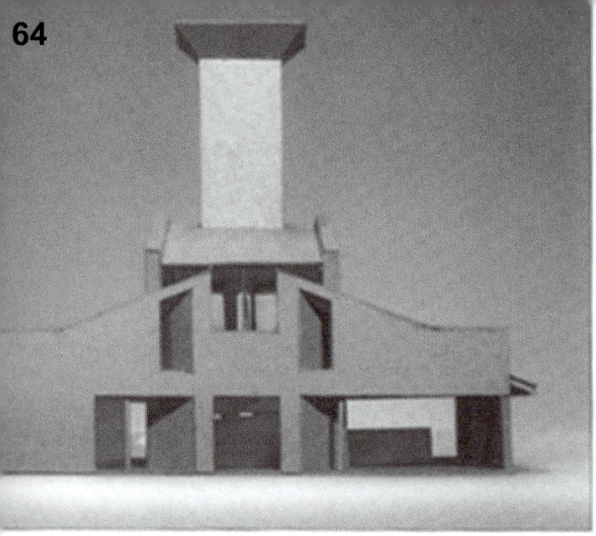

Up and Down Downtown

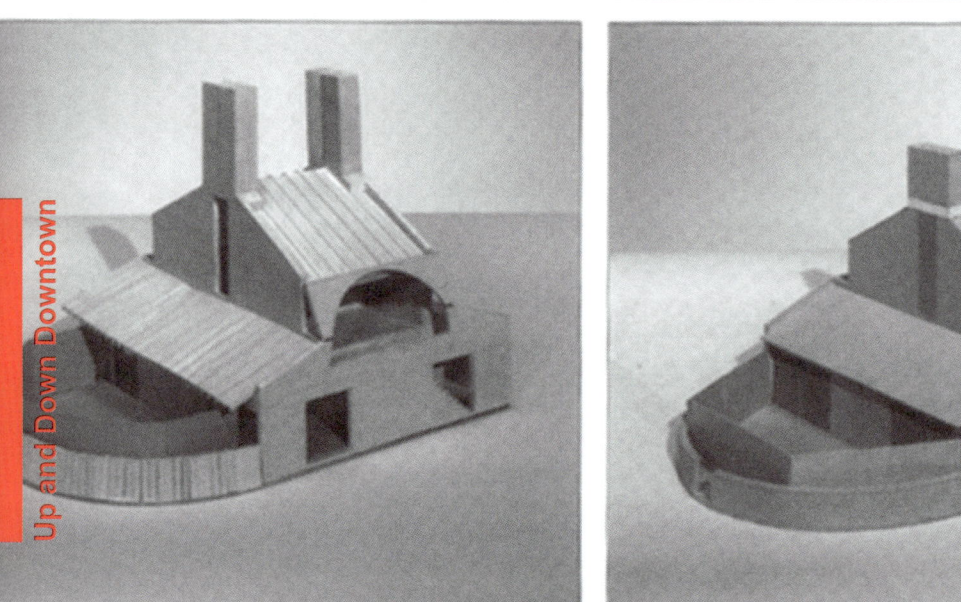

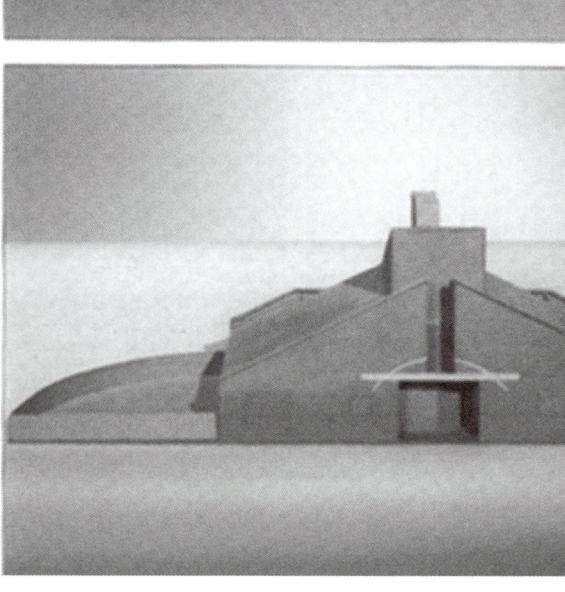

Vanna Venturi House
50. Chestnut Hill, Philadelphia, Pennsylvania (1964)

With **Bob's house for his mother**, it's fascinating to trace the migration of ideas – diagonal zoots, the nowhere stair, the big chimney, the melding of Michelangelo and Levitt, the consecration of stairways, the miniaturization and infantilization of suburbia, and the late arrival, after Bob and I began our work and life together, of the street through the building. I loved the contradictions, the broken rules, the strong juxtapositions that make it Mannerist and recall historical Mannerism. But I criticized the decoration.

Eyes That Do Not See!

Le Corbusier

DES YEUX QUI NE VOIENT PAS...

Une grande époque vient de commencer...

Nos yeux, malheureusement, ne savent pas le discerner.

On Urban Planning

There are many formulas: I don't look at any of them.

Your eyeglass prescription better be current – there's a lot to see in the windows of this optometrist's office! It's worth a closer look.

1960s America experienced tremendous social and cultural upheaval. Its cities, where poverty was concentrated, were epicenters of these tensions. Denise, then studying at the University of Pennsylvania's School of Planning, first began to explore city physics – the economic forces that shape cities as well as the lives within.

Central place theory, city physics, gravity and potential – all describe activity around points of high access or where the two main streets cross – where you get the greatest activity. It's where the most people want to be. It's as simple as that. There are many formulas: I don't look at any of them. I have the feeling of it, as I have the feeling of building structure in my body.

Central place theory is the most useful for me. Knowing that Chicago is a half-circle because of Lake Michigan, how does that half-circle guide urban development? Put a port on the lake, you'll get rings of concentric circles, roads radiate out, trains radiate out, development follows – you don't have to know the formula.

When I gave a lecture in Mexico City, I explained central place theory and the whole thing about roads that cross, and I showed them (*crosses her fingers at a 90 degree angle*). I said, "Just remember this, no formulas, just this!" And after the lecture as the students and teachers walked out, I saw them crossing their fingers!

I can tell the story of all the places where the peddlers walk and create certain patterns which become towns – but you can also start with a campus plan and relationships within your building, relationships between your buildings. When you're doing new city planning in a developing area, you're best advised to not be taken up too much with the familiarities you know from your own cities. Instead you can start by looking for new structures and how basic overall structures can make the town. When you're excited you're inspired – and that structure can provide that excitement.

Natural Structure

These are all human structures about natural form. I love to extend them.

Patterns: In the 1950s, a lot of people were talking about natural structure. My friend Wolfram [Schlote], who was **Robert [Scott Brown]**'s friend and then mine, photographed beautiful things you could find in natural structure: crystal structure, cliff structure, structure in fields. I loved that structure – but then I found the geometric structure of fish set out on the sidewalk of High Street, London – a beautiful structure. And so were the shoes and so were the glasses – these are all human structures about natural form. I love to extend them.

Urban patterns form through the particular kind of system where the building block is a grid for good reasons and a marketplace is at the crossroads for good reasons, along with other important things like a cathedral and the ruler's castle nearby.

You could take this system into a living room and ask what all these elements represent in a living room – or you could take it into New York and ask what do they mean there. In New York you have to deal with where the highest density should be, what size sites people are looking for, what size sites are needed in the future, what growth should be permitted and which prevented. If you allow for a building on this site now and you don't want it to invade everything around it, you allow channels for where it can grow and channels for where it can't. So you are allowing for the uncertainty of growth but you're channeling it. If you don't want something very important – socially or historically precious – to be swept away, you find ways to allow access where you want a lot of people to be and limit access by what you want to protect.

51. South Street, Philadelphia

52. South Africa

69

Up and Down Downtown

53. A typical beach, showing typical distribution

I Can Like Something Worse Than You Can Like

Look at That!

"Chaos is an order we have not understood."

While visiting Downtown, *you must play "I Can Like Something Worse Than You Can Like"! Just look around and take photos of the beautiful / strange / ugly / fascinating things you see – both fabulous scenes and behind the scenes – then post them to Instagram: **#uglyinstagram_azw**. They'll instagramagically be added to the exhibition's feed.*

Denise and Bob talk about "learning to love what you love to hate." It's the first step in approaching the world that "is" rather than "ought" to be – and designing based on principles that are practical and humane.

Bob and I played a game called **I Can Like Something Worse Than You Can Like**. We would drive around and I'd say, look at that! And he'd say, yeuuuch! And then, one way or another, we'd internalize these things we hated and they would come out somewhere while we were working. And we came to conclusions: there's a thing called "messy vitality."

I had a student who did a term paper on philosophy and I was pleased to have him do it because I wanted to learn more about philosophy. Somewhere he found someone who said, "Chaos is an order we have not understood." And that related to our game. Serendipity is now an overall concern in many fields; complexity was then: **Paul [Davidoff]** and I went to a biology lecture about organized complexity; **Ian McHarg** was showing complexity of natural systems, etc. And so that was part the game.

54. Southern California, 1966

55. Monterey, California, 1966

Sees Her Signs

We've made it to the far end of Downtown and – what's this magnificent Classical icon? Is it ancient Rome or...mid-century Las Vegas?! In fact, it's a sign fabrication shop cleverly named Sees Her Signs. Let's pause our tour around Downtown to check out its wonderful collection of photographs and texts.

The famous 1968 "Learning from Las Vegas" research studio was led by Denise, Bob, and Steven Izenour at Yale University. Nine students spent three weeks researching and four days visiting Los Angeles before launching into ten days in Las Vegas – a frantic candy-colored whirlwind of data collection, discussion, covert casino snapshots, and photography by land and air. Why? To understand, without prejudice, emerging American forms of urban sprawl, the auto-city, and their social impacts. They didn't seek to legitimize or promulgate but to "learn from." They returned to Yale and spent ten weeks processing the data they'd collected. In 1972 the book Learning from Las Vegas began to transform how we learn and understand architecture.

56. The LLV studio team, 1968

57. Texaco sign, 1968

1968

"The Lido Crew": Denise (center), Steve Izenour (left in sunglasses), and the Learning from Las Vegas studio students pose dramatically

SEES HER SIGNS

MINE IS AN AFRICAN VIEW OF LAS VEGAS
MEIN BLICK AUF LAS VEGAS IST EIN AFRIKANISCHER

1968 STUDIO • 1972 BOOK • 1977 2ND ED.

Up and Down Downtown

LEARNING FROM LAS

"Passing Through Las Vegas Is Route 91, the archetype of the commercial strip, the phenomenon at its purest and most intense. We believe a careful documentation and analysis of its physical form is as important to architects and urbanists today as were the studies of medieval Europe and ancient Rome and Greece to earlier generations. Such a study will help to define a new type of urban form emerging in America and Europe, radically different from that we have known; one that we have been ill-equipped to deal with and that, from ignorance, we define today as urban sprawl. An aim of this studio will be, through open-minded and nonjudgmental investigation, to come to understand this new form and to begin to evolve techniques for its handling."[1]

... was a research project, undertaken as a collaboration among three instructors, nine students of architecture, and two planning and two graphics students in graduate programs at Yale... We spent three weeks in the library, four days in Los Angeles, and ten days in Las Vegas. We returned to Yale and spent ten weeks analyzing and presenting our discoveries. Before this, we authors had visited Las Vegas several times and written "A Significance for A&P Parking Lots, or Learning from Las Vegas" (Architectural Forum, March 1968); this formed the basis for the research program that we drafted during the summer of 1968.[2]

war ein Forschungsprojekt, das in Zusammenarbeit mit drei Dozent*innen, neun Architekturstudent*innen, zwei Raumplanungsstudent*innen und zwei Grafikstudent*innen im Master- und Doktoratsprogramm in Yale durchgeführt wurde ... Wir verbrachten drei Wochen in der Bibliothek, vier Tage in Los Angeles und zehn Tage in Las Vegas. Nach unserer Rückkehr nach Yale analysierten wir zehn Wochen lang unsere Entdeckungen und präsentierten sie. Zuvor hatten wir, die Autor*innen, Las Vegas mehrmals besucht und „A Significance for A&P Parking Lots, or Learning from Las Vegas" veröffentlicht (Architectural Forum, März 1968). Dieser Artikel bildete die Grundlage für das Forschungsprogramm, das wir im Sommer 1968 entwickelten.[2]

FROM ROME
VON ROM NACH L

"Durch Las Vegas führt die Nationalstrasse 91, der Archetypus eines kommerziellen Strips in seiner reinsten und intensivsten Ausprägung. Wir glauben, dass die sorgfältige Dokumentation und Analyse seiner physischen Form für Architekt*innen und Stadtplaner*innen heute genauso wichtig ist wie das Studium des mittelalterlichen Europas, des antiken Roms und Griechenlands für frühere Generationen. So eine Studie wird dazu beitragen, einen neuen Typus von urbaner Form zu definieren, der in Nordamerika und Europa entsteht und sich grundlegend von allem unterscheidet, was wir bis jetzt kennen; auf den wir bislang schlecht vorbereitet waren und den wir bislang aus Unwissenheit heraus Zersiedelung nannten. Ziel des Studios ist es, durch aufgeschlossene und vorurteilslose Untersuchung ein Verständnis dieser neuen Form erlangen und Techniken zu entwickeln, um mit ihr umzugehen."[1]

What Did We Do?
The teams took slides and made several films of the Strip and Fremont Street. They also collected base maps, aerial photographs and publicity material about Las Vegas and the different hotels and casinos. To note change and permanence in the city, they gathered early photographs and made tape recordings of the memories of old-timers. They also recorded the views of planning officials on zoning and other regulations for the Strip. We visited the Young Electric Sign Co. plant, interviewed people there, and got from the Aladdin Sign designer a detailed description of his design philosophy.[?]

Was Haben Wir Gemacht?
Die Teams machten Dias und drehten mehrere Filme vom Strip und der Fremont Street. Weiters sammelten sie Kartenmaterial, Luftaufnahmen und Werbematerial über Las Vegas und die verschiedenen Hotels und Casinos. Um die Veränderung und Permanenz der Stadt zu dokumentieren, sammelten sie alte Fotos und machten Interviews mit langjährigen Einwohner*innen. Sie interviewten Planungsbeamt*innen über Flächennutzungs- und Bebauungsvorschriften für den Strip. Wir besuchten das Werk von Young Electric Sign Co., interviewten die Mitarbeiter*innen und erhielten vom Gestalter des Aladdin-Schildes eine detaillierte Beschreibung seiner Designphilosophie.[?]

Quite Unsuccessful
Ziemlich Erfolglos
Our attempts to find statistical information about the life of the city, its linkages and activity patterns were quite unsuccessful. Questions about land values brought forth the answer, "If you had that information, you would be the most powerful person in Las Vegas". We could not take photographs inside the casinos, and our one attempt to tape record inside a casino ended with the words "Get that guy". Our efforts to document how people used the Strip through tracking studies foundered on our inability to design studies we could perform.

Following people by car, riding with them in buses, and attempting to interview in their cars produced little information and several mishaps. Finally, we simply stationed students at the entries of several casinos, to observe which entrances cars used and where they parked in relation to the signs.[?]

Unsere Versuche, statistische Informationen über das Leben in der Stadt, über Verflechtungen und Aktivitätsmuster zu finden, verliefen ziemlich erfolglos. Fragen zu Grundstückspreisen wurden mit „Alle, die diese Informationen hätten, wären die mächtigste Person in Las Vegas" beantwortet. In den Casinos durften wir nicht fotografieren und bei unserem einzigen Versuch mit Tonbandaufnahmen im Casino wurden wir sofort aufgefordert, die Aufnahme zu stoppen. Unsere Bemühungen mittels Tracking Studies zu dokumentieren, wie die Menschen den Strip nutzten, scheiterten an unserer Unfähigkeit, das durchführbare Studie zu entwerfen.

Menschen mit dem Auto nachzufahren, mit ihnen im Bus zu sitzen oder Autoinsassen zu interviewen, brachte wenig Informationen und führte zu einigen Pannen. Schließlich positionierten wir die Student*innen an den Eingängen mehrerer Casinos an zu beobachten, welche Eingänge Autos benutzen und wo sie in Relation zu den Schildern parkten.[?]

DIRECTIONAL SPACE

SPACE SCALE SPEED SYMBOL

What Did You L

When asked, "What did you learn from Las Vegas?" a boss for an answer: An early reply was: "What did I learn from..."

"Architects, bar o be diehards, are coming to realize learned from Las Vegas, and what they by implicate too, is not to place neon signs on the Champs Elys "2 + 2 = 4" you the rest of the Mathematics Building, assess the role of symbolism in architecture, and, in learn a new receptivity to the tastes and values of other see modesty in our designs and in our perception as tools in society."

Today young architects are returning to these topics persons and graciousness weren't inherent. What replying from Las Vegas was in part a social tract, they in to be kidding: "It's antisocial!" But this generation the book carries a social message and responds to political movements of the 1960s.[?]

Learning from Las Vegas
Studio (1968)   Book 1st Ed (1972)   Book 2nd Ed (1977)   Book 1st Ed Facsimile (2017)

Up and Down Downtown

58. 1968

Las Vegas by day and night, ground and air, via analytic drawings (above) and sign design sketches (right)

Up and Down, Downtown

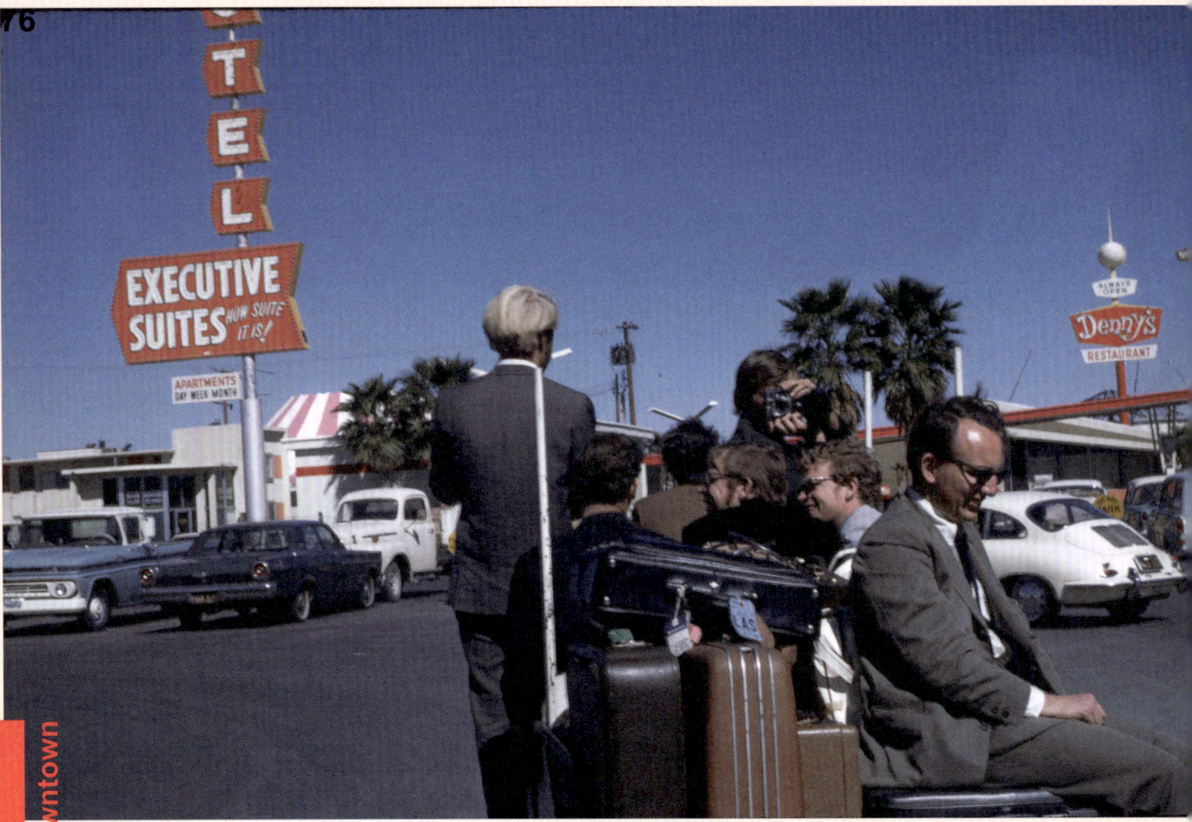
EXECUTIVE
SUITES
HOW SUITE IT IS!
APARTMENTS
DAY WEEK MONTH
ALWAYS OPEN
Denny's
RESTAURANT

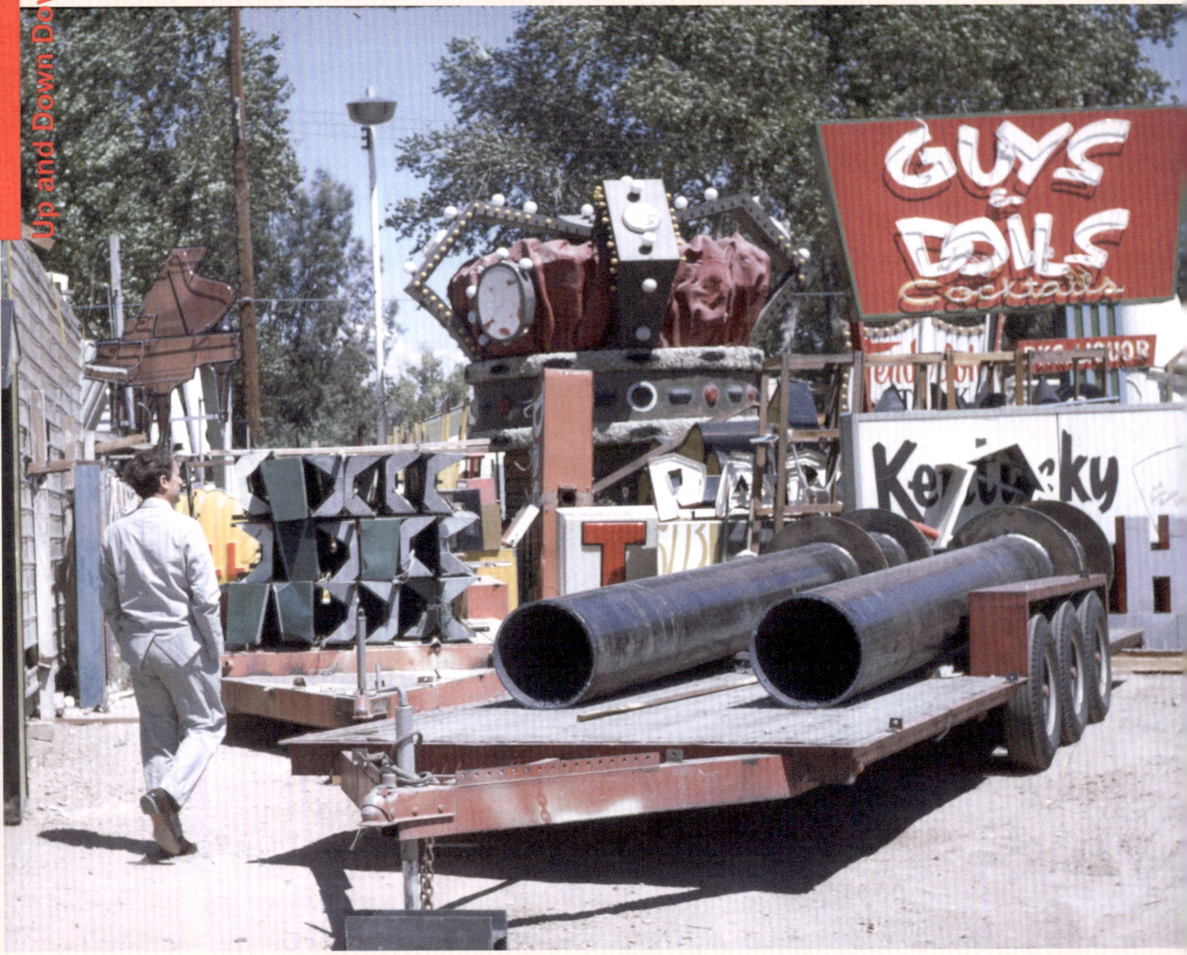
GUYS
&
DOLLS
Cocktails

59. 1968

Opposite page:
Traveling and signs

This page:
Documenting the auto city

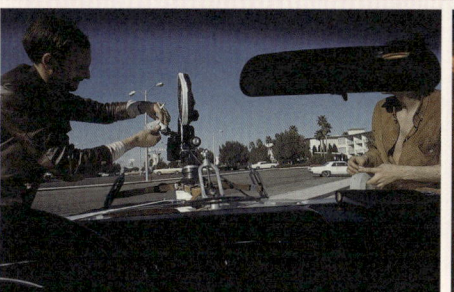

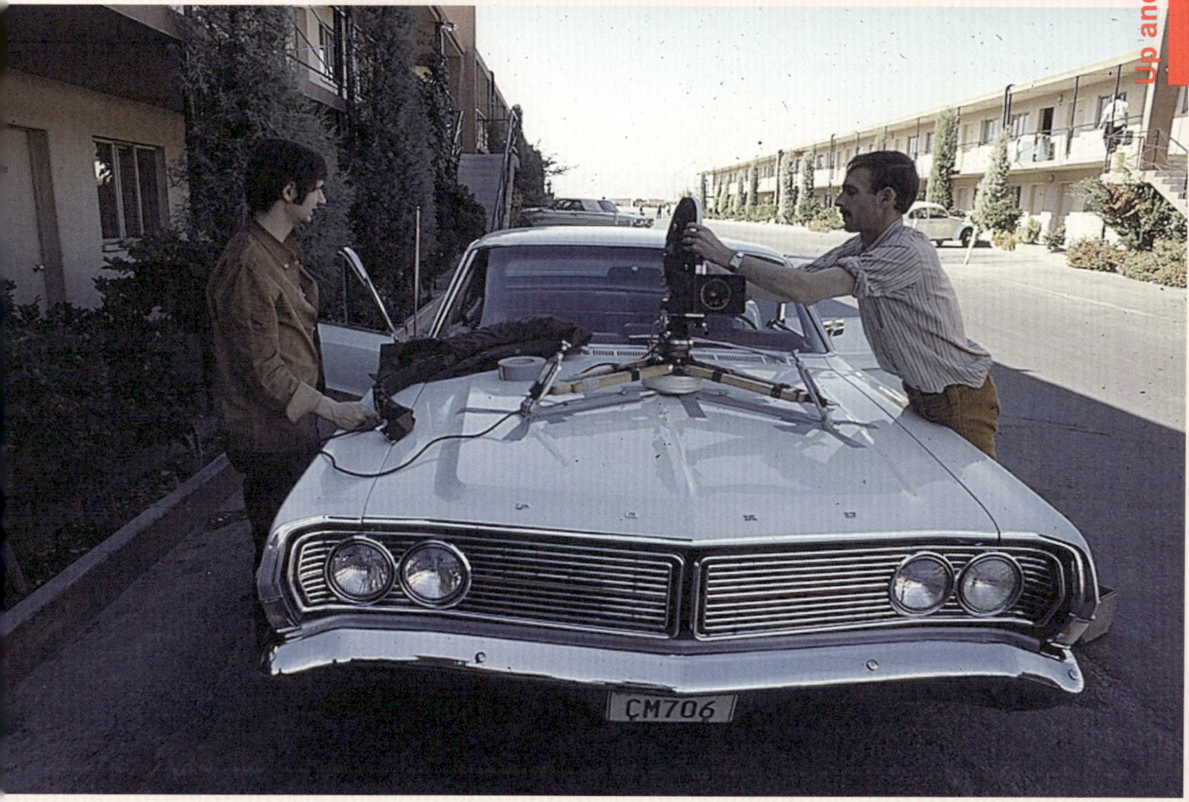

Up and Down Downtown

The Pad Lab

What Does This Room Need?

"How about Batman?"

What a groovy pad, man! Look at all this kooky stuff! Here at the far-out far end of Downtown you'll flip your lid to see this storefront jam-packed crazy with the hippest off-the-wall doo-dads, gewgaws, and bric-a-brac. Like wow!

Denise and Bob treat their home like a laboratory – experimenting with pattern, iconography, and organization. They're also designers of mugs and plates and silverware and earrings and fabrics and tea sets and cuckoo clocks. Bob is lead designer for most of their decorative arts – "about 70% / 30%," Denise says – but like all of their work together, these objects are based on ideas that Bob and Denise develop and share together. Now that their home is also a home office, Denise talks about the kooky way she designed for the change.

When we retired and created a new office in our house, I wondered: how am I going to get people comfortable in living room furniture? I said, I'm going to buy 15 pillows and 15 pillowcases. Now, what are they? They are very small, but 15 together suggest a *region*. They suggest a much bigger scale than their size. Very simple and rather cheap. Then I said, their design can't be Art Nouveau and it can't quite be *not* Art Nouveau, and it must have some scale differences and color differences. Charlette [Caldwell] said, "How about **Batman**?" And so we go to the catalogues and look at little boys' sheeting and there's Batman. Why Batman? Because it's Art Deco and Pop Culture – and I think it's beautiful. It achieves a sense of scale, comfort, flexibility, and welcome – and fun altogether.

60. "Batman" pillows, 2018

61. "Flower" place setting, 1984

62. "Grandmother" pattern bedding

PAD LAB

SCOTT BROWN & VENTURI

The Pad Lab

SEIT 1960

LIKE MANY ARCHITECTS, WE MADE OUR "PAD" OUR LAB¹
WIE VIELE ARCHITEKT*INNEN MACHTEN WIR UNSER WOHNZIMMER ZUM ARBEITSRAUM.¹

Up and Down Downtown

Desire Lines

Urbanism in Practice

I often think: how do you help form communities whose interdependencies are there, visible, appreciated, and lead to loving relationships?

The sign above this old shuttered shop reads "Desire Lines," but it's been closed for so long no one quite knows what was sold there. Still, the windows are amazing: a time capsule of evocative photos revealing cities and landscapes that span the globe.

Denise's urban planning practice began as activism and grew into planning for colleges and universities. At the outset of her planning career in 1969, Denise helped defeat plans for a new crosstown expressway that would have destroyed Philadelphia's vibrant South Street. In 1978, she crafted a plan to revitalize Washington Avenue in Miami Beach. And in 2005 as her last planning project, she worked with Tsinghua University in Beijing, China, to recommend ways its campus should evolve and become more student-friendly.

Philadelphia's South Street starts on the banks of the Delaware and heads west. Early settlers lived on the banks of the river. If you look where Philadelphia's immigration offices were, where the boats landed, it was on the banks at South Street. In parallel along South Street and Market Street were the traders, Italians and later blacks and Jews and Irish. When **Robert Scott Brown** and I got to Philadelphia, we saw a charming enclave just before the South Street Bridge, and there were some old people in aprons sitting on the steps, and they said, "Where y' folks from?" We said, "We come from a very long way away. We come from Africa." And they said, "We reckoned from yer accent youse from out of town." Then they went on to say, oh you don't want to go down that area, that's a very bad area. Of course, they meant where the black people lived. And we asked ourselves, are we in South Africa? I knew I was coming to a complex country but it really surprised me.

63. "Ruscha" street elevation photo montages of South Street, Philadelphia, 1969

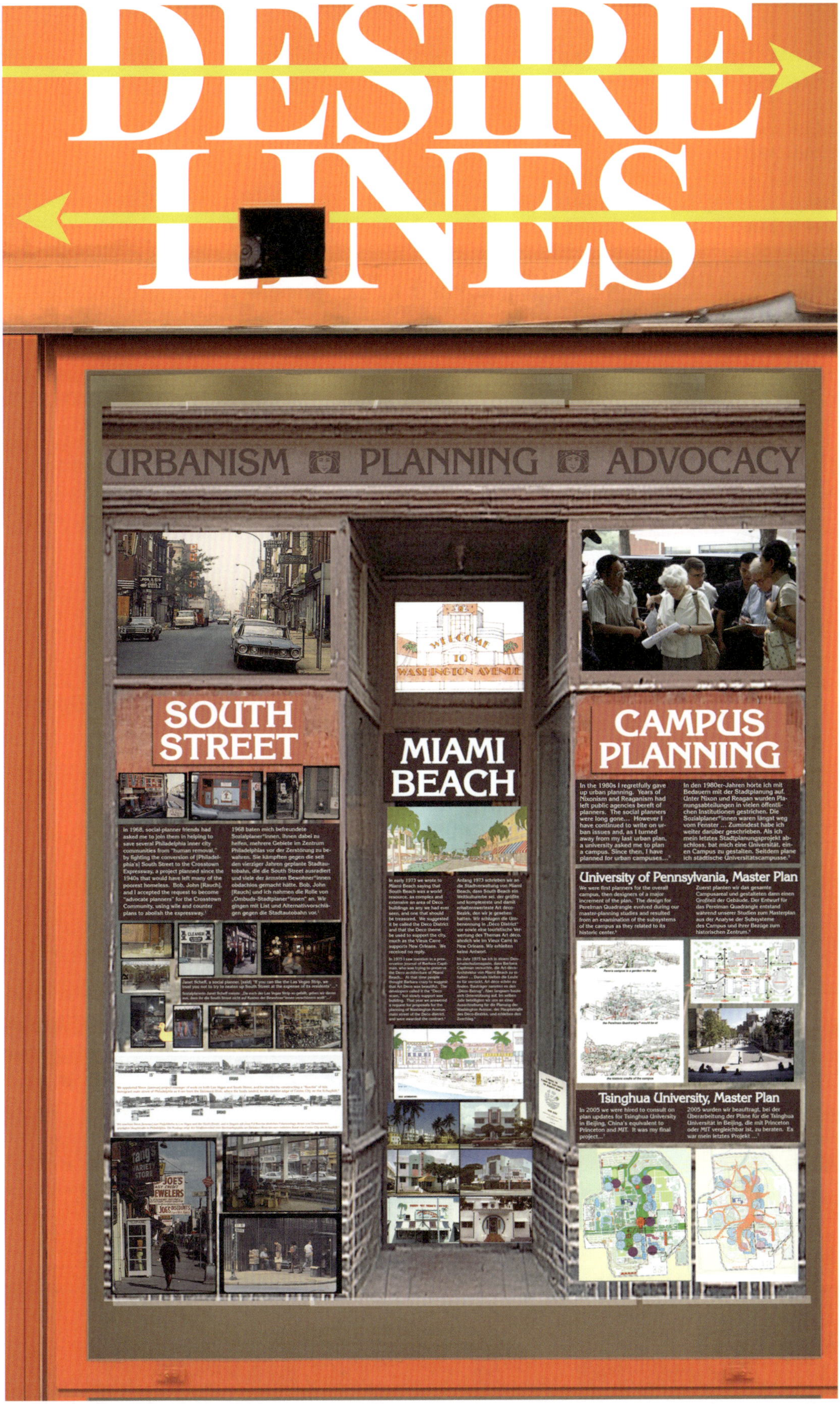
DESIRE LINES
URBANISM PLANNING ADVOCACY
SOUTH STREET
In 1968, social-planner friends had asked me to join them in helping to save several Philadelphia inner city communities from "human removal," by fighting the conversion of [Philadelphia's] South Street to the Crosstown Expressway, a project planned since the 1940s that would have left many of the poorest homeless. Bob, John [Rauch], and I accepted the request to become "advocate planners" for the Crosstown Community, using wile and counter plans to abolish the expressway.[1]
1968 baten mich befreundete Sozialplaner*innen, ihnen dabei zu helfen, mehrere Gebiete im Zentrum Philadelphias vor der Zerstörung zu bewahren. Sie kämpften gegen die seit den vierziger Jahren geplante Stadtautobahn, die die South Street ausradiert und viele der ärmsten Bewohner*innen obdachlos gemacht hätte. Bob, John [Rauch] und ich nahmen die Rolle von „Ombuds-Stadtplaner*innen" an. Wir gingen mit List und Alternativvorschlägen gegen die Stadtautobahn vor.[1]
CLEANER
JOE'S JEWELERS
MIAMI BEACH
WELCOME TO WASHINGTON AVENUE
In early 1973 we wrote to Miami Beach saying that South Beach was a world resource, as complex and extensive an area of Deco buildings as any we had ever seen, and one that should be treasured. We suggested it be called the Deco District and that the Deco theme be used to support the city, much as the Vieux Carre supports New Orleans. We received no reply.
Anfang 1973 schrieben wir an die Stadtverwaltung von Miami Beach, dass South Beach ein Weltkulturerbe sei, der größte und komplexeste und damit erhaltenswerteste Art deco-Bezirk, den wir je gesehen hatten. Wir schlugen die Umbenennung in „Deco District" vor sowie eine touristische Verwertung des Themas Art deco, ähnlich wie im Vieux Carré in New Orleans. Wir erhielten keine Antwort.
CAMPUS PLANNING
In the 1980s I regretfully gave up urban planning. Years of Nixonism and Reaganism had left public agencies bereft of planners. The social planners were long gone... However I have continued to write on urban issues and, as I turned away from my last urban plan, a university asked me to plan a campus. Since then, I have planned for urban campuses...[5]
In den 1980er-Jahren hörte ich mit Bedauern mit der Stadtplanung auf. Unter Nixon und Reagan wurden Planungsabteilungen in vielen öffentlichen Institutionen gestrichen. Die Sozialplaner*innen waren längst weg vom Fenster ... Zumindest habe ich weiter darüber geschrieben. Als ich mein letztes Stadtplanungsprojekt abschloss, bat mich eine Universität, einen Campus zu gestalten. Seitdem plane ich städtische Universitätscampusse.[5]
University of Pennsylvania, Master Plan
We were first planners for the overall campus, then designers of a major increment of the plan. The design for Perelman Quadrangle evolved during our master-planning studies and resulted from an examination of the subsystems of the campus as they related to its historic center.[6]
Zuerst planten wir das gesamte Campusareal und gestalteten dann einen Großteil der Gebäude. Der Entwurf für das Perelman Quadrangle entstand während unserer Studien zum Masterplan aus der Analyse der Subsysteme des Campus und ihrer Bezüge zum historischen Zentrum.[6]
Tsinghua University, Master Plan
In 2005 we were hired to consult on plan updates for Tsinghua University in Beijing, China's equivalent to Princeton and MIT. It was my final project...[7]
2005 wurden wir beauftragt, bei der Überarbeitung der Pläne für die Tsinghua Universität in Beijing, die mit Princeton oder MIT vergleichbar ist, zu beraten. Es war mein letztes Projekt ...[7]

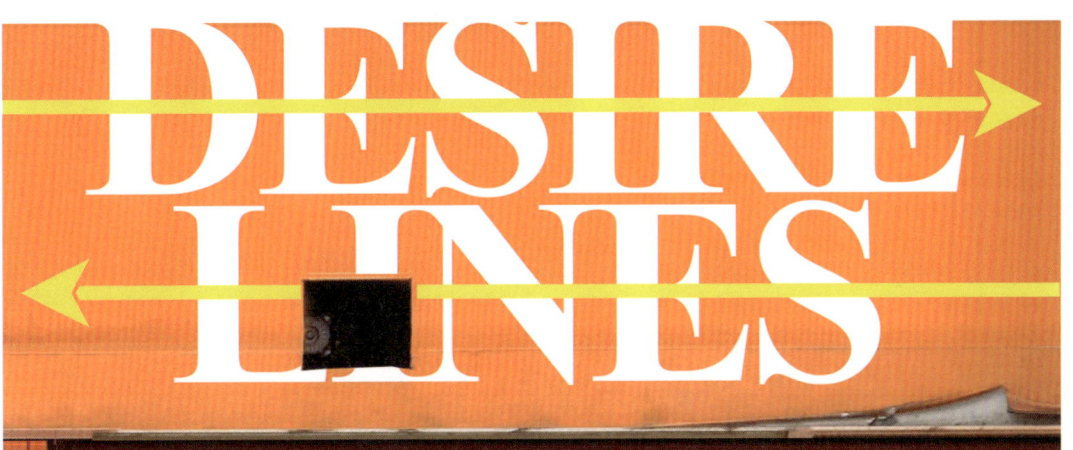

South Street communities were like beads on a string, ending in Grey's Ferry with Irish people. Well, everyone hated everyone – and I loved them all. One community was called The Forgotten Community: low-income black people at the end of South Street backed up against an Italian community. And they said, "No one ever thinks of us!" Everyone thinks of Bella Vista and they don't realize that there's a Forgotten Community on the riverfront.

When you put them together, they all had middle class value systems. I never found anything other than that. The only difference was, the white people didn't want the black people there. Now I had to exist within that, but they had a joint need that made them live and work together. You see it in other situations: if there's a catastrophe, people regardless of color are friends with each other. I often think: how do you help form communities whose interdependencies are there, visible, appreciated, and lead to loving relationships?

Crosstown Community Plan
64. South Street, Philadelphia, Pennsylvania (1970)

Up and Down Downtown

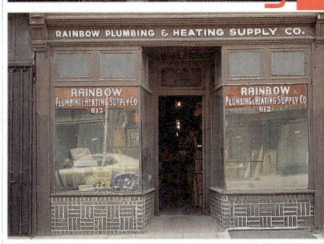

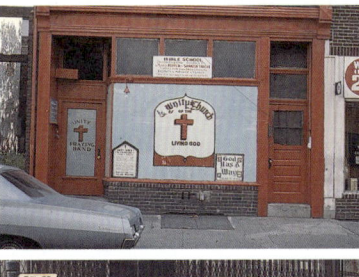

In 1972 I went to **Miami Beach** with Bob and we discovered South Beach: all Art Deco Cubist, small hotels in pastel colors, shapes like portholes and boomerangs, sunbursts. We wrote to the head of the Miami American Institute of Architects to say how very unique it was, in America and the world. We heard nothing. Then I read in *Preservation News* about the Miami Design Preservation League and **Barbara Capitman** who formed it, and she and I became fast friends. Well, three years later we submitted a proposal to replan part of South Beach and we gave it a name, the Deco District, akin to the Vieux Carré in New Orleans. Bisecting it was Washington Avenue, which was lined with discount outlets and convenience and cheap restaurants. Cuban supermarkets next to Kosher butchers, tawdry but vital. We recommended how to conserve the Deco but evolve, but critics called it the "Deco scam," they thought it threatened their economy. Afterward I saw the Deco District on TV: *Miami Vice*. Barbara Capitman was their design advisor!

POLICY RECOMMENDATIONS

Washington Avenue Corridor Project
City of Miami Beach, Florida

Washington Avenue Plan
65. Miami Beach, Florida (1978)

Up and Down Downtown

When I took Chinese administrators from **Tsinghua University** to see American campuses, particularly Princeton, they were very interested in how students use the landscape for studying. They realized that their laws, which kept people off the grass, made good grass but maybe not good education. They asked, what is the purpose of students all over the grass? I said, look there: students reading, students studying, writing, finding happy places to work.

Up and Down Downtown

Tsinghua's campus

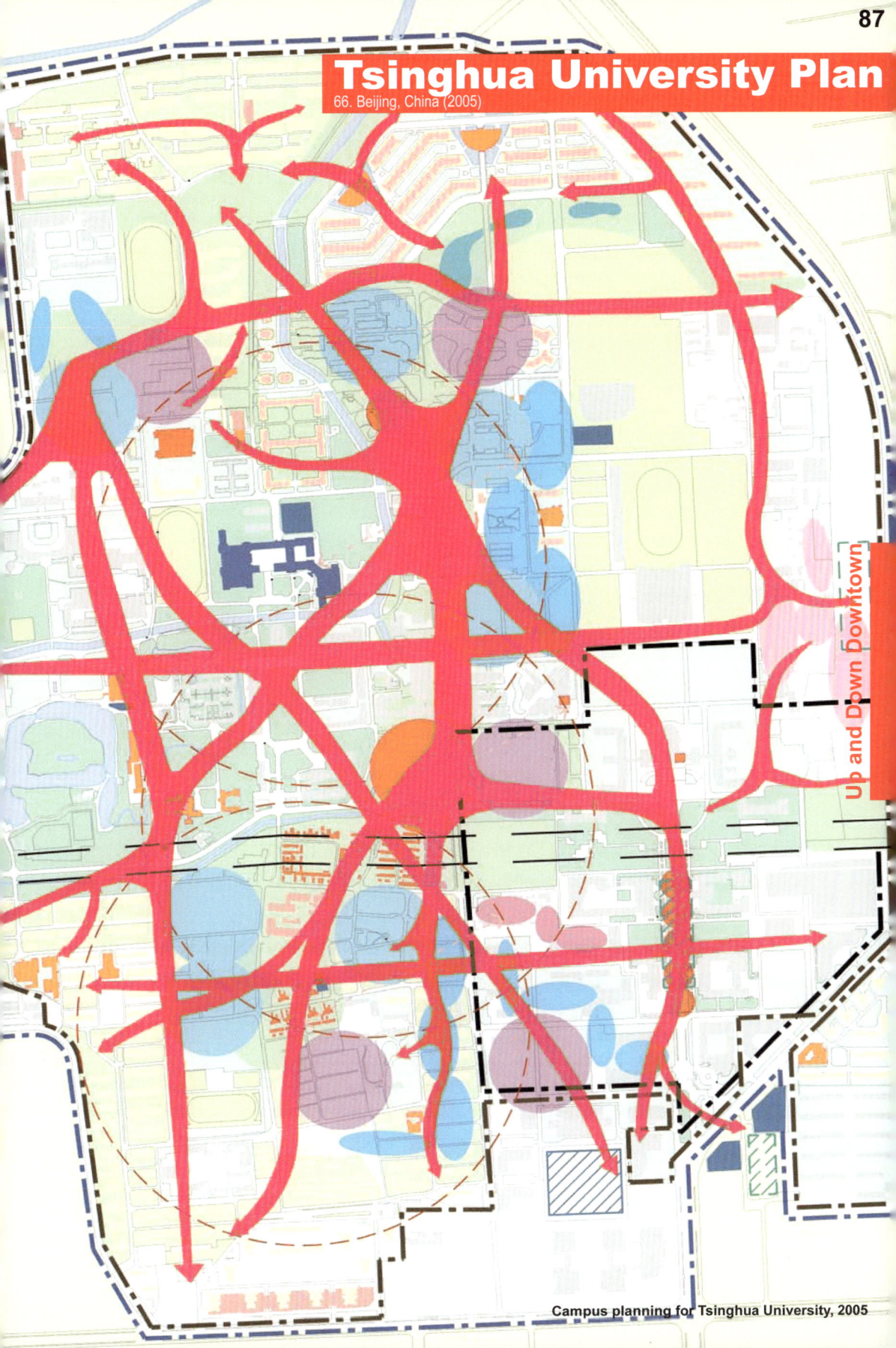

Tsinghua University Plan
66. Beijing, China (2005)

Up and Down Downtown

Campus planning for Tsinghua University, 2005

Kleine Big Ideas

Functionalism, Meet Mannerism

I see the beauty available through functionalism. Once you've followed all the rules and you've followed the truth of the machine -- and you don't take it to ridiculous lengths -- you see the challenge of bringing all systems together.

Everyone knows the best presents come in tiny packages. And you can't judge a book by its cover. And less is more. (Well maybe not that last one.) But what we're trying to say is: don't miss this little shop!

Denise and Bob have promulgated ideas spanning Mannerism, iconography, the duck and decorated shed, the vernacular, and much more. Through friendly humanistic approaches and without heavy-handed manifestoes, they've helped to instigate a sea-change in architecture and urbanism, restoring a freedom of expression lost in late Modernism. This impact radiates beyond into the arts, academic pedagogy, and countless other disciplines. Here, Denise reflects on her conceptions of functionalism and communication and how they evolved.

Functionalism: The first rule of Modernism is to accept all of these systems. Our second rule is to accept one new function, which belongs there and the early Moderns didn't think of: **communication**.

Now when you have all these systems and all their functions and all their rules, the only way of finding an optimum combination is by understanding *Mannerism*. Because you have to bend all of those systems, some more and some less, to get something that works – but it's also a very good way to look for beauty. It may be an unusual beauty and you may hate it at first; **Lou [Kahn]** says you hate it and you hate it until you love it because it's the way it's got to be.

That's my view of functionalism. It has a moral component which I uphold but it has an aesthetic component which I love.

What I can't stand is people saying it's functionalist and using that as an excuse for doing something they like the look of. Starting in the 1950s, I begin to get very mad at people for making things *look* functional when they're not. People kidded themselves into thinking that what they produced was functional, when really what they produced just looked Cubist – a nasty image of false functionalism.

67. "The Function of a Table":
Denise's students explore the use and symbolism of a table to show how diverse "functionality" really is.

Up and Down Downtown

I'd been taking photographs of High Street in London as well as factories. I was always disappointed that factory buildings in America had decoration on them. What a shame! I found the one that didn't: it looked like blocks of ice, very Cubist. Modern buildings were trying to look Cubist. Bob points out that some of the articulations mean nothing, have no functional reasons, even when you do them at the size of the building.

And then you start to think about change over time. Everyone in Europe was talking about, how do you deal with *change*? **Ernő Goldfinger** said to me around 1955, "I don't believe in functionalism because the functions *change*..." Kevin Lynch wrote "Environmental Adaptability," showing six different ways that buildings can change and the costs of change. **Dave Crane** gave it to us to read. And then you have the **glove and mitten** analogy, and you can't build it like a glove. So I began to realize you need to think about functional needs of change.

So you put all that together and all these little things that make a factory look delightfully Cubist don't work. Before the building is even finished its activities change, very common in a commercial building.

Then I began to look at where decoration *was* on some of these buildings – at first thinking, *they would be so wonderful if they didn't have it*. I thought, they're very changeable buildings so they're better than *imitation* Modern buildings. These are more functional.

And I remember Auguste Perret saying, "Decoration always hides a fault in construction." When you think of woodwork, and wood is going to shrink, and traditional woodwork leaves gaps and uses separate panels so parts can move a little and the whole thing doesn't crack up. Inevitably there will be fault – not because of you, but because wood shrinks. So you put decorative pieces over those gaps: that seems very functional to me. And then you think of roof eaves, where something that looks like decoration actually moves water away from the edge. So when Perret said it always hides a fault in construction – I didn't take it as a fault anymore.

If you're a craftsperson, you make things beautiful, you make things you love. If you're a Machine Age person, you get that joy but in different ways: maybe by making things shiny and flat – *extra* shiny and flat – but you still have to know about the tolerances you have to evolve between concrete columns and window frames – and that gives you a place for adding joy in the system.

And so I began to ask: where are they putting that decoration? They're putting it at a column's capital where it joins to a beam, or over a front door.

My father did a building in Johannesburg whose façade was a grid; he was very much in love with vertical window patterns in office buildings. I learned a lot from looking at them and thinking, "What *should* he do?" He produced a building where a window is straight above the doorway – it looks like a double doorway, very big and monumental. I said, well to hell with that! That's terrible! But now I would be apt to say, you *do* need to know where the doorway is, that *is* a communication device (though it doesn't have to be quite as gross as his was…).

68. Tastykake factory, Philadelphia, 2000s

69. Robert Venturi's sketch of palazzo forms

STROZZI   FARNESE

Up and Down Downtown

70. The glove and the mitten, early 200s

(He was very scornful of ESCOM House, which was built by all [University of the Witwatersrand] School of Architecture faculty – a beautiful Deco building. He says: "They made the corridors *much* too wide! And they took the stores off the level of the street!" Well sure enough, it was eventually demolished. He was probably right.)

Communication: The Modernists did have a form of communication and it still holds: the information that comes out of perceiving city physics. As you move through a city, you read density increasing and you know you're getting near the center. You read the physiognomy of different elevations: this one must be a hospital, this one an office. And then finally signage.

Bob and I wrote about the *meaning*, what you *understand* – signage and communication, forms in relation, messy vitality, impurity, mixed communications, scale differences. I first wrote about the broader elements.

But when Bob started to include communication on buildings I was horrified. I'd been taught you don't decorate buildings. And at the time he wasn't choosing the best way to do it, but it was the only way he could get to from his background. As he got to know more, he didn't need to stick little bits of wood on: every few years you need to take that arch off the **Vanna Venturi House** and put a new one on, it doesn't last so well.

> When Bob started to include communication on buildings I was horrified.

Outside Functionalism: The same way you learn to make relationships between rooms, there are many relationships outside the front door – which don't just have to do with aesthetics.

You go from this building you're designing and ask: what about the next building? If it's got a coffee shop, your people are going to be going there. What does that mean for you? What else can you be doing in your two buildings to link them? And then you get this idea of serendipitous meeting: if you make places where people can gather at the meeting of circulation routes, you will get interdisciplinary thinking. In labs we make the meeting place where vertical circulation meets the corridor. What use can you make there for interdisciplinary purposes? So when you get off on a floor other than your own and you go to the coffee lounge, you get talking with someone, maybe some new principle will come out of that? Life sciences love that idea and a lot of people are doing it now; I like to think I had something to do with starting that a long time ago.

It's part of a social-ethic for campuses.

71. North Penn Visiting Nurses Association, Ambler, Pennsylvania, 1962

72. Guild House, Philadelphia, built 1963, photo 2009

Deep Wörter

Pedagogy?

Architects didn't know the word.

"There's more to life than books, you know," sings Morrissey, "but not much more." This superb façade is a Downtown jewel, a gleaming gateway to a library of architectural books. And why not take some home with you?: several of Denise's publications are available at the Venturi Fruit and Produce Marketplace beside Café Nkana.

Denise and Bob are prolific and joyful writers. Many of their books are co-authored, allowing them to explore shared ideas from slightly different perspectives. Denise's own works include hundreds of books and articles, ranging from the intense disquisitions and case studies of Urban Concepts *to her diverse collected essays,* **Having Words**. *Like her planning and design, all her writings have a personable, human-sized quality, opening them to all readers.*

I've written a great deal about pedagogy and one of the first places was **Urban Concepts**. I use the word "pedagogy," which planners use when they're talking about teaching and particularly about studio; architects didn't know the word. I've written "Studio: Architecture's Gift to Academia"; there are many places I've written about architecture and I'd like to bring them together as a book of essays.

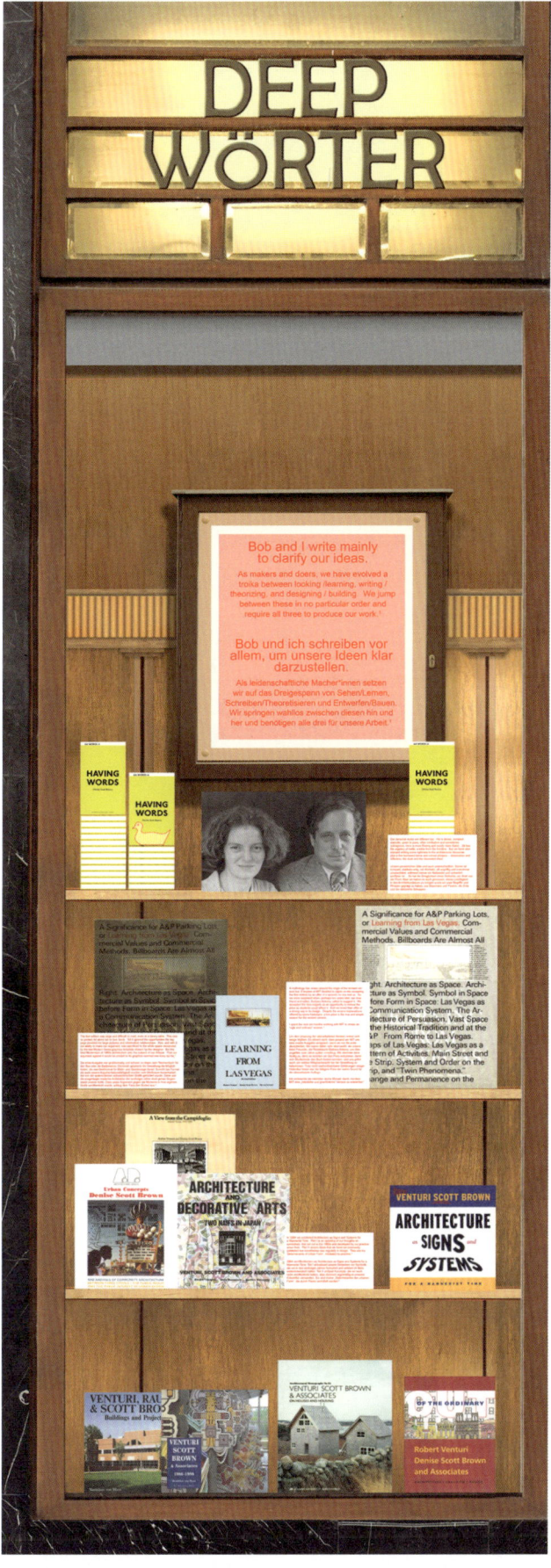

Up and Down Downtown

Manierismuseum

How to Bend the Rules

They used to say, Mannerism is just rich architects who are bored with the rules and breaking the rules. But then we began to say: look, we live in a complex society and *everyone's* going to break rules. When you put the systems of a city together, they clash.

Set among Downtown's predominantly 20th century storefronts, this imposing 18th century Baroque façade is home to Downtown's Manierismuseum, the Museum of Mannerism. Posters advertise current and upcoming exhibitions.

Denise and Bob have been called founders of "postmodernism" in architecture, but that isn't a term they would apply to their design philosophy. "Mannerism" was a 16th century art movement known for eccentricity and rule-breaking. While Denise and Bob certainly bend architectural rules, their Mannerism is also much more: it's an ethical approach to resolving conflict in a complex world. Here Denise articulates the basis for her approach while reminiscing about its 20th century origins and secret history.

If you're Mannerist, you love things that bend rules and clash with each other. In real life, things *need* to clash with each other. **Messy vitality** makes a city. But that doesn't mean you go out looking to create that; you go out looking for an opportunity to do the right thing, the thing that brings everything together, and if at first it looks ugly you look on that as an opportunity to see what beauty you can draw from it.

Rem [Koolhaas] works at the outskirts of the IIT campus where the railroad goes – and he puts the [McCormick Tribune] campus center there. He creatively puts the computer arcade under where the trains go, so the noise of student life goes with the noise of the trains and augments the atmosphere. And he uses what I call Take No Prisoners Materials, the kinds of materials you'd find in train stations and bathrooms.

They used to say, Mannerism is just rich architects who are bored with the rules and breaking the rules. But then we began to say: look, we live in a complex society and *everyone's* going to break rules. When you put the systems of a city together, they clash. Look at the train route from Philadelphia to New York: clashing systems all through that marshland – that's the playground of the gods. It's Saturday night on Mount Olympus! Everything falling over. And in that clashing of systems, I find Mannerism.

Mannerism was an art movement in the 16th century. It was called a movement of neurosis: only people with multiple problems liked that ugly rule-breaking. So it was pushed aside. Then, in the 1940s, **Nikolaus Pevsner** – a Germany-Jewish art historian who fled to England and became a Cambridge professor – he kind of resuscitated it. He wrote *The Englishness of English Art*. **Robin [Middleton]** came to be his student: Pevsner had visited South Africa and met Robin and thought he would be a bright student. Robin was working for an architect; he was one of the brightest architects I'd ever come across and he dropped the practice. So he went to Cambridge and got a doctorate out of Pevsner. I've seen the letters from Pevsner to Robin, telling him how to go and pip **John Summerson**: "You'll get him this way!" And between the two of them, Pevsner and Summerson resuscitated Mannerism as not the architecture of spoiled brat architects and neurotic architects but as something very vibrant and interesting.

Ten years before Bob discovered Mannerism, Pevsner and Summerson are writing about it, lecturing about it; I sat through Summerson's lectures about it twice. (In parallel, Donald Drew Egbert lectured to Bob two times at Princeton.) The **Smithsons**, someone turned them towards Mannerism, saying: when you're thinking about **New Brutalism**, not the one in **Le Corbusier** but to learn from it, get some help from Mannerism. I'm not sure, but there was a man called [Rudolf]

"**Denise believes in crap!**"

Wittkower, who later ended up at the Warburg Institute in London and ended up in America, and he wrote a book on Mannerism that the Smithsons were reading. Someone gave Bob that book; I suspect it was Jim Gresham. Another book that was very dear to the Smithsons, *The Idea of Space in Greek Architecture*, by a South African named Rex Martienssen – those two books were given to Bob as gifts. I find no evidence that he read them; I couldn't read the Wittkower book myself, but I could read the one by Martienssen. Scully was virulently against that book; he said *he* invented those ideas, who was this other guy?

So Mannerism was very well ensconced in England and the Smithsons made it even more so. We were full of enjoyment of the rule-breaking. Then Bob read [Sigfried] Giedion. Giedion sent young, privileged architects to travel and look at Baroque architecture. And then there was John Winter in England, who called me his best friend for personal reasons, but abhorred what I believe in: he said, "Denise believes in crap!" John said, look, in the 1950s we all believed that everything good came out of America – Ian Hamilton and the International Group and looking at advertising. But there's an Italian named **[Eduardo] Paolozzi** who started that. His Pop Art precedes American Pop Art. (And there's a man called something like Saunders even before that in the '40s.) Bob wouldn't believe me; we had a huge argument. He said, "Of course America started it! And the artists were leading!" and I said, "It's nice to see the artists in America catching up." And finally a book on Paolozzi came out and he saw what I meant. It's not as deep as the American Pop Art, but they stand on his shoulders, and it's very vital, interesting stuff. And Ian Hamilton doing the same thing; he's married to Judith Henderson, who's a sociologist. So now a sociologist begins to introduce Peter Smithson to ideas like those of **Herb Gans**.

Finally something happens with the Smithsons and they depart from Pop Art and they depart from sociology and they become Miesian and less interesting to us. In fact not interesting at all. In fact really hostile to us. Alison Smithson became *extremely* hostile to me and she had been a very good friend to my sister. Peter said, "The sociologists will have to extend their thought before I can work with them," but I know what he meant; you try working with Herb Gans – he's churlish as all get-out!

So anyway, I knew all about that when I met Bob – I'd been fighting with **Paul Davidoff** for two years by the time I'd met Bob and I continued to as he taught the theories course. Now it's very interesting: there was a group of people meeting to discuss curriculum at Penn as I was a student and then when I joined the faculty. They were not architects, they were planners. Bret Harris, for example, had long experience planning things to allow for creativity. And **Dave Crane** knew about such things. So I was listening to

> **In Europe, everyone was using the word "Mannerism"; in America, no one was using it.**

all this and also dealing with the Mannerist side of things when I met Bob at a faculty meeting over the preservation or use of this very Mannerist building [Penn's Fisher Fine Arts Library]. It breaks all the rules and I loved it. I was the only one. I said, "You mustn't demolish it! Paint it white inside and use it." And Bob came up afterward and said, "I agreed with everything you said (except the paint it white part). My name's **Robert Venturi**." And I said, "Why didn't you say something?" We were friends from then. Then Bob, when he got back from **[the American Academy in] Rome**, started to work as an assistant to **Lou [Kahn]**, and he started to share his ideas with Lou. Just two weeks before he left Rome – not before then – he decided Mannerism was for him.

Colin Rowe had been at the English Academy in Rome and lectured frequently. He said, "Denise, you must admit I was Mr. Mannerist of the 1950s." They'd heard him lecture on Mannerism. I think someone heard a talk from Colin Rowe, and Colin had probably discovered Brasini's buildings and said "Let's go on an expedition." So Bob went and saw the Brasini buildings and decided, "This is latter-day Mannerism."

In Europe, everyone was using the word "Mannerism"; in America, no one was using it. That word didn't just come out of Bob. He'll say it did.

Jointkreativität

Ping-Pong

Take a mix of creative people from different backgrounds and put them around a table looking at a design and building on each other's suggestions. I call that ping-pong.

The *Guru*

But sometimes, when they go into public, no one will admit to this joint creativity. Those same architects say, it was all our guru and I stand beside the *guru*.

Here's Downtown's arthouse cinema, Jointkreativität. Films are so complex, you know; the overall team can consist of several thousand people! Jointkreativität honors both stars and crew. Take a moment to read the window posters advertising some of these amazing collaborations.

Denise and Bob were awarded the 2016 Gold Medal by the American Institute of Architects – the first collaborators (and first living woman) to be so recognized – after decades of being denied the right to even apply because only individual applicants were permitted. Beyond the importance of their work, Denise and Bob have brought recognition and celebration to joint collaboration and the diversity of authorship.

Architecture is so complex. The overall team can consist of several thousand people, and it's an economy, and there are so many dimensions, and my joy is to keep all those dimensions in play and related to that physical thing and yet make it beautiful. All of that stuff has to come together and be made beautiful or else you're pushing things under the rug, and when you do that you lose tension. If you think that way, you probably need a little help. You need two people to span everything.

(I look at **Le Corbusier**'s work and I see those very beautiful drawings and I look at his earliest drawings and it's as if his pencil were a nail. I don't think he learned to draw; I think tucked away somewhere there was someone who did drawings for him, and maybe more than drawings for him. And the specialness of it came from two people, though he never admitted it.)

Take a mix of creative people from different backgrounds and put them around a table looking at a design and building on each other's suggestions. I call that **ping-pong**, a ping-pong of ideas. Someone has an idea and one says, here's a terrible idea, but if you take yours and you add it to mine it could come out like this – maybe it comes out looking rather like an Edwardian lady's hat? There's a lot of creativity going on in that ping-pong and in that conclusion (which is all metaphor; the building will come out looking like a building). But the point is, there are two people, three or four people, building an idea – the first person says it's terrible, the second person sees some joy in it, and everyone who gets up from that table has a sense of relation. And it works best when people trust each other and feel they will be welcome. This is a kind of creativity well known in architecture.

JOINTKREATIVITÄT

Robert Venturi
"I think it's one of the luckiest, best things of my life -- working together and coming together."
„Ich glaube, mit [Denise] zusammenzuarbeiten und zusammenzukommen war eines der glücklichsten und besten Dinge in meinem Leben."

Denise Scott Brown
"Being a married couple and partners in work produces maximum possibility for abrasion."[1]
„Verheiratet zu sein und zusammen zu arbeiten, bietet die größtmögliche Reibungsfläche."[1]

Denise Scott Brown
Robert Venturi and I met as faculty members at Penn in 1960 at my first School of Fine Arts faculty meeting, when I made an impassioned plea that the university not tear down the Furness Library,--can you imagine they were considering it?[2]

Robert Venturi
Denise made a beautiful plea. She said, "Yes, we must take a stand, this building should not come down!" Afterwards I went up to her, I had seen her around a lot, of course, but we had not met. I said, "I want to introduce myself, my name is Robert Venturi, and I want to tell you how much I agree with what you just said." And her first words to me were, "Why didn't you say something?" And it's kind of been that way ever since.[3]

Denise Scott Brown
Robert Venturi und ich lernten uns bei meiner ersten Fakultätsversammlung 1960 an der Penn kennen, bei der ich ein leidenschaftliches Plädoyer für den Erhalt der Furness Bibliothek hielt. Kaum zu glauben, dass sie einen Abriss in Betracht zogen![2]

Robert Venturi
Denise hielt ein wunderbares Plädoyer. Sie sagte damals: „Wir müssen Stellung beziehen! Dieses Gebäude darf nicht abgerissen werden!" Danach sprach ich sie an. Ich hatte sie zwar schon öfters gesehen, aber nicht kennengelernt. Ich sagte zu ihr: „Ich heiße Robert Venturi, und ich möchte Ihnen sagen, dass ich ganz Ihrer Meinung bin." Sie antwortete nur: „Und warum haben Sie dann nichts gesagt?" Seitdem läuft es irgendwie immer so zwischen uns.[3]

Bob and I have probably learned as much from each other as from anyone else. And those influences go both ways.[4]

Bob und ich haben wahrscheinlich so viel voneinander gelernt wie von anderen Menschen. Und diese Einflüsse wirken wechselseitig.[4]

Our commonality
had to do with design, architectural and urban, and how we might respond as designers to concerns we held in common -- pluralism, multiculturalism, social activism, symbolism, iconography, impure art, Pop Art, popular culture, the everyday American landscape, Italy, Mannerism, the uses and misuses of history, the uncomfortably direct design solution, and the uncomfortably indirect design solution.[5]

Unsere Herangehensweise
an Architektur und Urbanismus und deren jeweilige Herausforderungen stimmten überein -- Pluralismus, Multikulturalismus, sozialer Aktivismus, Symbolik, Ikonographie, Unreine Kunst, Pop Art, Massenkultur, die amerikanische Alltagskultur, Italien, Manierismus, der Ge- und Missbrauch von Geschichte, beunruhigend direkte und indirekte Entwurfslösungen.[5]

JOINTKREATIV   **JOINTKREATIV**   **JOINTKREATIV**

Up, and Down, and Downtown

When not to collaborate?
Wann sollte man nicht zusammenarbeiten?

"I've learned we shouldn't talk when we're hungry"[6]
„Ich habe festgestellt, dass wir nicht diskutieren sollten, wenn wir Hunger haben."[6]

Bob and I had worked out basic ideas together during our years of collaboration at Penn before Venturi and Rauch, or the Vienna Venturi House, or Complexity and Contradiction existed, and this continued away from the office when we taught. These were all taken to Bob's, and many were. But many were not, including "Venturi's Duck," which was "Denise's Duck" by origin, though Bob's and Denise's by use. Bob and I are two work horses, not a horse and a pony. When we go in tandem we do our best architecture. The burden of these early contretemps turned my thoughts to joint creativity and this is a battle now taken up in the profession.[7]

Bob und ich hatten während unserer jahrelangen Zusammenarbeit auf der Penn gemeinsame Grundsätze erarbeitet, noch vor Venturi und Rauch, vor dem Vienna Venturi House, noch vor Complexity and Contradiction. Das setzten wir auch außerhalb des Büros, im Unterricht fort. Alles wurde Bob zugeschrieben, und vieles stammte auch von ihm. Anderes aber auch nicht, darunter „Venturis Ente", die eigentlich „Denises Ente" ist, aber von Bob und Denise verwendet wurden. Bob und ich sind zwei Arbeitspferde, nicht ein Pferd und ein Pony. Wenn wir im Tandem arbeiten, entsteht unsere beste Architektur. Diese frühe Missachtung war belastend und ich begann über gemeinsame Kreativität nachzudenken – ein Kampf, der in unserer Profession aktuell ausgetragen wird.[7]

It's difficult ... to get architects to believe that an idea can originate and grow through the contribution of two or more minds -- to conceive of the notion of joint creativity. Yet with us, each idea has its antecedents in our shared past. It's hard to say that it originates in one, not the other, because we've been through so much together. We may both think of it at the same time, or one may suggest it and the other see its value and add what makes it important in the design. The original thought may be inappropriate but when capped by a second thought it may become central. Both contributions, plus a ping-pong back and forth, may be needed to make it great.[8]

Es ist schwierig ... Architekt*innen zu überzeugen, dass eine Idee sich aus zwei oder mehreren klugen Köpfen heraus entwickeln kann -- zu verstehen, was gemeinsame Kreativität ist. Bei uns hat jede Idee ihren Ursprung in unserer gemeinsamen Vergangenheit. Schwer zu sagen, ob eine Idee von der einen oder „dem anderen" herrührt, da wir so viel zusammen durchlebt haben. Wir können gleichzeitig denselben Gedanken haben, oder einer von uns macht einen Vorschlag und der andere hält ihn für wertvoll und fügt ein wichtiges Element hinzu. Der ursprüngliche Gedanke mag unpassend sein, wird aber durch eine hinzukommende Idee zum zentralen Element. Es braucht beide Beiträge und ein anschließendes Ping-Pong, um etwas Großartiges zu schaffen.[8]

[T]he American Institute of Architects rethought its stance on collaborators as candidate for the Gold Medal.
Recognizing the evidence for joint creativity in architecture, they debated whether and how to award it without obscuring its worthy focus on design creativity and design leadership... And joy followed when the long list of couples in line for the Medal signaled change for years to come ... More should now be learned about joint creativity and the types of collaboration that produce it. I wish the Pritzkers would help extend thought on this subject by funding an introductory conference...[9]

Das American Institute of Architects hat seine Haltung gegenüber Architekturteams für die Goldmedaille überdacht.
In Anerkennung kreativer Zusammenarbeit diskutierten sie, ob und wie die Auszeichnung vergeben werden kann, ohne den Fokus auf entwerferische und kreative Leitung zu verwässern ... Wir freuten uns über die lange Liste von Paaren, die für die Medaille in Frage kamen und die Wandel, der sich damit für die nächsten Jahre abzeichnet. Es sollte mehr über gemeinsame Kreativität und Formen der Zusammenarbeit gelernt werden. Ich wünschte, die Pritzker-Organisation würde eine Konferenz finanzieren, um dieses Thema auszuloten.[9]

JOINTKREATIV   **JOINTKREATIV**   **JOINTKREATIV**

Mayhew's

Petition Comments

"Denise Scott Brown is my inspiring and equal partner."
- Robert Venturi

"It's the right thing to do"

"It's high time the Pritzker Committee shed its sexism."

"Denise Scott Brown as an equal partner deserves equal recognition."

"The fact that one of the most creative and productive partnerships we have ever seen in architecture was separated rather than celebrated by a prize has been an embarrassing injustice."
- Rem Koolhaas

"1 + 1 > 2"

Mayhew's is a secret Downtown treasure – but unfairly "secret." It's too often overlooked amongst Downtown's other attractions. Help correct this sorry situation: during your visit, spend some time at Mayhew's.

In 1991, Bob Venturi was awarded the Pritzker Prize for work that he and Denise created together. They both objected – but their young firm needed the prize money, so they agreed that Bob would accept but Denise would stay home from the award ceremony in protest. In 1975, Denise wrote an essay cataloging the marginalization of women in architecture, the process by which singular male gurus are manufactured while female architects and collaborators are denigrated, forgotten, and openly attacked. Again to preserve the firm, "Room at the Top? Sexism and the Star System in Architecture" would remain unpublished until 1989. Have things changed? How will they?

All of the things I talk about – the morality, the patterns that make social life, the whole – I say it's a **four-leg table** and you bring the four legs together and they contribute to making a beautiful table. You do all those things; that's design.

That's a very feminine outlook, I think. Saying that this person, that person helped me – that may be a very feminine outlook, while a man may say, "All that came out of me (and I do it for you, my darling)." It's a whole different view of the origin of creativity. And I feel that a women's view is a very useful one – not saying everyone should feel that way.

If you start with the idea, I'm going into architecture and I intend to earn a **Pritzker Prize** – I don't think that's a very productive way. But if you start by searching for your passions, getting to be very good at some things and learning how to support yourself, in an office they will want you for the things you can do. And learning all of that should also make you a good feminist supporter. There's an old feminist who says, *for a woman to do as well as a man in the world she has to be twice as clever and work twice as hard, but luckily this is not difficult*. So if you start this way and get *very good*, showing people all the working drawings they think you can't do (you're just a girl!) and you love it, the thing you love is what they will want to hire you for.

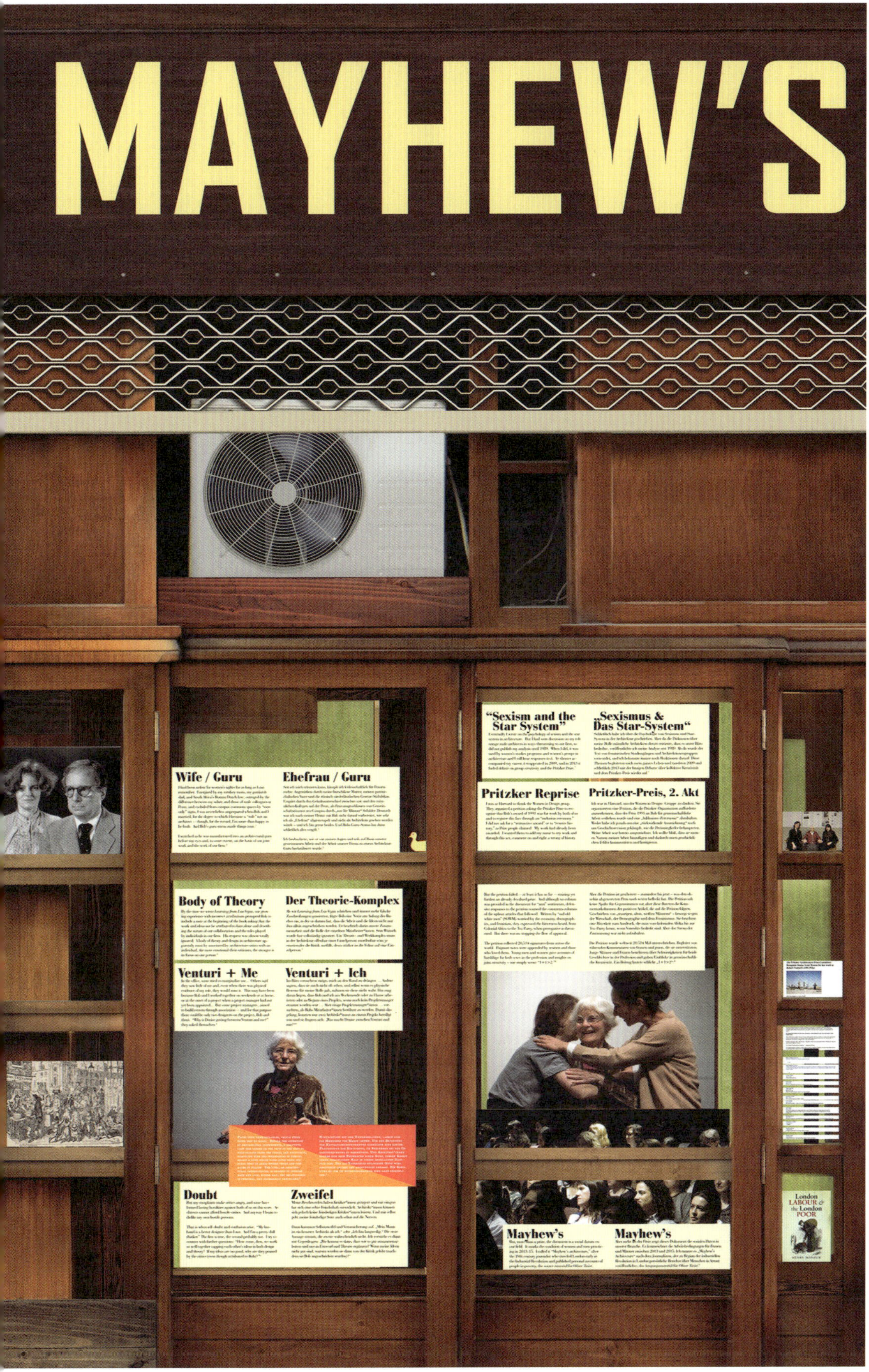
MAYHEW'S
"Sexism and the Star System"
„Sexismus & Das Star-System"
Wife / Guru
Ehefrau / Guru
Pritzker Reprise
Pritzker-Preis, 2. Akt
Body of Theory
Der Theorie-Komplex
Venturi + Me
Venturi + Ich
Doubt
Zweifel
Mayhew's
Mayhew's
London LABOUR & the London POOR

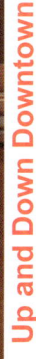

There's a way of not starting with, *oh all the hard things I'm going to have to face*, but rather, *here are the strengths I have – now let's start dealing with this problem*.

Young women who say they don't need feminism, they come out of school, where they're the most equal they'll ever be. And if they keep on that way and don't build their strengths and enjoyments, they'll just fail. And they won't know what hit them when they find there's a glass ceiling.

I was, at some point of my life, suffering from a sense of structurelessness. I think it goes with some form of depression, and I think you'll find the whole line of our family has some form of depression. I don't think I have it now, but at some point I felt very lost, not knowing what was coming next. And I should have been more patient, because now, as I look at my whole career, I see such structure – one part amazingly nesting into the next, one part in Africa, one in England, one in Europe, one in America, and one now – but I didn't see it then and I should have been more hopeful than I was.

And thank goodness I was helped by **Arthur Korn**, and then I got so involved and passionate with New Brutalism that I forgot about things like structurelessness. And I had fun and worked very hard and traveled and met wonderful people – particularly people in Italy who looked at our enthusiasm and remembered their own of the 1930s. They looked at you with love: "You're very young, we had to learn, but we remember when we felt the way you do," big smiles on their faces. Albini said, "Modern architecture was the beacon that supported me all throughout the war"; it was very moving. So we learned something about passion and how it helps you and where you go.

So I say, if anyone has feelings of structurelessness, have patience, because it works itself out. After a presentation one young woman said to me, "I am having those feelings that you were having." And as she started trying to explain, her boyfriend interrupted: "Well, what she actually means is..." And I thought to myself: there's the problem. But then I thought, no, you can't say that aloud: he might be all she has? So I held him by the hand and said: "Look, you're doing a wonderful job and it's really important for her what you're doing, but if you don't let her speak for herself she's never going to find out what she wants." I just hope it helped.

73. With Arielle Assouline-Lichten and Caroline James, Women in Design, Harvard Graduate School of Design, 2013

74. Harvard Graduate School of Design, 2013

P. M. Clock Shop

"Postmodern" versus "PoMo"

I don't think there's a good example of good PoMo.

Nowhere Downtown is more au courant than the P. M. Clock Shop. It carries all manner of timepieces, from historical to modern and beyond.

Bob Venturi is unambiguous: "I am not now nor have I ever been a Postmodernist and I unequivocally disavow fatherhood of this architectural movement." (Note that Denise is never called the mother *of postmodernism; in her marginalization, Denise is rarely even credited with participation in the ideas that critics abhor.) And yet Denise here takes a softer, more nuanced stance, distinguishing between the potential richness of "postmodernism" and the degeneracy of "PoMo."*

I approved of "**postmodernism**" because of its origins in theology. It was very much in line with the social planners and it had been part of the early Modern movement.

I learned in my two-year-old form: life is now completely changed since World War I and the change means we have to produce an architecture that goes with our era – that is true to the machine and true to materials. Based in this new-era thought and away from the wicked ways of the pre-war and Beaux Arts architecture – and that we must make things that fit like a glove to our new lives, our new activities. (In the end, I questioned the "glove" part because it seemed too tight a fit for change over time.)

"**PoMo**," on the other hand, is basically a degradation by architects who don't understand postmodernism. Philip Johnson was a *good* example of *lousy* PoMo. Michael Graves was boilerplate. I don't think there's a good example of good PoMo.

A+ You

On the Sainsbury Wing and Trafalgar Square

Our design spans these influences but in urbanistic ways.

Architecture plus urbanism is the only way to go! This ornate window features a special display of Denise's buildings all around the world – each exemplifying an insightful union of architecture and urbanism.

Denise says, "You have to think of urbanism as well as architecture, and then the ideas will come." All of her projects celebrate the fusion of these two disciplines, revealing a continuity of thought from the economic interests of a region down to a child's needs. The different ways Denise resolves these twin ideas throughout her work reveal her cultural and contextual sensitivity and her inexhaustible imagination.

Up and Down Downtown

The **National Gallery's Sainsbury Wing** is a modern building, but it's also a link in the Classical chain. Trafalgar Square's Classicism, you can see it in its columns and cornice lines, in the National Gallery's porticoes and pilasters. Our design spans these influences but in urbanistic ways. It goes Modern or historical with allusion and Mannerist rule-bending: Palladio and Modernism fight it out on the main façade. Our allusions tie in to Trafalgar Square and adjacent areas, matching in materials, borrowing elements such as Wilkins's columns but in syncopated bunched-up ways. They're jazz not minuet. But both Modern and historical camps weren't happy. The English press accused us of spreading a "vulgar, American, Postmodernist, Mannerist, pastiche" like "slime" over our façade.

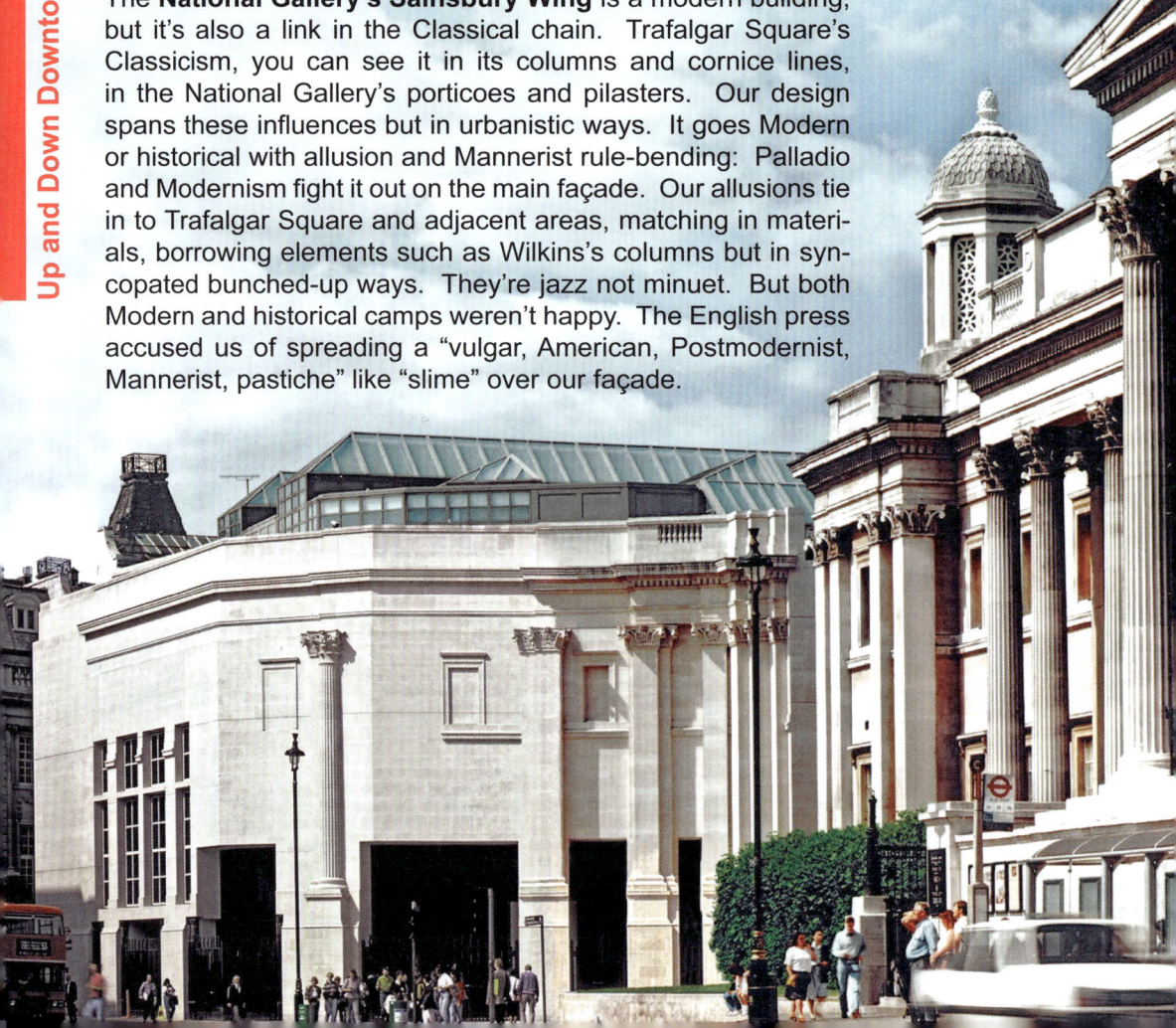

75. National Gallery, London, England, 1991

Up and Down Downtown

Sainsbury Wing, National Gallery
76. London, England (1991)

Up and Down Downtown

Nikko Kirifuri Hotel & Spa
77. Nikko, Japan (1997)

We learned many lessons from Las Vegas. One of the most important was to reassess symbolism and the use of representation and decoration. When we did our **hotel and spa in central Japan**, we made the lobby into a Japanese village street — in depiction, with store windows and signs and banners. These elements of the cultural landscape created a setting that was part Main Street, part museum, part fairytale.

Mielparque Nikko Kirifuri Hotel and Spa, Nikko, Japan, c. 1997 all photos

Up and Down Downtown

Signs of Life, Symbols in the City was our ambitious exhibition for the Smithsonian's Renwick Gallery, going along with the Bicentennial in 1976. It was a *catalogue raisonné* of visual communication. It derived from our "Learning from Las Vegas" and "Learning from Levittown" studios but focused on communication rather than social or pedagogical elements. We wanted to educate and liberate aesthetically but in a fun way, without shaking people by the lapels. At the same we had encyclopedic information to purvey. We wanted a big simple framework to enliven our dense information. Here we had some roadside dinosaurs: a Los Angeles freeway billboard with a California "golden girl" – luscious lips beyond belief – and McDonald's arches – and a "76" gas station ball. This was "The Strip" and it contrasted with "The Street" and "The Home," which focused on suburbia.

"Signs of Life"
78. Renwick Gallery, Smithsonian Institution (1976)

Up and Down Downtown

Up and Down Downtown

79. High Point Cafe, Philadelphia, c. 2017

Food and Drink: Café Nkana

Welcome to Café Nkana! As a satellite of the Architekturzentrum's Wien's Café Corbaci, Café Nkana brings you a delicious selection of drinks and snacks – but with a suitably Denisian spin. Try the Denisuccino, prepared just the way Denise likes at her favorite Philadelphia café. When you arrive Downtown, be sure to stop by Café Nkana and get a treat to take with you as you tour.

What made Denise Scott Brown? What did she "learn from..."? When she says, "I stand on the shoulders of a lot of people," this isn't only humility but also memory and perspective: tracing the elements that composed her. Denise's South African childhood, her family life, and her school years were at turns wondrous, privileged, painful, strange, and occasionally as common as ours.

A Modern life: I became a Modernist at two years old. My mother was a Modernist: I was born from a Modernist and I accepted the dogma. I have a visual memory of a blue paper with white lines...

As a child, what did you think about America?

Magic.

Magic...

I looked at America as Coney Island.

Up and Down Downtown

80. Denise about two years old, c. 1933

English upbringing: I very much had an English upbringing. I was born British. My mother was British. My grandmother and grandfather were naturalized British citizens. Teachers in my school were mostly from England. I was alive during the coronation of George VI and somewhat present during the abdication of Edward VIII; I knew the meaning of the word "Morganatic" at the age of four. English ceremony was a part of my life – as well as bar mitzvahs and all of that. My grandmother used to say, "You children must go *home* to England," and we understood that was the unnecessary snobbery of my grandmother. I felt myself to be totally rusticated in South Africa, far away from all the things that interested me, though arguably I was leading a richer life than many.

Family business: **Nkana** was a mine in Rhodesia and later a town. Parts of Rhodesia had little towns, a synagogue in each town, pretty little synagogues all bolted up now. In our town my dad had a concessions store on the mine. Most of its clientele were black mine workers. He had worked in a store in Johannesburg with a poor black miner clientele, so he learned to sell to them and he learned to give people good bargains. He said he managed to give them half the price charged in the regular retail stores and still do himself a better favor than when he was working in Johannesburg. (He was a clever little...)

And also there was a kind of zest in it. The British may have a law system there that's not going to help a small Jewish merchant very much; it's all to do with mining housing and things like that, and they bring back all the loot to England. So when you're working without legal or economic protection, you bring a member of your family, common all over there (and common in La Cosa Nostra): you get loyalty and trust where there's no legal system. My dad needed that and so he imported his brother, my Uncle Max. They built this wooden-iron shed with a porch on it and they spent all day fitting it out. They went to bed that night on stretchers inside the shed. And at 4:00 in the morning they heard this great commotion: here were masses of Africans coming to buy! And they opened the doors and they worked until about 2:00 the next morning. So it was success just like that.

Jewish, bullied, and something else: I was Jewish. The school welcomed that. The kids, though – kids of white South Africans who made money in God knows what – they were dreadful, some of them – just mean and nasty, sometimes an interracial thing, but for some of them it was the tension of country, it was the war. Many of them bullied me. I was easy to bully: I was Jewish but also shorter than everyone, smaller, younger. One kid – a year younger and six inches taller – she got her hands on my shoulders and got her foot and banged it into my stomach, winded me. No one noticed. I held onto a wall and gathered my breath. Nothing ever came of it. I think she was being bullied by her older sister. Very often bullying comes in a line.

My teachers were totally weak and didn't help. When I got to about 13, teachers began to notice me. I was always known as a clever child, but there were cleverer than me. The cleverest girl in the class, of her everyone said, "She can't help being clever." Of course, she was getting records for playing sports.

81. The Lakofskis' "Modern" home in Johannesburg, 1930s

82. 1940s Johannesburg:
Extended family and many family friends, including refugees from the war

It was difficult for me to find friends there, and some of the friends I found were later lost. It was difficult to be friends with me: the other kids would say, "Why do you want to be friends with *her?*" I became close friends with someone and we went on holiday together. When we got back to school, one of the kids said to her, "Do you like Denise?" And she looked at me, and looked at them, and said, "A bit." All that friendship had turned into "a bit."

An English teacher gave us an essay: "An Afternoon at the Public Swimming Pool." I didn't write in my own persona; I assumed the persona of an elderly gentleman with a fat stomach! Heavens knows why. And he says he's "swimming about peacefully" – I got his language, you see – and then the schoolchildren come and he objects to them leaping and landing on his stomach! Well, the teacher said to the class, "You all didn't write good stories." And I said, "I know, mine was awful." And she said, "No, yours was the only good one. I'm going to read it to the class." Well, she starts. I know the funny parts before they're read aloud and I start having fits of laughter. Somehow that really helped me.

And then other teachers, the same. And then the headmistress **[D. V. Thompson]** saw something in me. She taught the Scripture classes; Jews didn't have to go when it became the New Testament, but we all did, it was so interesting. She asked us to produce an interpretation of "man does not live by bread alone but by every word out of the mouth of God." I sat and I thought hours and hours, what could this mean? I thought: maybe it's got to do with popularity? And maybe the bread is achievement, but popularity is something else that you need too, an unmeasurable, and hard to get? Well of course it isn't, but the teacher sent me a note and asked, "Did you think of this yourself? Come to tell me." And I *had* thought of it myself. She gave me the highest mark you could get; people almost never gave me that grade. And then she said, "I have real hopes for you – and when you learn to concentrate and pull yourself together, you should do very well indeed." It really got me.

Our beginnings and our ends: Look at me as a baby: I spoke very early, I laughed, most beautiful baby – I think that's my personality. And then I started to grow up and I had a very difficult father, subject to towering anger and scary as hell. We had to be like little mice on certain days when we saw the atmosphere around him. It made me very suppressed. He was bipolar? He has to have been: he was also very brilliant and did very well. I look back and think there must still be things I didn't realize. And I had a mother who was pretty neurotic, so she couldn't stand up against that, she was just scared of it.

I didn't have the support I need – so my uncles and aunts became so important. Some of them suffered from my dad's bullying when they were children. I remember when I was about four, an aunt drawing a picture, and she left a little space between the face and neck. I took my pencil and said, "You have to put this line up to there." She then turns to someone and says, "See, she finishes off things for me." That defined me. I thought later, do I really just want to be someone who finishes off things for someone? Can I escape from that? And I think I have. I make things.

83. Late 1930s / early 1940s

84. Robert Charles Venturi, Sr.'s produce shop on South Street, Philadelphia

The Marketplace: Venturi Fruit & Produce

Don't be fooled: Venturi Fruit and Produce isn't a vegetable stand but a market of charming gifts! Check out mugs, books, clothing, and snowglobes – each item emblazoned with a brilliant quote. The Marketplace is located directly beside Café Nkana. Remember, your friends will never forgive you if you go home empty-handed – so bring home a piece of Downtown!

The Venturi Fruit and Produce Marketplace is a loving homage to Bob's father's shop on Philadelphia's South Street. It also hints at "Venturi shops," bric-a-brac stores that Bob adored during his visits to Japan. This is more than just a gift shop: all items contain quotes about humanism in Denise and Bob's work. No other part of the exhibition deals so directly with the subject. These items aren't conceived as "souvenirs" but pieces of the actual exhibition that you can take home. Of all the information Downtown conveys, humanism is surely the most universally applicable and important – and just what you would want to hold close?

How conscious are you of humanistic issues as you work?: Very much so. Because you can't be South African and not be conscious of it. Because of my schooling, the kind of school I went to. Because of the fact of racism in South Africa and how we had to live within that and were torn – because we had the privilege, and were scared of losing it, and yet had to say *you can't do that*. People point out that Jews in South Africa – despite the metaphor of slavery, and the reality of slavery, and the reality of losing all their relatives to the Nazis – still wanted to be top dog. What are you going to do to contain that internal impulse?

I had a good indoctrination in our school. I hope it's still as good as it was, because it was very unusual. The headmistress [D. V. Thompson] was a tower of strength. She was very against racism and she was very happy to have Jewish children in the school; there was a lot of anti-Semitism and she really protected us. She wasn't allowed to admit black people, she wasn't allowed to admit Indian people, she was barely allowed to admit Chinese people *but she did*. And that was a very good thing: it made us all more human. Later, private schools were the ones that broke down apartheid and admitted all people and the nationalists were no longer strong enough to object. Catholic schools came first: my mother says, when she was in boarding school in the 1910s, 1920s, there was a mix of races and no one dared take the school on.

Humanistic Roots

In the end, in Johannesburg, I began to see a few things and I began to think:

Maybe I can't stay here.

It'll destroy me.

Well, in the end, in Johannesburg, I began to see a few things and I began to think: maybe I can't stay here. It'll destroy me.

I took math with the engineers. A black man came in to scrub off the blackboard and the engineering students in the back of the room had great fun throwing chalk at him. Just for fun. Just a black man. And the professor came in, and he had been in a concentration camp in Denmark, not Jewish, and he escaped. And he turned and looked up at the engineering students and he said, "This working man here tells me that as he works you throw chalk at him." And he looks at them and says, "Members...of a white... master race." Of course, they didn't care. I cared very much.

Then, **Robert [Scott Brown]** and I went to the post office down the road. Didn't have room for separate white and black entrances. Only room for one counter. So we're two big healthy white people that walk into this room and there's a very, very old black person, barefoot and wearing rags, and he was mailing a parcel, and he's at "our" counter because there isn't any other, and he sees us coming and he gets terribly, terribly scared. Of us. So he slides along the counter, away from us, and slides until he reaches a wall. And he's stuck there and he can't go any farther. He's trapped there, shivering. I can't live with that.

Robert very much intended to come back to South Africa after travels, and I did too. But **Professor [I. Douglas] MacCrone** saw through that. He said: you're not going to come back.

A big fight: I wasn't brave enough to do anything about apartheid while living South Africa. I felt I wasn't strong enough. Many people *were* fighting apartheid. But with my family around me...

My father was pretty racist. There was a big fight between generations in South Africa, as there was between generations after Hitler. You found your father had been a Nazi and you'd break with him. Well I had a huge fight with my dad in a café in London. We were having dinner. Students at my university had an integrated medical school, because there was a law that said blacks could be admitted if there was no other alternative but a white university, because the training was not given at a black university. But the government said, we can't change the law but we can refuse to pay the scholarship. Well, the students got together to pay the scholarship, adding to their own fees.

My father said they should not continue those scholarships because those students would get out into the real world and find out how terrible the world was about segregation. But he was *causing* segregation! And it became very bitter. My dad said to me, you're a cynic. I said, segregation's a bad problem, but the problem of not getting education is even worse – and with education they can surmount segregation. He said, you're just a cynic, you don't believe in anything! That was 1953. He had come to England for the Coronation.

So in 1983, maybe later, he said to me: I agree with you now. I said, about what? He said, don't you remember the argument we had in the Acropolis Café? And

85. Robert Scott Brown and Denise, early 1950s

you said this and I said that? Well, I agree with you now. By then he had left my mother. He had found a wonderful girlfriend, a South African woman. And by then I'd developed another belief: people have the politics they can afford. So I felt very cynical about his apology. It's nice that he came to believe that, but what about believing it when it was hard?

Social planning and Penn: In terms of ethics, at Penn the only ones sympathetic to my sympathies were the social planners, who were all about ethics.

After **Jane Jacobs**, architects were suddenly feeling freedom, they could really do good for society. (You should hear what the planners say about naïve do-gooders and how dangerous that is; a lot of my education came from that, from **Paul Davidoff** and all those people). So the architects in 1956 say, *we can do all these great things*, and they start – and within two years **Herb Gans** and Jane Jacobs are excoriating them. They say, you're doing terrible things! Architects *hear* what the planners say, they form Architects for Humanity and such, but they continue to do the same things and they've never changed.

So I begin to say, look, there are things we can do which are softer toward the environment, and softer toward humanity, and they can be beautiful. At Penn, Holmes Perkins fired everyone who could have helped do that. They were building

> **There are things we can do which are softer toward the environment, and softer toward humanity, and they can be beautiful.**

up a school where social planners were getting to speak with architects. Paul was beginning to say, Denise, I see why you say **Lou [Kahn]** is a humanist, all of those interesting relationships – well Holmes fires all of them. They all went into other programs, because Holmes wanted none of that and Nixon was taking away their funding.

Since that time, no one's put together anything convincing. **Bill Menking** tried. For years he tried to teach architects the same thing I did. In the end he gave up; he said he just couldn't get any interest. Paul would have helped make it interesting.

[In a conciliatory voice] Later, poor Paul admitted I made his life very difficult. He never complained. But I said, look, I've *done* some planning, you've never *done* any, it wouldn't work that way! Yes, in principle you're right, but in detail it doesn't work. And I'd take him on about democracy, too. I'd ask him difficult questions he couldn't answer. As a South African. Like, if you're living in Algeria and the French vote about your future, you are a citizen of Greater France but you are likely to lose your life through a theoretical vote on the basis of principle – is that right? Should you have more of a vote? He had no answer for that. I challenged everything. I felt very bad later. I thought of myself as his former student; he thought of me as a difficult colleague.

86. Denise and Bob teaching, possibly at the University of Pennsylvania, early 1960s

Street Lounge

"So Now You Owe It To Others To Teach"

First, go to Café Nkana and get a Denisuccino or a Learning from Café Latte. Then pick up a copy of Downtown's free newspaper, "So Now You Owe It To Others To Teach"; it's available at various locations around the plaza. Finally, find an open table and relax and read – sit and sip and study.

Denise once told Arthur Korn, her mentor and studio critic at the Architectural Association, that she "felt guilty, even as a child, that I had privilege beyond what I deserved in South Africa." He responded, "So now you owe it to others to teach." Downtown's free newspaper is dedicated to Denise's teaching – her philosophy, pedagogical process, and studios. It reproduces her actual class handouts as well as materials related to her "Learning from Levittown" studio. Denise talked with us about how she learned to learn via studio education. She reminiscences about her early studios in South Africa, Wales, and Peru.

I stand on the shoulders of a lot of people. The sources for my pedagogy came from all sorts of experiences and a lot of people.

The first team studio I worked on was in South Africa. Every year they had a team research studio. The first one we did on hospital kitchens. We got into teams of five people and surveyed various hospital kitchens. (That teaching style was like **Le Corbusier** telling his students to see how a train kitchen is organized.) I think we looked at hotels, too. The Grand Hotel in Johannesburg. It was fun and we produced a beautiful report.

Then I got to England and I was a part of a group that took on the Rhondda Valley in Wales and lots of little towns that are now all destroyed. Little green mining villages, hard modernism, unpretty, Welsh, sheds, mighty sheds. Have you seen the film *How Green Was My Valley*? Well, we produced hillside row housing that was connected housing. It was a lovely thing: there was a courtyard and the houses wrapped around it, one above the other like towers on the slope.

87. Denise and Bob, possibly at the University of Pennsylvania, early 1960s

Then Ernesto Paredes and **Robert Scott Brown** and I worked in a group for a linear town in Peru. The linear town gives you access to greenery on either side. I thought of Sienna in Italy: I had previously taken photos of Sienna from the marketplace where you see a hill, a wall, and the city goes around it, at a few levels on the contour. It's shaped like a starfish, maybe with more legs, so agriculture can come right up to the marketplace. And it allows straight streets that donkey carts can go along. I took a photo of that because it seemed indicative of a kind of urbanism like a ribbon, springing out. In my [forthcoming] photography book, I've got a photo that shows the tops of San Francisco hills, long lines of houses you can see from the road: it's interesting to compare to Sienna for the same reason: the donkey cart needs a little path to go up and down the hills, though in San Francisco the slope might be a bit much for it…

Street Art

> "Then there are graffiti. Endlessly creative... Where do they get their fecund fonts, unlike any others?"

Local graffiti artists love the secret passage through Downtown Fountain: it's private, it offers two great wall canvases, and the local authorities never seem to paint over their creations. (They never graffiti the digital monitor where Denise's personal video message plays.) As you pass through, take a moment to admire the vital, talented designs of Downtown's street artists! Also, speaking of street art, we noticed posters posted around the plaza suggesting the circus is coming to town?

Inside Downtown Fountain's secret passage, you'll find a lively graffiti riot, sayings and aphorisms lifted from Denise's writing and life. Elsewhere around Downtown, posters expound on what Denise means when she calls herself a "circus-horse rider," riding and reining the twin beasts of architecture and urbanism.

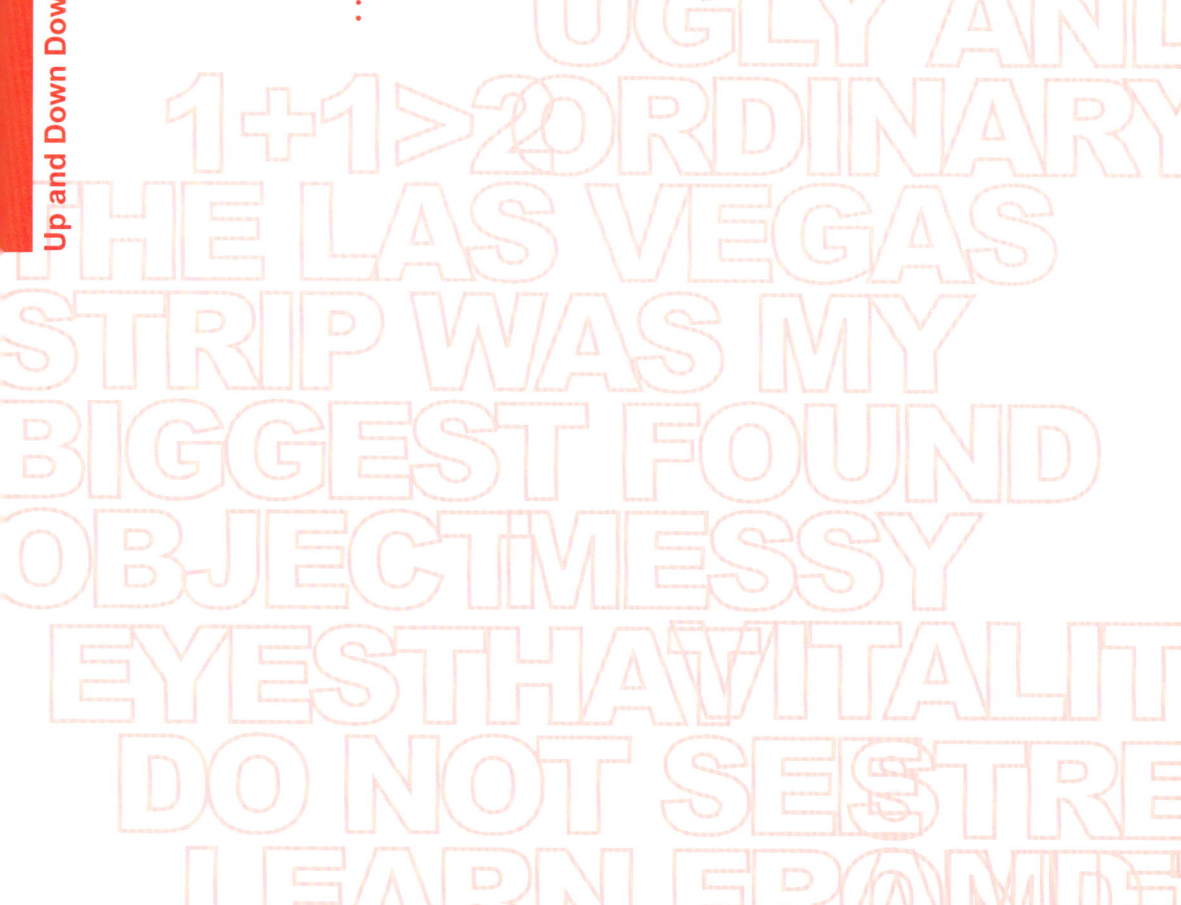

CIRCUS HORSE RIDER
I HAVE BEEN A
ZIRKUSPFERD REITERIN
ICH WAR EINE

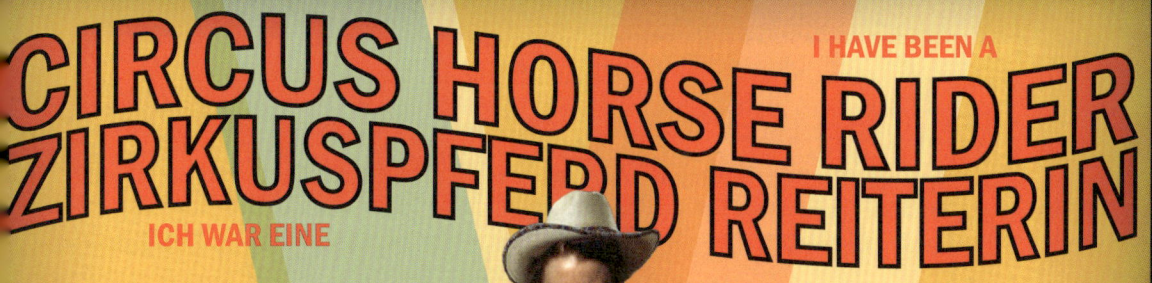

I have been a circus horse rider between architecture and urbanism most of my life. But reining together animals that have been tugging apart over five decades has made for a bumpy ride. My role as an architect and planner takes in more than physical planning or urban design.

Most of my career has been spent applying an urban outlook to the practice of architecture and, when feasible, the type of urban planning that I helped to evolve during the social movements of the 1960s.

But I have also penetrated beyond both architecture and planning toward the social sciences at one end and art and iconography at the other...

Spanning the two major disciplines of architecture and planning and the semi-discipline of urban design, my issues are many and varied. They come from the early history I brought with me to America; received a galvanising and organising jolt from planning school, and merged via the issues that Bob and I melded into our variegated way of being architects and planners.

I have also straddled continents. The 1930s and '40s saw me in Africa, mainly South Africa, the 1950s in England and Europe, and from 1958 my life has been spent in the United States, mostly Philadelphia with a stint in California, 1965-67...

'A]rchitecture schools on three continents provided the point of departure for a career that has taken me across the United States and to England, Europe, and Asia. My intimacy with several cultures, while young, helped me to do my work in these places – though the African in me still asks, "What am I doing here?" ¹

I [grew up] Jewish in a country where anti-Semitism was just one of many group animosities. Where black-white segregation blanketed everything, I was by no means as beset by racism as black children were, but bullying, some of it racial, hung over my early school life. It put me in internal conflict. Neither my family nor I would have considered leaving Judaism, and with Hitler, our loyalty increased. However, loyal as I felt, I did not want to be sealed in to one group, by either prejudice at school or culture and custom at home. A wide and exciting world waited...

That part of inner diversity I resolved by leaving home – although it had not been my intention. And I did not escape. I felt guilty for leaving and also for living with racism in America.

Nor was my marginality, my wanting to be both inside and out, resolved. But at some point I realized it would never be and should not be...

Our inner diversity, our conflict about marginality, is both close at hand and deep in our being. Living with it is hard, but it stirs our drives, hones our sensitivities and makes us unique. It's key to our creativity. ²

Die meiste Zeit meines Lebens bin ich auf zwei Zirkuspferden – Architektur und Stadtplanung – gleichzeitig geritten. Aber das Zusammenhalten von zwei Tieren, die seit fünf Jahrzehnten auseinanderdriften, war eine holprige Angelegenheit. Meine Rolle als Architektin und Stadtplanerin umfasst mehr als nur physische Planung oder Städtebau.

Den Großteil meines Berufslebens verbrachte ich damit, in die Architektur städtebauliche Perspektiven einzubringen, und wenn möglich jene Perspektiven, die ich während der sozialen Bewegungen in den sechziger Jahren mitentwickelt habe.

Aber abseits von Architektur und Stadtplanung bin ich auch in Gebiete der Sozialwissenschaften, der Kunst und der Ikonographie vorgedrungen ...

Ich habe auch Kontinente überspannt. Die 1930er- und 40er-Jahre in Afrika, hauptsächlich in Südafrika, die 1950er-Jahre in England und Europa und seit 1958 in den USA, wo ich, abgesehen von meiner Zeit in Kalifornien 1965 bis 1967, hauptsächlich in Philadelphia lebe ...

Gemeinsam mit einer Architekturausbildung auf drei Kontinenten ist dies der Ausgangspunkt für eine Karriere, die mich durch die USA und nach England, Europa und Asien geführt hat. Meine frühe Vertrautheit mit verschiedenen Kulturen half mir an diesen Orten zu arbeiten – obwohl die Afrikanerin in mir sich immer noch fragt: „Was mache ich hier?" ¹

Ich wuchs als Jüdin in einem Land auf, in dem der Antisemitismus nur eine von vielen Feindseligkeiten zwischen Gruppen darstellte. Die Rassentrennung überlagerte alles. Natürlich war ich vom Rassismus nicht so betroffen wie schwarze Kinder, dennoch sind meine ersten Schuljahre von Mobbing überschattet, was bei mir einen inneren Konflikt auslöste. Weder meine Familie noch ich hätten daran gedacht, vom Judentum abzugehen und als Hitler an die Macht kam, hat sich unsere Loyalität noch verstärkt. Doch so zugehörig ich mich auch fühlte, wollte ich nicht auf eine Gruppe festgeschrieben werden, weder durch die Vorurteile in der Schule noch durch Kultur oder Tradition zu Hause. Eine weite und aufregende Welt erwartete mich ...

Diese Frage der inneren Vielfalt löste ich, indem ich wegging – obwohl dies nicht meine Absicht gewesen war. Und ich bin auch nicht geflüchtet. Ich fühlte mich schuldig, weil ich gegangen bin und auch weil ich in einem rassistischen Amerika lebte.

Auch war damit mein am-Rand-sein, mein Wunsch, sowohl drinnen als auch draußen zu sein, nicht gelöst. Aber irgendwann wurde mir klar, dass das nie der Fall sein würde und auch nicht sein sollte ...

Unsere innere Vielfalt, unsere Konflikte rund um Ausgrenzungen finden sich sowohl an der Oberfläche als auch tief in unserem Wesen. Damit zu leben ist schwer, treibt uns aber an, schärft unsere Sensibilität und macht uns einzigartig. Es ist der Schlüssel zu unserer Kreativität. ²

THOUGH THE AFRICAN IN ME STILL ASKS
OBWOHL DIE AFRIKANERIN IN MIR SICH IMMER NOCH FRAGT:
"WHAT AM I DOING HERE?"
„WAS MACHE ICH HIER?"

Up and Down Downtown

88. The circus comes to Downtown

Up and Down Downtown

89. First office, Pine Street, Philadelphia, 1974

Street Life

Every part of Downtown tells the story of Denise's life – from storefronts to street signs, monuments to post boxes. Look everywhere; learn from everything.

Today is October 3, 2018. It's Denise's 87th birthday. She continues to write and work passionately, with two books and countless interviews and manuscripts and people demanding her time. The adventure of her life continues. We asked Denise to reflect on her life's accomplishments and her ongoing dreams.

What are your great achievements?: I had to live through a great tragedy. I had to live through, in some ways, a difficult childhood, not given to self-esteem. I had to find gumption to do the things I needed to do and I thought I couldn't.

Somehow I got through all that and made an oeuvre I can be proud of, sort of. Having said all that, I think I've managed to find a way to live with uncertainty, which was difficult for me. And I think I've managed to help other people to do that. I think I've managed to think through the issues of being a form-loving, design-loving, communication-loving –

Bob, crying loudly from the other room: Hi, honey!

Hi, honey! – *along with Bob*, and I've been able to bring all that together into what I describe as "a beautiful table with four legs." That makes me proud – that I can say, out of all that I've drawn a beauty from what was agonized beauty. And the kinds of people I seem to associate best with are the ones with a certain striving for the same. If they're not a little complex, I'm not very intrigued.

That's on the one side. On the other side, I'm happy to have helped to define advocacy architecture and to have practiced some of it. I'm happy to have helped promote women in architecture. I'm happy now to be ending my career by summing up what needs to be summed up. I'm missing the thing I became addicted to, which was design. That was my great joy – but it was complex with me.

> I can say, out of all that I've drawn a beauty from what was agonized beauty.

Up and Down Downtown

I'm also very very happy to have lived beside Bob and to have managed the *Sturm und Drang* – and to have brought out of that a relatively happy Bob and a relatively happy self and an oeuvre we can both be proud of. To have produced a son who's as much *Sturm und Drang* as my husband, who seems to be having a great career too, who has found his passion now, who will go on finding passions.

We've worked in this house all our lives and now it's being run for the first time as it needs to be run because we've got all this care in here. And in every room you find someone working, tucked in a chair here or there. One person here has said, "I've never lived in a house where every person is living and working." So we've made a Peaceable Kingdom of an unusual type. And I'm very proud of the stewardship of our landscape, and people don't know how much of my time I've given to that – ideas from urbanism but they have to do with where the sun reaches and where the paving should go.

The retirement that others look forward to is not the retirement you want for yourself?: Well I've got too many things to do! All these people coming to talk to me and I love talking with them. They say, make room to smell the roses, and I say, the roses are right on my drawing board. Look at my life: I get to go to Japan, not as a tourist but as someone who shares the secrets of people I'm planning for – isn't that better than being a tourist? So I'm getting those rewards in another way.

I've got too many things to do!... They say, make room to smell the roses, and I say, the roses are right on my drawing board.

Look at what I'm doing now in this house – which we bought so there would be room for all my family when they came here – and how we found that having handypeople helped us run it and made life nice for both of us, because we both like students, so for many reasons. So I'm calling my house **The Peaceable Kingdom**.

I said to **Barney Horowitz**: "Look, Bob and I aren't going to go on cruises, that's what old people do when they retire if they have the money to do it – well, we're not doing to do that. We just want to keep on with an academic life." He said, "Well, if you do go, would you please consider going on a tramp steamer and not the QEII? Don't buy the QEII!" So I keep asking, am I buying the QEII? But what we're doing here is giving Bob around the clock care, having an office that helps me finish off the things I began early in life but could not finish because of the interlude of professional work – I'm going to take all of that and interpret it, which is what I'm doing now. And at the same time we're giving employment and running an organic garden, maintaining a landscape, and I'm hoping these things are making us useful to our locality. I have a feeling it's better than paying a lot of NGOs where the administrators would get a third of the money.

I'm thinking of this house as a prototype, but it's a very difficult one to reproduce: you could find a couple of elderly people with pensions and a little bit of income who need the support; you could put a daycare center in here for old people and young people. But if you want to repro-

0. 1969

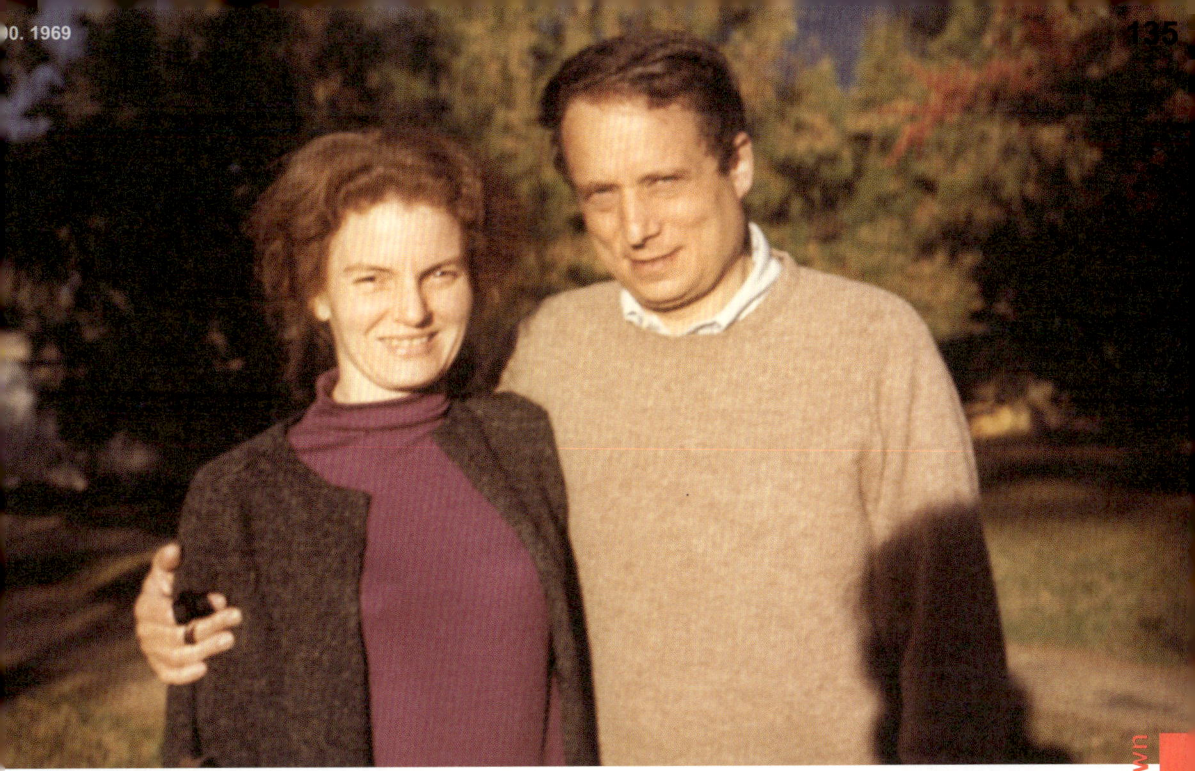

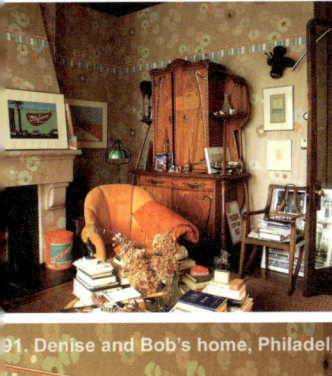

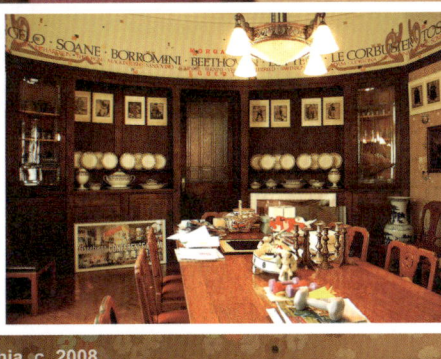

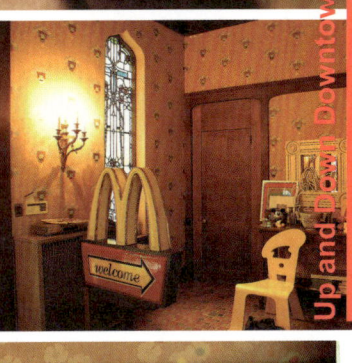

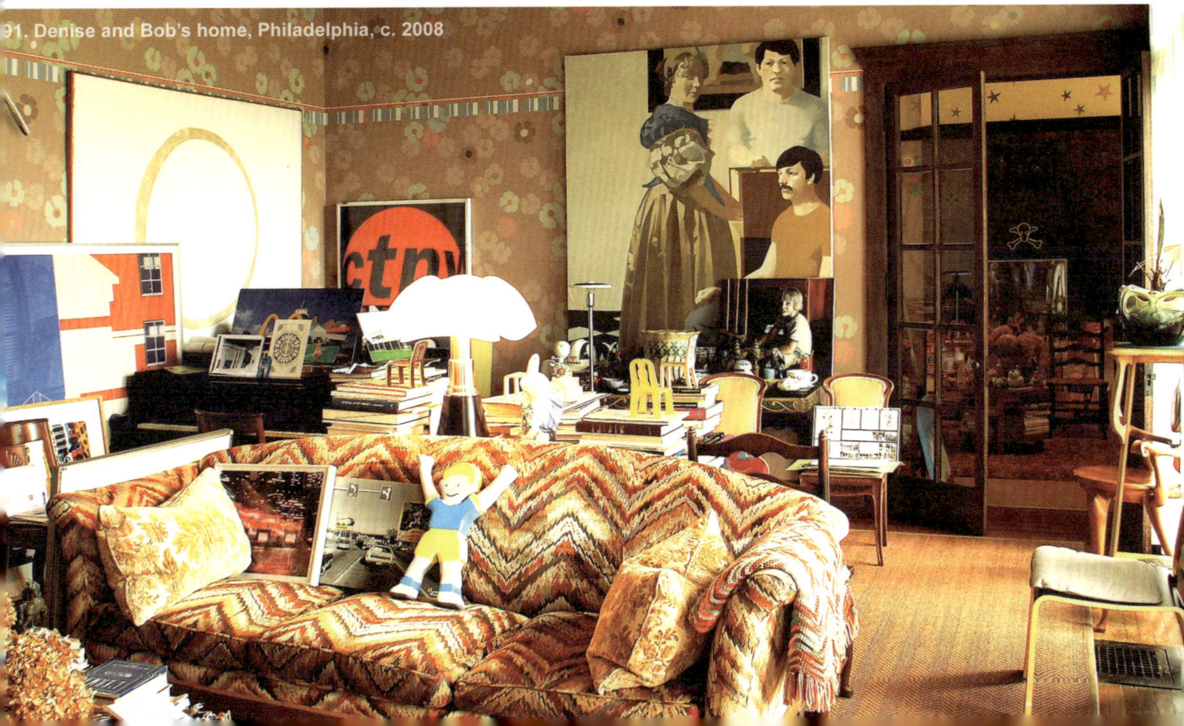

91. Denise and Bob's home, Philadelphia, c. 2008

duce that system at a scale you have to have a supervision system, and as soon as you get that, it breaks down. So I don't know what to do about that.

Now, at the end of it all, we gave money to charity as much as we could. I've given money to my old school in South Africa. When I was 13, my father bought 100 shares of a platinum stock (he was very much in favor of platinum and very much against gold) for each member of the family. Suddenly, one day in the office, I answer the phone and there's a South African accent: "Is this Mrs. Ventuuuri?" And I said yes and he said, "Do you know you have an account in South Africa...?"

This sounds like such a scam!

It *was* a scam. He was a bounty hunter. He said, "You have to sign this document and let me take a third of the money." And I talked to Barney and he said, you can do nothing else. So I did that – and then he disappeared. He obviously took all the interest that had accrued. The rest of the money waited in the account. And **Morris Kellett** helped me, and he did it pro bono, because he's a religious Christian, and we were very very good friends. We have a level of love between us and our lawyers which is very nice.

So one weekend Morris helped me to get this money and give it to my school [Kingsmead College]. It was $122,000

It's a nice story.

by that time, accruing from 1945 to 1985 or so, and I said I wanted it to go to a student whose teachers thought she could do *better*. A B-grade student they thought could be an A-grade student. When I went there, the headmistress – I saw her take kids who were, let's say, very raw and rough, and by the time they were with her a few years they too would get into medical school. She believed academic intelligence is one kind of intelligence but not the only kind. Have you heard me say that? I got it from her. And she had other ways of teaching for people who didn't need to go to college but, as she put it, would do very well. And so she had many ways of maintaining students' self-esteem and teaching people. And she did it for me – she discovered things about me that she really appreciated and her appreciation really helped me grow. I'm hoping the school will still be like that, with that sense of community.

So they did what I requested, they found a girl, **Gugu Ndlovu**, daughter of a Zulu teacher. And she finished there and did very well, and in the end she applied to all the medical schools in South Africa. And she got into every one. And for me...it was...

[Silence. Denise cries. She clutches her dress with her hands, looking down.]

Funny things are...moving. Some things are moving...

92. Robert Scott Brown and Denise, Rome, 1955

So, anyway [Denise's voice clears], nevertheless, I didn't hear from the school for a while. And apparently, after a great depression, the platinum stocks lost much of their value and never improved again.

Now recently I met a young Africaans woman traveling with her Venezuelan boyfriend, both going back to South Africa. He was a faculty member at ETH in Zurich and she was a student, beautiful young woman, sent to an English-speaking boarding school by her parents. Just wonderful, warm people. And he had some planning work in Johannesburg. And I said, please, when you go to my school, talk to them. And they did. Then a lawyer for the school contacted me and I told him this whole story about the platinum money and he said, "Wow that's such a story. Now let's see what we can do about it. Would you let this money be put in with the school's other bursary money?" I said yes, if it would be given under the conditions that I ask and in the name of **Robert Scott Brown**. And so they do that now. And so this is solved at the end of my life. It's a nice story.

93. Selfie, 1960s

Your Guide to Denise Scott Brown
is dedicated to

Robert Venturi

Robert Venturi died on a Tuesday evening, September 18, 2018.

Bob and Denise retired from practice in 2012. After 54 years of architectural work, Bob eagerly took to life back home, while Denise continued writing, designing exhibitions, and exploring their ideas.

Bob spent his retirement with happiness and high spirits. His last days were spent surrounded by his wife, his son, and his devoted caregivers. Lifelong friends visited; his room was filled with adored Beethoven.

Bob died as this book was going to print. We dedicate it to his memory -- joined forever with Denise Scott Brown, his partner in work and life. May we all find such joy on our own Grand Tours.

Az W Public Funding:

  Bundeskanzleramt

Media partners:

Supported by:

ARCHITECTURE LOUNGE
Architekturzentrum Wien

A good part of the Az W's comprehensive programme is supported by the contributions from its membership programme, particularly the contributions from its Architecture Lounge partners. This platform for highly committed companies and associations attributes top priority to knowledge exchanges and networking. Learning, networking, and hospitality are the notions that best describe this field of communication at the nexus of architecture, business and politics.

Credits & Citations

Front Cover. Denise Scott Brown and Robert Venturi, montage component photos
Inside Front Cover, 1.-2. Denise Scott Brown

YOUR QUICK GUIDE
3. Robert Scott Brown, montage component photo; Venturi, Scott Brown and Associates, Inc., drawing; Jeremy Tenenbaum, montage
4. Photographer unknown
5. Robert Venturi
6. Denise Scott Brown
7. Venturi, Scott Brown and Associates, Inc.
8. Denise Scott Brown
9. Photographer unknown
10. Robert Scott Brown, likely
11. Robert Venturi, montage component photo; Jeremy Tenenbaum, montage
12. Photographer unknown
13. Jeremy Tenenbaum, drawing, based on Robert Venturi sketch, based on photo in Peter Blake's God's Own Junkyard

WELCOME DOWNTOWN
14. Denise Scott Brown, montage component photos; Jeremy Tenenbaum, montage
15. Denise Scott Brown
16.-25. Photographer unknown
26. Learning from Las Vegas studio members
27.-28. Photographer unknown
29.-30. Matt Wargo
31. Kawasumi Architectural Photograph Office
32. Photographer unknown
33. Matt Wargo
34. Jeremy Tenenbaum
35. Matt Wargo
36. Az W, screen capture
37.-38. Jeremy Tenenbaum
39. George Pohl

UP AND DOWN DOWNTOWN
40. Denise Scott Brown, montage component photos; Jeremy Tenenbaum, montage
41. Robert Venturi, drawing
42.-43. Denise Scott Brown
44.-47. Denise Scott Brown, all photos
48. Matt Wargo, all photos except lower right by unknown photographer; Venturi, Scott Brown and Associates, Inc., drawing
49. Matt Wargo, all photos
50. Unknown photographer, models; Rollin LaFrance, elevation; Venturi, Scott Brown and Associates, Inc., drawing
51.-52. Denise Scott Brown
53. Photographer unknown
54.-55. Denise Scott Brown
56. Photographer unknown
57. Denise Scott Brown
58. Denise Scott Brown and members of the Learning from Las Vegas studio, all photos except aerial by unknown photographer; Venturi, Scott Brown and Associates, Inc., drawing
59. Denise Scott Brown and members of the Learning from Las Vegas studio, all photos
60. Jeremy Tenenbaum
61. Photographer unknown
62. Graydon Wood
63. Steven Izenour
64. Photographer unknown, top left photo; Denise Scott Brown, all other photos
65. Denise Scott Brown, all photos; Venturi, Scott Brown and Associates, Inc., drawings
66. Unknown photographer, all photos; Venturi, Scott Brown and Associates, Inc., drawing
67. The Historical Society of Pennsylvania
68. Venturi, Scott Brown and Associates, Inc.
69. Robert Venturi
70. Lauren Jacobi based on Denise Scott Brown's idea
71. George Pohl
72. Matt Wargo
73.-74. Photographer unknown
75. Matt Wargo
76. Matt Wargo, all photos except Richard Bryant, lower left photo of stairs
77. Kawasumi Architectural Photograph Office, all photos
78. Tom Bernard, all photos; Venturi, Scott Brown and Associates, Inc., drawing
79. Venturi, Scott Brown and Associates, Inc.
80.-83. Photographer unknown
84. Photographer unknown, both photos; image credit unknown
85.-87. Photographer unknown
88. Robert Venturi and unknown illustrator, montage components; Jeremy Tenenbaum, montage
89.-90. Photographer unknown
91. Mark Sfirri, house photos
92. Photographer unknown
93. Denise Scott Brown
94. Jeremy Tenenbaum

DSB A TO Z
95. Clive Hicks
96. Richard Pain
97.-98. Denise Scott Brown
99. Venturi, Scott Brown and Associates, Inc.
100. Tom Bernard
101. Denise Scott Brown
102. Tom Bernard
103. Photographer unknown

BEYOND DOWNTOWN
104. Denise Scott Brown, montage component photo and text; Jeremy Tenenbaum, montage
105. Photographer unknown
106. Denise Scott Brown
107. Mead Hunt
108. Pablo Leiva
109. Photographer unknown

Inside Back Cover: Denise Scott Brown
Back Cover: Denise Scott Brown

109. Denise and Bob at home, late 2010s

Team Az W

Director: Angelika Fitz
Executive Director: Karin Lux

Program Coordination: Katharina Ritter
Events: Lene Benz
Education: Anne Wübben
Excursions and Tourism: Anneke Essl

Archive and Collection: Monika Platzer (Lead), Sonja Pisarik,
  Katrin Stingl
Holdings Hans Hollein: Mechthild Ebert
Margherita Spiluttini Photo Archive: Iris Ranzinger

Press and Public Relations: Maria Falkner, Ines Purtauf
Marketing and Sponsoring: Alexandra Viehhauser
Website: Maria Falkner
Event Service: Daniela Zistler

Office Management: Evelyn Spindler
Secretary's Office and Proofreading: Lisa Kusebauch-Kaiser
Assistance to the Executive Board and E-Shop:
  Katharina Baumgartner
Accounting: Heidelinde Josifek
Library: Dietlinde Neubarth
Shop: Christoph Prammer
Workshop: Wolfgang Ahrer and Philipp Aschenberger

About the Az W

108. The Az W

The Architekturzentrum Wien (Az W) in Vienna's MuseumsQuartier is the Austrian museum of architecture. It researches and presents ways in which architecture and urban development influence and shape our daily lives.

The Architekturzentrum Wien's broad program is a bridge between the specialist world and everyday experts. With a floor area of 2000 square meters, the Az W presents international theme-related exhibitions, a permanent exhibition offering an overview of Austrian architecture, and over 500 annual events ranging from symposia, workshops, and lectures to guided tours, city expeditions, film series, and hands-on experiences.

The Az W has established itself internationally, acquiring a reputation as an outstanding institution where architecture is researched and communicated. It provides a comprehensive service for researchers and all those interested in architecture. Its facilities include a public reference library, the online building database Architektur Austria Gegenwart (Architecture Austria Contemporary), the online Lexicon of Architects, as well as a unique collection of material on Austrian architecture of the 20th and 21st century.

What can architecture do?

As an architecture museum, the Az W sees itself as an institution of the future, in which knowledge is not only collected but also shared. With a focus on the social dimensions of architecture, the Az W asks questions about just distribution in built form, living together in an increasingly diverse society, and the economic use of resources. A look behind the scenes and the incorporation of users' perspectives allow us to experience how architecture shapes our daily lives. Let's ask together: *what can architecture do?*

106. Las Vegas, late 1960s

107. The Neon Boneyard, Las Vegas, 2009

Beyond Downtown

> So now Downtown Denise Scott Brown is closed for the night.

VISIT: Nothing compares to experiencing their projects in person:

In Europe, visit the **National Gallery** in London, England, and the **Provincial Capitol** of Haute-Garonne in Toulouse, France.

In Japan, visit the Mielparque Nikko Kirifuri Resort (called **Oedo Onsen Monogatari Nikko Kirifuri**) in Nikko.

In the United States, the best cities to see publically-accessible projects include **Philadelphia**, **Seattle**, **Trenton**, **Houston**, and **Washington, DC**. Several projects exist for **Disney** campuses in California and Florida. Colleges and universities with their buildings include **Harvard**, **Yale**, **Princeton**, **Dartmouth**, **Bard**, **Oberlin**, **UCLA**, and the **Universities of Michigan**, **Kentucky**, **Delaware**, and **Pennsylvania**. And when in Philadelphia, stop by the **Fabric Workshop and Museum** to buy rolls of fabric they designed.

Also visit places that Denise and Bob helped to preserve. You won't see their architecture but you'll experience vibrant places they loved and helped to protect: **Jim Thorpe**, Pennsylvania; the **Deco District** in Miami Beach, Florida; **Wildwood**, New Jersey (a Steve Izenour labor of love), and **South Street**, Philadelphia – which I visit every week.

So now Downtown Denise Scott Brown is closed for the night. We go our separate ways, eyes alert for new things to learn from and love. As Denise says – *go well*.

Beyond Downtown

Now evening's twilight has grown into night. Downtown Denise Scott Brown is almost empty; the shops are closed, Café Nkana and the Marketplace are packing up; the fountain is still and quiet. As we linger, two staff members give us the wayward eye. Come on then, you and I. It's time to leave Downtown.

But this can't be the end? Beyond every storefront, every subject, every photograph, doesn't a whole universe demand to be uncovered? We have more talks to talk, more good fights to fight! Where do we go from here? What's beyond Downtown?

Our travels are just starting. Here's a brief guide on what to read and where to go to find more about Denise and Bob, their ideas, and their work.

CLICK: Much information is available online. First, see **AZW.at** for information about the exhibition. Then head to **VenturiScottBrown.org**, Denise and Bob's official site. It's fairly basic but it contains a database of projects, full résumés, and an up-to-date **bibliography** listing all publications by and about Denise, Bob, and their work. Also, why not drop by **VSBA.com** to see what the firm's next generation is working on now?

READ: The bibliography should be your first stop when drafting your Denise Scott Brown reading list but it can be overwhelming. Here are useful places to start:

Having Words (2009): This essay collection spans decades and topics, variously funny, dense, and inspirational. Includes the iconic "Room at the Top?: Sexism and the Star System."

Architecture as Signs and Systems for a Mannerist Time (with Robert Venturi; 2004): Based on their Massey lectures at Harvard, this is an accessible summation of their theory and work.

Wayward Eye (coming soon): Denise's forthcoming photo collection will show off hundreds of photos, many never published, while featuring her personal continent-hopping commentaries throughout.

Learning from Las Vegas (with Robert Venturi and Steven Izenour; 1972, revised edition 1977, first edition facsimile 2017): A foundation for all their subsequent work and theory. The Camus of their oeuvre: simultaneously difficult and daring, it's a wonderful book to show off in a pub.

In addition to books, thousands of articles and interviews are available. Again, the bibliography is a great resource.

105. Las Vegas

se in no particular order and require all three to pr
preferred medium). And setting down an idea helps
describe, direct and explain projects, to
from measured definitions of science and law,
scriptions. Polemics are personal and passiona
oes. Polemicists say 'is' or 'will' when they m
...' And they are braggarts. I know of only one
he nonlinear, poetic aspects of language that Seeger
flat indeed, and we protest, 'Yes, architecture must
it'. The same applies to the design guidelines that pl
matic or nuanced and allusive. They can rule heavy
accordingly, will find them coercive and constricti
brief is a verbal statement. It may provide merely a schedule
of creating the physical from the verbal. Moving from wor
intermediary images derived from cultural or personal value
while designing, including our own personal and poetic asso
reativity wor osyncratically and a hat may initiate the
rams as thes lve. The patterns of brief and context
mmars of form which architects use (largely unconsc
an in the earlier flights of association, is the critical location for
or the quality of outcome. And of course the finished b ldi
tween form a art and scien ate a publ
ple poetry cation, a yout entio
uch of hi
nother brin

Beyond Downtown

104. Las Vegas, late-1960s, meets "Words about Architecture" by Denise Scott Brown

BEYOND DOWNTOWN

103. Bob and Denise in front of the office, Manayunk, Philadelphia

Palimpsest		A half-erased document on which the original can still be detected. Denise uses the word to note old urban systems and forces that shape or manifest through contemporary building.
Peaceable Kingdom		Denise's term for her household – a community of family members, office employees, caretakers, researchers, house staff, guests, and visitors.
Philadelphia School		A loosely-defined generation of idiosyncratic and early postmodern architects associated with the city and University of Pennsylvania. Included Denise and Bob, Louis Kahn, and others.
Ping-Pong		Denise describes joint creativity as a *ping-pong* of people and ideas.
Postmodernism / PoMo		Denise and Bob initially embraced a *postmodernism* representing a return to early Modernism but enriched by theology and social planning. They reject *PoMo* as degraded commercial Modernism drained of social responsibility. Confusion between the terms required rejecting both; they call their work Mannerist.
Pritzker Prize		The Hyatt Foundation's prominent recognition of a living architect. Bob was awarded the 1991 prize for work he and Denise completed together. Women in Design at Harvard started a Change.org petition to recognize her.
Sad Old White Men (SOWM)		Denise's term for those who angrily oppose equal recognition of women and joint collaboration in architecture.
Team 10 (Team X)		An informal movement of architects sharing reformist ideas about design and urbanism. Incepted July 1953 at the 9th Congress of the International Congresses of Modern Architecture.
Venturi Fruit and Vegetable		Robert Venturi, Sr.'s shop on South Street, Philadelphia.
Ville Radieuse		Le Corbusier's unbuilt "Radiant City" explores utopian methods of social reform.
VSBA		Refers to both Venturi, Scott Brown and Associates, Inc. and its successor firm, VSBA Architects & Planners.

101. Mapoch Village, Mpumalanga, South Africa

102. Oberlin College, Allen Memorial Art Museum, Oberlin, Ohio, 1976

Handypeople	Denise and Bob's live-in assistant. In 1975, Fred Schwartz became their first; by 2018 they had passed their 50th.
Independent Group	1950s association of artists and writers critiquing Modernism and celebrating popular / mass culture.
Kraals	In South Africa, a traditional circular configuration of huts for residences and livestock.
"Learning from…"	An intensive and immersive process that Denise and Bob developed for their studios and studies. Since "Learning from Las Vegas" and "Learning from Levittown," the formulation has been used by countless others to name their own research projects or, more broadly, any process of "learning from" others.
Linear City	A linear city, largely conceptual, is a highly structured and scalable urban form in which functions are zoned following a line, as along a river.
Mannerism	A 16th century art movement noted for expressive eccentricity. Denise and Bob embrace a contemporary Mannerism that bends rules to address clashing requirements or systems.
Mapoch	A village 200 km northeast of Johannesburg. The resident Ndebele people decorate their structures with geometric abstractions of Western culture, which Denise photographed.
Mini-University	Denise's term for architectural assistants and collaborators, both within the office and at home in her "retirement."
Neue Sachlichkeit	"New Objectivity" was a Modernist reformation movement of the 1920s and 1930s primarily among German-speaking architects, including early Bauhaus.
New Brutalism	The Smithsons' term for Le Corbusier's monumentalism. The 1950s to mid-1970s movement involved imposing forms expressing adherence to functionalism.
Outside Functionalism	Denise extends traditional ideas about functionalism – as physical accommodation to program – into the spaces surrounding buildings and beyond, creating a continuum of functionality.

99. The Big Duck, Long Island, New York

100. Best Products Showroom, Langhorne, Pennsylvania, 1979

Learning from the Lingo

Active Socioplastics	Peter and Alison Smithson's term for the relationship between social / economic forces and physical forms, and how to maintain and strengthen those relationships.
Big Duck	A duck-shaped building in Long Island, New York, originally used to sell duck-related products. An abstract conception of a building as tailored to its specific function ("duck"), versus a building generically designed with applied information marking its function ("decorated shed").
City Physics / Central Place Theory	"City physics" is a planning term for the interrelation of urban forms based on their impacts and needs. "Central place theory," one aspect, shows intense urban development at the crossroads of major economic routes.
Congrès International d'Architecture Moderne (CIAM)	Conclaves of architects who discussed and promulgated Modern principals. Denise and Robert Scott Brown attended the 1956 CIAM summer school in Venice.
Desire Lines	In transportation planning, a path indicating the shortest or easiest route along either a formal or informal way.
Duck and Decorated Shed	An abstract conception of a building as either tailored to its specific function ("duck") or generically designed with applied information marking its function ("decorated shed").
Form, Forces and Functions	Denise taught planning studios as explorations of form, forces, and functions (FFF). In addition to built architectural contexts, they encompassed natural, economic, social, and technological systems as important determinants.
Functionalism	"Bob and I are dour functionalists. We see the Modern Movement's belief in functionalism as one of its glories. While Postmodern and Neomodern architects have departed from early Modern doctrines on function, we have remained functionalists for both moral and aesthetic reasons."
Glove and Mitten	A functionality metaphor: a glove will fit a specific program in a specific way while a mitten allows "wiggle room" for changing programs. Denise and Bob often prefer the mitten.

97. Traymore Hotel (in distance beyond Tanya billboard), Atlantic City, New Jersey

98. Santa Monica, 1967

Philadelphia, Pennsylvania	Location of Denise and Bob's home, office, and many of their projects.
South Street, Philadelphia, Pennsylvania	Historic working class commercial strip. Denise helped save it from destruction for a new crosstown expressway. Location of Bob's father's produce shop.
Traymore Hotel, Atlantic City, New Jersey	When this famous resort hotel was demolished in 1972, Denise and Bob acquired some of its furnishings for their new house.
University of Pennsylvania ("Penn," "UPenn") Philadelphia, Pennsylvania	Denise and Robert Scott Brown attended its planning school. Denise and Bob taught there, separately and together. They met during a faculty meeting after Denise argued for the preservation of the campus's Fisher Fine Arts Library. Denise and Bob completed several plans and buildings on campus.
Vanna Venturi House, Philadelphia, Pennsylvania	Bob's second built project was a home for his mother. Often cited as a progenitor of "postmodern" design.
Yale University, New Haven, Connecticut	Denise taught as Visiting Professor in Urban Design. Bob taught as Professor of Architecture. Together they taught the "Learning from Las Vegas" and "Learning from Levittown" studios.

USA: WEST COAST

Las Vegas, Nevada	Subject of the "Learning from Las Vegas" study and book. Throughout the 20th century the city evolved from a desert town to a gambling oasis to a family resort amid a suburban metropolis.
Santa Monica, California	Denise lived in a beach-side cottage here while teaching in Southern California.
University of California Berkeley, Berkeley, California	Denise left teaching at the University of Pennsylvania to teach at UC Berkeley as a visiting professor in the School of Environmental Design.
UCLA, Los Angeles, California	Denise taught as associate professor in UCLA's School of Architecture and Urban Planning, where she was named co-chair of the urban design program.

Learning from Where's Where

AFRICA

Johannesburg, South Africa — Denise was raised here from the age of two to twenty.

Kingsmead College — Denise's grade school in Johannesburg.

Nkana, Rhodesia (now Zambia) — Denise's birthplace. Nkana began as a copper mine and evolved into a mining town.

Temple of Karnak, Thebes, Egypt — Complex of ancient ruins. For a student project, Denise designed a visitor path into the center of the complex – but found no easy route back out.

University of the Witwatersrand, Johannesburg, South Africa — Denise's undergraduate university, where she studied both liberal arts and architecture.

EUROPE

Architectural Association, London, England — Denise attended in the early 1950s.

London, England — Leaving Johannesburg at twenty, Denise traveled to London first to seek architectural work then to attend the Architectural Association.

Rome, Italy — While traveling, Denise and Robert Scott Brown worked for Giuseppe Vaccaro in Rome. Shortly after, Bob Venturi attended the American Academy in Rome.

Venice, Italy — Denise and Robert Scott Brown attended CIAM Summer School in Venice.

USA: EAST COAST

Chicago, Illinois — Denise often references the urban development of Chicago, in part for love of the *1909 Plan of Chicago* by Daniel Burnham and Edward Bennett.

Levittown, Pennsylvania — Post-WWII planned suburb in Philadelphia. Denise and Bob's "Learning from Levittown" Yale studio proved more controversial than "Learning from Las Vegas."

Paul and Linda Davidoff	Social planners and activists. As a University of Pennsylvania planning department teacher, Paul was Denise's mentor.
Peter and Alison Smithson	English architects associated with New Brutalism, Team X, and the Independent Group. Peter advised Denise and Robert Scott Brown to study at the University of Pennsylvania.
Phyllis Lakofski	Denise's mother.
Robert Scott Brown	African architecture student and Denise's first husband. Died in a car accident in Philadelphia 1959.
Robert Venturi, Sr.	Bob's father. Operated Venturi Fruit and Produce on South Street in Philadelphia.
Robin Middleton	Architecture teacher at Columbia University. Denise's close friend at the University of the Witwatersrand.
Shim Lakofski	Denise's father.
Steven Izenour	Architect, co-author of *Learning from Las Vegas*, and principal of Venturi, Scott Brown and Associates.
Vanna Venturi	Bob's mother. Quaker, liberal, and feminist. Bob's second built project was a house for her.
Vincent Scully	Architectural teacher, writer, and historian.
Walter Gropius	German architect, Bauhaus founder, and pioneer of Modern architecture.
Walter Isard	American economist, writer, and pioneer of regional science. Denise cites as influence.

CREW

Angelika Fitz	Director of the Architekturzentrum Wien. Initiated the *Downtown Denise Scott Brown* exhibition.
Katharina Ritter	Curator of the Architekturzentrum Wien and *Downtown Denise Scott Brown*.
Karin Lux	Executive Director of the Architekturzentrum Wien
Philipp Aschenberger	Head of the Architekturzentrum Wien's Workshop / Exhibition Construction for *Downtown Denise Scott Brown*.
Jeremy Eric Tenenbaum	Designer of *Downtown Denise Scott Brown* and author of the accompanying *Your Guide to…* (this book!).

Henry Mayhew	19th century English social researcher and reformer. "Mayhew's Architecture," Denise's lecture at the Harvard Graduate School of Design, urged greater social consciousness relating to women and collaboration in architecture.
Herbert Gans	University of Pennsylvania social planning teacher, writer, and advocate. Taught and influenced Denise.
Ian Douglas MacCrone	University of the Witwatersrand psychology teacher and Vice Chancellor. When Denise and Robert Scott Brown left for England, he asked, "If young people like you leave, what will South Africa do?"
Ian McHarg	Landscape architect and regional planning pioneer who studied natural systems. University of Pennsylvania teacher and founder of department of landscape architecture. Denise audited his course, "Man and the Environment."
James Venturi	Denise and Bob's son. Filmmaker, technology entrepreneur, transportation planner.
Jane Jacobs	Urbanist, activist, and writer who injected sociology and economic analysis into urban studies and planning.
John Summerson	British architectural historian and writer. In parallel with Nikolaus Pevsner, helped reintroduce Mannerism in 1960s England.
Le Corbusier	Swiss-French architect who greatly shaped Modern architecture and urban planning.
Louis Kahn	Highly influential American architect of the Philadelphia School and University of Pennsylvania teacher.
Morris Kellett	Denise and Bob's lawyer.
Muriel Cooper	Noted MIT Press designer who created the 1972 first edition of *Learning from Las Vegas* – much-disliked by Denise, Bob, and Steven Izenour.
Nikolaus Pevsner	German-Jewish architect, historian, and writer. In parallel with John Summerson, helped reintroduce mannerism in 1960s England.
O. R. Lumpkin	1970s automobile mechanic, West Philadelphia. Denise photographed his shop sign ("We Take The Dent Out Of Accident") and called it a "sonnet."

Barney Horowitz	Family friend and financial advisor. Denise's father and Horowitz's father were business partners in Johannesburg. His son, Daniel, worked for Denise and Bob's firm.
Charles Seeger	Ethno-musicologist, father of folk singer Pete Seeger, friend to Denise.
Colin Rowe	British-American architectural historian and writer. Self-professed "Mr. Mannerist of 1950." Denise says he influenced Bob's turn towards Mannerism.
Daniel McCoubrey	President and principal of VSBA Architects & Planners, successor firm to Venturi, Scott Brown and Associates.
David Crane	University of Pennsylvania urban design teacher. Student advisor and mentor to Denise and Robert Scott Brown.
Doris Vera Thompson	Founder (1933) and headmistress of Kingsmead College, Johannesburg.
Ed Ruscha	Painter and multimedia artist. His streetscape photos influenced Denise, Bob, and Steven Izenour to create "Ruschas" during their urban studies.
Ernö Goldfinger	Hungarian-British Modern architect. Briefly employed Denise in London.
Frank Furness	Idiosyncratic Philadelphia Victorian architect. Denise first met Bob while arguing for the preservation of Furness's Fisher Fine Arts Library at the University of Pennsylvania.
George Holmes Perkins	Architect and educator. From 1951 to 1971 led and reshaped the University of Pennsylvania's School of Fine Arts.
Giambattista Nolli	18th century Italian architect whose influential map of Rome delineated public and private space. Denise and Bob created "Nolli" maps during campus planning.
Giuseppe Vaccaro	Italian architect who employed Denise and Robert Scott Brown in Rome.
Henri Cartier-Bresson	Pioneering French photographer whom Denise admires and studies.

Learning from Who's Who

"Learning from..." is an intensive and immersive process that Denise Scott Brown and Bob Venturi developed for their studios and studies. Since "Learning from Las Vegas" and "Learning from Levittown," the formulation has been used by countless others to name their own research projects or, more broadly, any process of "learning from" others.

How did I know that? I looked it up below! Here's a helpful glossary of the people, places, and ideas you'll encounter Downtown.

It is rather curious that Denise married two Roberts. In the lists below, her first husband "Robert Scott Brown" is written fully while "Robert Venturi" is abbreviated "Bob."

STARS

Denise Scott Brown — Born Denise Lakofski, 1931, in Nkana, Rhodesia (now Zambia). Architect, urbanist, writer, teacher. Founding principal of Venturi, Scott Brown and Associates. Married to Robert Scott Brown then Robert Venturi.

Robert Venturi — Born 1925 in Philadelphia. Architect, writer, teacher. Founding principal of Venturi, Scott Brown and Associates. Married to Denise Scott Brown.

SUPPORTING CAST

Aalto — Denise and Bob's dog. Also an architect.

Arielle Assouline-Lichten and Caroline James — As students of Harvard's Graduate School Design and founders of Women in Design, started a Change.org petition urging the Pritzker Architecture Prize Committee to acknowledge Denise's joint work with Bob, who was awarded the prize alone.

Arthur Korn — Architectural Association teacher. Denise's mentor and studio critic.

Barbara Capitman — Founder of the Miami Design Preservation League and collaborator with Denise in the preservation of Miami's Deco District.

96. Aalto the dog

DSB A TO Z

95. Building a tennis shelter at the University of the Witwatersrand, 1950

Denise Lakofski

94. High Point Cafe, Philadelphia, 2018

www.ingramcontent.com/pod-product-compliance
Ingram Content Group UK Ltd.
Pitfield, Milton Keynes, MK11 3LW, UK
UKHW020838250326
469204UK00022B/126

Snyder, John, 'Film and Classical Genre: Rules for Interpreting *The Rules of the Game*', *Literature and Film Quarterly* (10:3, July 1982), pp. 162–79.

Vanoye, Francis, *La Règle du jeu: Jean Renoir* (Paris: Nathan, 1989 and 1995).

Vincendeau, Ginette, 'Daddy's Girls: Oedipal Narratives in 1930s French Films', *Iris* 8, Cinéma et Narration 2 (5:1, January 1989).

Wilson, Emma, *Alain Resnais* (Manchester/New York: Manchester University Press, 2006).

Wollen, Peter, '*La Règle du jeu* and modernity', *Film Studies* (no. 1, spring 1999), pp. 5–13.

The Rules of the Game', *Film Quarterly* (21:2, winter 1967–68), pp. 2–9.

Lacan, Jacques, *Le Séminaire VIII: Le Transfert* (Paris: Seuil, 1991 and 2001).

Leahy, James, in *Senses of Cinema* (2003) (www.sensesofcinema.com/contents/directors/03/renoir.html) – accessed 6 May 2006.

Liselotte, *Le Guide des convenances* (Paris: 1915, 10th edition – no publisher given).

Macnab, Geoffrey, review of Altman's *Short Cuts*, *Sight and Sound* (12:2, February 2002), p. 46.

Mast, Gerald, *The Comic Mind: Comedy and the Movies* (Chicago/London: University of Chicago Press, 1972 and 1979).

Nancy, Jean-Luc, 'La Règle du jeu dans *La Règle du jeu*', in Antoine de Baecque and Christian Delage (eds), *De l'histoire au cinéma* (Paris: Éditions Complexe, 1998).

Neupert, Richard, *A History of the French New Wave Cinema* (Madison/London: University of Wisconsin Press, 2003).

O'Shaughnessy, Martin, *Jean Renoir* (Manchester/New York: Manchester University Press, 2000).

Passek, Jean-Loup (ed.), *Dictionnaire du cinéma français* (Paris: Larousse, 1987).

Poulle, François, *Renoir 1938 ou Jean Renoir pour rien?: enquête sur un cinéaste* (Paris: Cerf, 1969).

Powrie, Phil, and Keith Reader, *French Cinema: A Student's Guide* (London: Arnold, 2002).

Premier Plan: Jean Renoir (Lyon: 1962).

Reader, Keith, 'Chaos, Contradiction and Order in Jean Renoir's *La Règle du jeu*', *Australian Journal of French Studies* (xxxvi:1, January–April 1999), pp. 26–38.

Renoir, Jean (trans. Carol Volk), *Renoir on Renoir* (Cambridge: Cambridge University Press, 1989).

Renoir, Jean, *Ma vie et mes films* (Paris: Flammarion, 1974).

Resnais, Alain, 'Alain Resnais and Jean Renoir' (interview between Resnais and Richard Roud), in Renoir, Jean (trans. John McGrath and Maureen Teitelbaum) *The Rules of the Game* (London: Lorrimer, 1970).

Roud, Richard, *Cinema: a Critical Dictionary* (London: Martin Secker and Warburg, 1980).

Sartre, Jean-Paul, *Réflexions sur la question juive* (Paris: Gallimard, 1954).

Serceau, Daniel, *Jean Renoir l'insurgé* (Paris: Sycomore, 1981).

Serceau, Daniel, *Jean Renoir: la sagesse du plaisir* (Paris: Cerf, 1985).

Serceau, Daniel, *La Règle du jeu* (Limonest: L'Interdisciplinaire, 1989).

Sesonske, Alexander, *Jean Renoir: the French Films* (Cambridge, Massachusetts and London: Harvard University Press, 1980).

Simsolo, Noël, *La Règle du jeu*, *Revue du cinéma* (244, 1970), pp. 117–25.

Cauliez, Armand-Jean, *Jean Renoir* (Paris: Éditions Universitaires, 1962).

Chabrol, Claude, 'Renoir, "La Règle du jeu" et moi', *Positif* (no 537, November 2005), p. 100.

Crisp, Colin, *The Classic French Cinema, 1930–1960* (Bloomington/Indianapolis, Indiana University Press, 1993).

Crisp, Colin, *Genre, Myth, and Convention in the French Cinema, 1929–1939* (Bloomington/Indianapolis: Indiana University Press, 2003).

Curchod, Olivier and Christopher Faulkner, La Règle du jeu: *scénario original de Jean Renoir* (Paris: Nathan, 1999).

Curchod, Olivier, *Jean Renoir:* La Règle du jeu (Paris: Livre de Poche, 1998).

Dalio, Marcel, *Mes années folles* (Paris: J-C. Lattès, 1976).

Damour, Jean-Pierre, *Renoir:* La Règle du jeu (Paris: Ellipses, 1993).

Davis, Colin, 'État présent: Hauntology, Spectres and Phantoms', *French Studies* (lix:3, July 2005), pp. 373–9.

Deleuze, Gilles, *Cinéma 2: L'Image-Temps* (Paris: Minuit, 1985).

Durgnat, Raymond, *Jean Renoir* (Berkeley/Los Angeles: University of California Press, 1974).

Entretiens et propos, special issue of *Cahiers du cinéma*, 1979.

Esnault, Philippe, *L'Avant-scène du cinéma* (lii:1, 1 October 1965).

Faulkner, Christopher, *The Social Cinema of Jean Renoir* (Princeton, Princeton University Press, 1986).

Faulkner, Christopher, 'Un cocktail surprenant: la projection et la réception de *La Règle du jeu* dans l'après-guerre en France', in Frank Curot (ed.), *Renoir en France* (Montpellier: Université Paul Valéry, 1999).

Fofi, Goffredo, 'The Cinema of the Popular Front in France (1934–1938)', in *Screen Reader I* (London: Society for Education in Film and Television, 1977), pp. 172–221.

Forbes, Jill, '*La Règle du jeu*', in Jill Forbes and Sarah Street (eds), *European Cinema: An Introduction* (Basingstoke/New York: Palgrave, 2000).

Gauteur, Claude, '*La Règle du jeu* et la critique en 1939', *Image et son* (282, March 1974), pp. 49–73.

Gauteur, Claude, *Jean Renoir: la double méprise* (Paris: Les Éditeurs Français Réunis, 1980). (Republished as *D'un Renoir l'autre*, Pantin, Le Temps des cerises, 2005.)

Godier, Rose-Marie, *L'Automate et le cinéma* (Paris: L'Harmattan, 2005).

Grelier, Robert, 'Dialogue avec une salle', *Cinéma 68* (124), p. 22.

Guislain, Pierre (ed.), *La Règle du jeu, 1939, Jean Renoir* (Paris: Hatier, 1998).

Guislain, Pierre et al., *La Règle du jeu: profil d'une œuvre* (Paris: Hatier, 1998).

Guislain, Pierre, *La Règle du jeu: Jean Renoir* (Paris: Hatier, 1990).

Jeancolas, Jean-Pierre, *Quinze ans d'années trente* (Paris: Stock, 1983).

Joly, Jacques (trans. Randall Conrad), 'Between Theatre and Life: Jean Renoir and

Appendix 3: Bibliography

This includes all works from which direct quotation is made in the text, along with others relevant to Renoir to which reference is made.

Baillon, Jean-François, *Jean Renoir:* La Règle du jeu (Paris: Ellipses, 1998).

Bardèche, Maurice, and Robert Brasillach, *Histoire du cinéma* (vol. 2), (Paris: Les Sept Couleurs, 1965 – originally published 1943).

Bates, Robin, 'Audiences on the Verge of a Fascist Breakdown: Male Anxieties and Late 1930s French Film', *Cinema Journal* (36:3, 1997), pp. 25–55.

Bazin, André (trans. W.W. Halsey II and William H. Simon), *Jean Renoir* (New York: Simon and Schuster, 1973).

Bessy, Maurice and Claude Beylie, *Jean Renoir* (Paris: Pygmalion, 1989).

Bordwell, David and Kristin Thompson, *Film Art: An Introduction* (New York: McGraw-Hill, 1993).

Bove, Carol, 'Revisiting modernism with Kristeva: De Beauvoir, Truffaut, and Renoir', *Journal of Modern Literature* (25:3–4, summer 2002), 114–26.

Brassel, Domenica and Joël Magny, *Jean Renoir:* La Règle du jeu: *lecture accompagnée* (Paris: Gallimard, 1998).

Braudy, Leo, *Jean Renoir: The World of His Films* (London: Robson Books, 1977).

Bron, Jean-Albert, *Jean Renoir:* La Règle du jeu (Paris, Ellipses/Résonances, 1998).

Bron, Jean-Albert and Daniel Serceau, *Contre bande:* La Règle du jeu *de Jean Renoir* (Paris: Université de Paris I – Panthéon – Sorbonne, 1999).

Browne, Nick, 'Deflections of Desire in *The Rules of the Game*: Reflections on the Theatre of History', *Quarterly Review of Film Studies* (VII3, summer 1982), pp. 251–61.

Burch, Noël and Geneviève Sellier, *La Drôle de guerre des sexes du cinéma français, 1930–1956* (Paris: Nathan, 1996).

120   LA RÈGLE DU JEU

1937: *La Marseillaise*
1938: *La Bête humaine*
1939: *La Règle du jeu*
1941: *Swamp Water*
1943: *This Land Is Mine*
1944: *Salute to France*
1945: *The Southerner*
1946: *The Diary of a Chambermaid*
1946: *The Woman on the Beach*
1950: *The River*
1952: *Le Carrosse d'or*
1954: *French Cancan*
1956: *Eléna et les hommes*
1959: *Le Testament du Docteur Cordelier*
1959: *Le Déjeuner sur l'herbe*
1962: *Le Caporal épinglé*
1969: *Le Petit Théâtre de Jean Renoir*

Appendix 2: Filmography

This lists all films directed by Renoir. I have provided date, director and such other details as seemed relevant for other films to which reference is made in the text, so have not listed them here.

1924: *La Fille de l'eau*
1926: *Nana*
1927: *Charleston/Sur un air de Charleston*
1927: *Marquitta*
1928: *La Petite Marchande d'allumettes*
1928: *Tire-au-flanc*
1928: *Le Tournoi/Le Tournoi dans la cité)*
1929: *Le Bled*
(All of the above are silent.)

1931: *On purge bébé*
1931: *La Chienne*
1932: *La Nuit du carrefour*
1932: *Boudu sauvé des eaux*
1932: *Chotard et cie*
1933: *Madame Bovary*
1934: *Toni*
1935: *Le Crime de Monsieur Lange*
1936: *La Vie est à nous*
1936 (released 1946): *Partie de campagne/Une Partie de campagne*
1936: *Les Bas-Fonds*
1937: *La Grande Illusion*

In front of the camera

Robert de la Chesnaye: Marcel Dalio
Christine de la Chesnaye: Nora Gregor
Octave: Jean Renoir
André Jurieux: Roland Toutain
Geneviève de Maras: Mila Parély
Lisette Schumacher: Paulette Dubost
Schumacher: Gaston Modot
Marceau: Julien Carette
Jackie: Anne Mayne
Saint-Aubin: Pierre Nay
The General: Pierre Magnier
Charlotte de la Plante: Odette Talazac
Dick: Georges Forster
La Bruyère: Richard Francoeur
Madame La Bruyère: Claire Gérard
Berthelin: Tony Corteggiani
Cava: Nicolas Amato
Corneille: Eddy Debray
The Chef: Léon Larive
Adolphe: Jacques Beauvais
Germaine: Jenny Hélia
La Chesnaye's driver: Bob Mathieu
Christine's driver: Marcel Melrac
Mitzi: Gitta Hardy
William: Henri Cartier-Bresson
First keeper: Maurice Marceau
Pointard: Ernest Pointard
Radio reporter: Lise Élina
Caudron engineer: André Zwobada

Shooting details

Shot between 22 February and early June 1939, in the Pathé-Joinville and Billancourt studios near Paris. Location scenes filmed in and near La Ferté Saint-Aubin, outside Fontainebleau and at Le Bourget Airport. The running time of currently distributed versions is between 110 and 113 minutes.

Appendix 1: Credits

Behind the camera

Director and scriptwriter: Jean Renoir
Assistant scriptwriter: Carl Koch
Assistant directors: André Zwobada, Henri Cartier-Bresson
Script-girl: Dido Freire
Set designer: Eugène Lourié
Assistant set designer: Max Douy
Costumes: Maison Chanel
Make-up: Paul Ralph
Hairdresser: Suzy Berton
Properties: Laure Lourié, Christofle
Studio manager: Raymond Pillion
Cameraman: Jean Bachelet
Assistant cameramen: Jean-Paul Alphen, Alain Renoir
Camera operator: Jacques Lemare
Sound: Joseph de Bretagne
Editor: Marguerite Houllé-Renoir
Assistant editor: Marthe Huguet
Music: Roger Désormières
Adviser for hunt scene: Tony Corteggiani
Production manager: Claude Renoir
Production administrator: Camille François
Still photographer: Sam Levin

of living in a society that is 'dancing on a volcano' has emphatically not dissipated. I hope that this book will help new generations of viewers to understand and appreciate a film whose Mozartian interplay of simplicity and complexity has, for me at least, grown ever deeper on the by now countless occasions I have seen it.

Conclusion

To formulate any kind of conclusion to a film as rich, both textually and contextually, as *La Règle du jeu* is a difficult, even presumptuous, exercise. It has been almost unanimously hailed as a masterpiece since its 1959 re-release, give or take a few dissenting (for which read uncomprehending) voices from the United States. My personal favourite among these is one who opines at the end of his review, 'This is strictly one for the buzzards.' This is not exactly surprising; the film's iconic position as the finest work of one of the greatest directors appears self-evident, reinforced by its early status as a *film maudit* and the widespread agreement that Renoir's wartime and post-war work did not reach the same heights. *Citizen Kane* – as we have seen, the only film consistently to beat it in critics' polls – likewise benefits from a mythical aura nourished by the view that Welles's career started at the top and worked its way down.

More generally, what is most astonishing about *La Règle du jeu* today is its Janus-faced quality, its reconstitution of a world almost inconceivably old-fashioned in a cinematic style of breathtaking modernity. The film's oscillation between comedy and tragedy, its distribution of attention across a wide range of characters none of whom truly deserves the label of hero(ine) or villain, its vertiginous sense of what can only be termed organized chaos – schematically, chaos at the level of the profilmic, organization at the level of the filming – make it at once a film (*the* film?) of its time and one for all time. Nearer 70 than 60 years after *La Règle du jeu* was made, the sense

114   LA RÈGLE DU JEU

Gosford Park deserves particular attention because no major film known to me is so closely patterned on *La Règle du jeu*. Given that it was the first film Altman – who based himself for many years in Paris – had shot in the UK in a career almost 50 years long, the audacity of so evident a tribute should not be underestimated. So iconic has Renoir's film become that any hunting scene – certainly in a French film – is all but certain to summon up intertextual memories of it. The films mentioned here are by no means the only ones of which that is true, nor, inevitably, will they be the last.

Notes

1   Neupert, Richard, *A History of the French New Wave Cinema* (Madison/London: University of Wisconsin Press, 2002), p. 280.

2   Bove, Carol, 'Revisiting modernism with Kristeva: De Beauvoir, Truffaut, and Renoir', *Journal of Modern Literature* (summer 2002), 25:3-4, pp. 114–26.

3   For a more detailed treatment of Resnais's film in its historical context, see Reader, Keith, 'Giscardian Desiring Machines: Alain Resnais's *Mon oncle d'amérique*', *Journal of European Studies* (xxvi, 1996), pp. 175–84.

4   Wilson, Emma, *Alain Resnais* (Manchester/New York: Manchester University Press, 2006), p. 154.

5   Macnab, Geoffrey, in *Sight and Sound* (12:2, February 2002), p. 46.

life – and the American film producer Weissman are 'commoners,' there respectively to entertain and be admired by a star-struck audience and to garner material for a forthcoming film. Their roles in that sense are perhaps parallel to those of Jurieux and Octave, the former of whom is the cynosure of the La Colinière guests and, via the radio broadcast at the beginning, is connected to the nascent world of the media while the latter, at least if we know that he is played by the film's director, provides a link to the world of the cinema. The financial circumstances of Weissman and Octave are at opposite extremes – Weissman does not join in the shooting because he is a principled vegetarian (which causes consternation below stairs similar to Madame de la Bruyère's refusal to eat salted food in *La Règle du jeu*), whereas Octave's reason is, in all probability, that he cannot afford a gun. It is still intriguing to note the presence of characters in both films whose class position does not fit smoothly into the quasi-feudal division between masters and servants that otherwise prevails. The upper class in *Gosford Park* may have no imminent fear of war and invasion but the prominence of the 'new aristocracy' of entertainment and the media nevertheless suggests that its dominance is unmistakably under threat.

The two sequences in *Gosford Park* that most explicitly evoke Renoir's film are, as already mentioned, the arrival of the guests in limousines amid pouring rain and the hunt scene, which occurs about a third of the way through the film much as in *La Règle du jeu*. Altman's hunt scene closely follows the beginning of Renoir's, concentrating on the shooting of pheasants (no rabbits here) and, like Renoir's, makes the dangers of the hunt for pursuers as well as pursued evident through an accident, though, in the Altman, perhaps only an apparent one. Renoir's General, we recall, relates to widespread hilarity the tale of a hunter who, the previous year, inadvertently shot himself in the thigh and was dead within 20 minutes. Altman's 'accident' is at once more dramatic – we see it on screen – and less – Sir William is merely hit in the ear by a bullet, quite possibly fired by a resentful guest such as Meredith whom he is threatening with financial ruin. It assumes greater dramatic significance after Sir William's murder, which raises the suspicion that it might have been a deliberate attempt to hurt or even kill him – 'a new definition of the word accident' indeed.

112   LA RÈGLE DU JEU

involved with servants – or at least so they believe. Sir William, a lecher in his younger days and still a roué (at least) now, is having an affair with the housemaid Elsie (Emily Watson), which becomes apparent when she blurts out his given name at table and is instantly dismissed. His wife Lady Sylvia (Kristin Scott Thomas) now sleeps in a separate room, though the couple were at least sexually active enough in the past to produce a daughter, Isobel (Camilla Rutherford) – a departure from *La Règle du jeu* in which, as already noted, parents are conspicuous by their absence. Sylvia makes unmistakable overtures to Henry Denton (Ryan Philippe), ostensibly the manservant of the Hollywood film producer Morris Weissman (Bob Balaban), though it turns out that he is sailing under false colours, being in fact an actor researching a role – a pretence that is to earn him the undisguised opprobrium of the 'real' servants. Denton – a faux Mellors to Sylvia's Lady Chatterley? – responds enthusiastically to her while also making a less successful play for Elsie. More endogamous activity is represented by a (heterosexual) couple of servants caught in flagrante delicto in the laundry. Censorship would obviously have made such goings-on – whose filming in the laundry scene at least is more reminiscent of the bawdy English seaside postcard than of anything more erotic – impossible to show in Renoir's time but Guitry's *Désiré*, as its very title implies, illustrates how it was possible to suggest even cross-class sexual attraction within the bounds of visual and linguistic propriety. The inhibition increasingly dominant in Renoir's world would seem to confine its denizens within what would nowadays be called their own peer group. An alternative, and less gloomy, way of looking at this would, of course, be to say that La Chesnaye is far too decent to engage in the serial sexual harassment characteristic of Sir William, even if he had the subservient female workforce at the factory owner's disposal. Sir William, indeed, resembles nothing so much as an Anglicized version of the lascivious publisher Batala in *Le Crime de Monsieur Lange* – an importation from another Renoir film that is surely not inadvertent.

In *Gosford Park* as in *La Règle du jeu*, we find two characters whose relationship to the world of the aristocracy is a somewhat tangential one. The singer and songwriter Ivor Novello – who of course existed in real

gitimate son Robert Parks (Clive Owen), he was already dead when that occurred. It was Parks's mother, Mrs Wilson (Helen Mirren), employed in her youth as a worker in one of Sir William's factories where she was seduced and discarded and now as his housekeeper, who, suspecting that Parks was planning to kill his father, pre-emptively poisoned Sir William's whisky to save her son – who still does not know who his mother is – from possible legal retribution.

That sentence, perhaps inevitably as convoluted as the intrigue it unfolds, suggests why *Gosford Park* has been described as 'Renoir's *La Règle du jeu* crossed with Agatha Christie's *Ten Little Indians*'.[5] The element missing from that amalgam is the melodrama or family romance – a quintessential Hollywood genre to go with the English country-house murder mystery and the European art-house film and one which the emotionally charged revelations of *Gosford Park*'s final half-hour or so unmistakably evoke. That, in turn, helps to explain why Altman's film is far removed from a 'merry drama' – so too, of course, in many respects, is Renoir's but in more devious and generically subversive ways. On-screen tears in *La Règle du jeu* are few and far between – Schumacher weeps discreetly in Marceau's presence when he has been dismissed from La Colinière and Jackie's distress after André has been shot may well manifest itself in the same way – but Renoir's film has nothing to compare with Mrs Wilson's anguished sobs as she realizes that her son will never know her or the sacrifice she has been prepared to make. The world of *La Règle du jeu* is tragic precisely because it is terminally trapped in what Henri Laborit would call the mode of inhibition, in which the catharsis afforded by Mrs Wilson's tears, and by the melodramatic genre in general, is finally unattainable.

Another significant respect in which *Gosford Park* differs greatly from *La Règle du jeu* is in its much freer treatment of illicit sexual activity. The erotic chemistry between Lisette and 'Madame' notwithstanding, there is no suggestion of any 'upstairs–downstairs' sexual relationship in the Renoir. The flirtatiousness between Octave and Lisette might seem to suggest the contrary but, within the film at least, it remains at the level of badinage and Octave's own class position is, as we have seen, highly ambivalent. Both members of Altman's central couple, on the other hand, are

Altman film, and Altman has spoken warmly of how much he learned about the film-maker's craft from Renoir's work. Like *La Règle du jeu*, *Gosford Park* uses a weekend house- and hunting-party – this time set in the English Home Counties – as the setting for an overlapping series of social and emotional rivalries at a time when society in general and the aristocracy in particular is in crisis. Altman's film is set somewhat earlier than Renoir's, in 1932 – after the Wall Street crash that plunged Europe into economic turmoil (two of Altman's minor aristocratic characters spend the film trying, with suave desperation, to manoeuvre their way out of impending financial ruin), and at a time when the 'old' landed aristocracy were losing ground to the upstart 'new' money of the rising industrial bourgeoisie. Sir William McCordle (Michael Gambon), the boorish factory owner on whose estate the film takes place, is resented by many members of the more traditional aristocracy almost as much as La Chesnaye, though of course without the undercurrents of racism manifest in some of Renoir's characters. From its opening shot – of guests arriving for the house-party in the pouring rain – through its pheasant-hunting scene to the parallels between masters and servants, made more explicit here by the fact that below stairs the guests' servants are called by their masters' names, the film pays explicit and repeated homage to *La Règle du jeu*.

Yet there are important differences between the two films, which it is important to note before beginning an analysis of their echoes and similarities. Altman's film has a less overt political sting to it than Renoir's – perhaps the result of the collaboration between the avowedly left-wing director and his Oscar-winning scriptwriter, Julian Fellowes, who is no less avowedly a Conservative and, indeed, has written speeches for the former Tory Party leader Iain Duncan Smith. Whereas Renoir's film, we have seen, includes none of the really major French stars of its time, Altman, obviously with a much larger budget, fields a pantheon of top British names. Despite a host of witty and amusing moments, *Gosford Park* could not really be described as the 'merry drama' Renoir sought to make with *La Règle du jeu*. The death on which the film hinges – that of Sir William McCordle, found murdered in his study – is anything but an accident. We learn at the end that, while McCordle had indeed been stabbed by his abandoned ille-

LA RÈGLE DU JEU AS FILMIC PRE-TEXT   109

kind of return of the animal repressed, in which escape becomes impossible (Jurieux's gunning-down), combat initially proves disastrous (Schumacher's cutting loose in the château) and the gloomily frozen solemnity of the ending can be read as the terminal assertion of inhibition on both a personal and a societal level.

The hunt scene on which *Mon oncle d'Amérique* closes involves the shooting of wild boar, in which an aristocratic acquaintance has invited Jean to take part. Janine, with whom Jean had been living until his wife prevailed upon her to give him up on the (spurious) grounds that she was terminally ill, tracks down her erstwhile lover, whose indecisiveness is reminiscent of La Chesnaye's, and the film's narrative concludes with her beating furiously and ineffectually at him. To quote Emma Wilson:

> In these images, Resnais pays homage to Renoir's shooting scene in *La Règle du jeu*. Cutting between the shot boar and Janine herself, he allows the viewer to reconsider the sentience and the pathos conjured in shots of a dying creature.[84]

The hunting of animals and the pursuit of love, less pivotally but in this scene no less unmistakably than in *La Règle du jeu*, coincide with and reinforce each other in a doubling of ironies whose narrative result, here as in Renoir's film, is likely to be the assertion of the status quo for no better reason than that there appears no alternative. A comparison of *La Règle du jeu* with *Mon oncle d'Amérique* brings out the desolating and entropic triumph – if indeed it can be called that – of inhibition in the closure of both films.

Robert Altman's *Gosford Park*

The similarities between *Gosford Park* and *La Règle du jeu* are far more obvious than those between Renoir's film and *Mon oncle d'Amérique* and have been pointed out by a great many writers on the film. Bertrand Tavernier, in the booklet that accompanies the American DVD of *La Règle du jeu*, metaleptically compares Renoir's opening sequence to a Robert

108   LA RÈGLE DU JEU

the two films which make the hunting reference more than a token tribute. Both films anatomize, at once amusingly and cruelly, a France in social and political crisis, though the Giscardian modernizing frenzy of the late 1970s depicted in *Mon oncle d'Amérique* was obviously a less threatening phenomenon than the desperately compromised pre-war world of *La Règle du jeu*.[3] Both also cast some of their main actors against type. Gérard Depardieu, who plays the hapless textile-factory manager René Ragueneau for Resnais, had at this comparatively early stage of his career featured primarily in less 'respectable' roles, most notably for Bertrand Blier – *Les Valseuses* (1974) and *Préparez vos mouchoirs* (1978) – while Roger Pierre, the broadcasting executive and aspirant politician Jean Le Gall (intriguingly the actor's real name), has worked almost exclusively as a comic actor in boulevard theatre, middle-brow movies and television series. *Mon oncle d'Amérique*'s three principal characters – the two already mentioned plus Nicole Garcia as the fringe actress turned hard-nosed executive Janine Garnier – all refer at moments of crisis in their lives to favourite actors of their youth (Jean Gabin for René, Danielle Darrieux for Jean and Jean Marais for Janine), thus making the film a many-layered reflection on theatricality and role-playing, a description we have seen to be applicable to *La Règle du jeu*.

Mon oncle d'Amérique also uses animals to provide an ironic meta-textual commentary on human activity, by courtesy of the neurobiologist and behavioural scientist Henri Laborit (playing himself). Laborit assimilates human behaviour to that of animals – particularly in this film, laboratory rats – classifying human responses under one of four headings: consumption/gratification, escape, combat (the 'fight-or-flight' response) and inhibition, the last named being responsible for neurotic and self-aggressing phenomena such as the renal colic and stomach ulcers from which Jean and René respectively suffer. This view – more fashionable perhaps now than at the time of the film's release, when loftier Freudian perspectives tended to hold sway – is by no means unequivocally endorsed by Resnais and Gruault, who indeed come close to burlesquing it in scenes where we see characters repeating earlier actions while wearing rat masks over their heads. Yet the breakdown of civilized behaviour which increasingly characterizes *La Règle du jeu* could not implausibly be viewed as a

are made; questions of the propriety of slaughter and the breaking of society's rules loom large in the intrigue. For all these superficial similarities, however, *The Shooting Party* belongs firmly in the British heritage film genre, concerned, like the films of Merchant and Ivory, with lavish period reconstruction involving major stars and a large costume budget. Hunting in the UK has always been more of an upper-class preserve than in France, in whose more rural society it is far more widely practised though, as we have seen, the Sologne represents something of an exception; and *The Shooting Party*'s somewhat fustian tone doubtless reflects this. The film's rather pious final voice-over, hammering home the parallel between hunting and war and reminding us of the bloodshed to come, would scarcely have been appropriate, or even thinkable, in the very different historical and generic context of Renoir's film.

I propose here to concentrate in greater detail on two films both of which bear the imprint of Renoir's masterpiece and which have the twofold advantage of being, in my view at least, of outstanding quality and (indisputably) readily available on DVD. These are Alain Resnais's 1980 *Mon oncle d'amérique* (issued by MK2 in France, but with English subtitles, and obtainable online from Amazon – www.amazon.fr) and Robert Altman's 2001 *Gosford Park*. The intertextual similarities are more clearly marked with the Altman but I hope to show in what follows that the Resnais too bears the trace of *La Règle du jeu* in a variety of ways.

Alain Resnais's *Mon oncle d'amérique*

This film, scripted by Jean Gruault who had co-scripted *Jules et Jim* with Truffaut and was to write two more films for Resnais – *La Vie est un roman* (1983) and *L'Amour à mort* (1984) – concludes its narrative on a hunting scene, thereby all but automatically signalling a homage to *La Règle du jeu* whose shattering impact on the young Resnais we have already seen. Comparatively few critics have dwelt on this resemblance, though Penelope Houston drew attention to it in her *Sight and Sound* review (50:1, winter 1980, pp. 62–3); yet there seem to be significant points in common between

Bernadette Lafont and was the first film to feature a score by Serge Gainsbourg. If, as Richard Neupert maintains, Doniol-Valcroze's 'social satire owes more to the Renoir of *Rules of the Game* than to any of his contemporaries',[1] the corollary of that, alas, is that the film has dated badly in comparison with many of its contemporaries from the *annus mirabilis* of the New Wave. Among these is Rohmer's first feature, *Le Signe du lion* (1959), which tells the tale of a rotund and good-natured, but feckless and over-trusting, musician Pierre Wesselrin (Jess Hahn), whose rash reliance on a rumoured inheritance leads him to the brink of destitution, if not derangement. It does not seem fanciful to see in Pierre a descendant of that Octave with whom he has so much in common. Truffaut in his 1961 *Jules et Jim* puts before us a woman – Catherine (Jeanne Moreau) – whose hesitation between the two title characters, German and French respectively, and a cast of minor lovers has been likened by Carol Bove to that of Christine in *La Règle du jeu*.[2] Catherine, to be sure, has no compunction about acting out desires that for Christine seem condemned to remain at the level of fantasy, but both women have in common that they are, in the last resort, defined by and through those who desire them – the mainspring, it could be argued, of the films' gender politics. *Jules et Jim* is also significant as a *mise en scène* of Franco-German relations between the belle époque and the approach to the Second War – a concern prominent in *La Grande Illusion* but also, we have seen, figured throughout *La Règle du jeu*. Finally, Godard counterposes a clip from the *danse macabre* sequence to a shot of the concentration camps in his mammoth 1988–1998 *Histoire(s) du cinéma*, making the sequence appear indeed like dancing on a volcano, and worse.

Among non-French films Alan Bridges's *The Shooting Party* (1984), starring James Mason, John Gielgud and Dorothy Tutin, is, as its title indicates, an obvious intertext. Its similarities to *La Règle du jeu* were bizarrely emphasized for me by the fact that the only viewing copy I could find, in the Bibliothèque de France, was dubbed into French. Bridges's film, set on the eve of the First War, deploys – in a considerably more laboured form than Renoir's – the analogies between hunting, the pursuit of love and the impending global conflict. A poacher is recruited to be a gamekeeper; emotional tensions are played out at a fancy-dress ball; anti-Semitic remarks

5   *La Règle du jeu* as filmic pre-text

The list of films that bear the influence of *La Règle du jeu* is scarcely less daunting than that of the film's literary and artistic pre-texts, for all that that influence did not start to become widely apparent until after the 1959 re-release. Perhaps the major exception, as suggested in the previous chapter, is Jean Grémillon's *Lumière d'été* (1942), in which a masked ball, filmed in bravura style, forms the linchpin of the action. The strain of what might be called decadence is much more marked in *Lumière d'été* than in Renoir's film, as evidenced by the fact that the corrupt aristocrat Patrice, played by Paul Bernard, has earlier shot his wife – an inconvenient obstacle to his extra-curricular *amours*. Grémillon's narrative resolution, on the other hand, is several degrees more optimistic than Renoir's, enabling the film's heroine, Michèle (Madeleine Robinson), to find happiness, in approved Pétainist or indeed Stalinist fashion, in the arms of a clean-cut engineer working on a nearby dam. Grémillon can be counted among the great unknown masters of French cinema; only the 1939–1940 *Remorques*, thanks to one of Jean Gabin's major roles, is currently widely available on DVD, but for which I should assuredly have devoted more attention to *Lumière d'été* than I have done.

The increased influence of *La Règle du jeu* after 1959 owes a great deal to the *Cahiers* critics who later became the leading New Wave directors. Jacques Doniol-Valcroze, a co-founder of *Cahiers*, directed the comedy of manners *L'Eau à la bouche* (1959), which gave an early major role to

104   LA RÈGLE DU JEU

44   O'Shaughnessy, *Jean Renoir*, p. 56.

45   Durgnat, Raymond, *Jean Renoir* (Berkeley/Los Angeles: University of California Press, 1974), p. 203.

46   Ibid., p. 209.

47   Ibid., p. 211.

48   Braudy, Leo, *Jean Renoir: The World of His Films* (London: Robson Books, 1977), p. 133.

49   Ibid., p. 134.

50   Sesonske: *Jean Renoir: The French Films, 1924–1939*, p. 389.

51   Ibid., p. 408.

52   Ibid., p. 410.

53   Ibid., p. 414.

54   Ibid., p. 421.

55   O'Shaughnessy: *Jean Renoir*, p. 48.

56   Serceau: *Jean Renoir, l'insurgé*, p. 125.

57   Ibid., p. 130.

58   Ibid., p. 131.

59   Ibid., p. 136.

60   Ibid., p. 145.

61   Ibid., p. 147.

62   Serceau, Daniel, 'La Pomme et la marguerite: la question sexuelle', in Bron and Serceau, *Contrebande:* La Règle du jeu *de Jean Renoir*, p. 91.

63   Serceau: 'La Pomme et la marguerite', p. 95.

64   Ibid., p. 97.

65   O'Shaughnessy: *Jean Renoir*, p. 54.

66   Bessy and Beylie: *Jean Renoir*, p. 179.

67   Deleuze: *Cinema 2: The Time-Image*, p. 85.

16   Ibid., p. 116.
17   Ibid.
18   Ibid., p. 118.
19   Ibid., p. 119.
20   Ibid., p. 124.
21   Simsolo, Noël, '*La Règle du jeu*', *La Revue du cinéma* (no. 244, 1970), pp. 117–25, p. 123.
22   Ibid., p. 124.
23   Gauteur, Claude, *Jean Renoir: la double méprise* (Paris: Les Éditeurs Français Réunis, 1980), p. 173.
24   Ibid. (The use of the expression 'guard-dogs' is a clear reference to Paul Nizan's diatribe against political neutrality, *Les Chiens de garde*.)
25   Faulkner: *The Social Cinema of Jean Renoir*, p. 110.
26   Ibid., p. 111.
27   Ibid., p. 119.
28   Burch and Sellier: *La Drôle de guerre des sexes du cinéma français, 1930–1956*, p. 74.
29   Ibid., p. 77.
30   Browne, Nick, 'Deflections of Desire in *The Rules of the Game*: Reflections on the Theatre of History', *Quarterly Review of Film Studies* (VII:3, summer 1982), pp. 251–61, p. 257.
31   Burch and Sellier: *La Drôle de guerre des sexes du cinéma français, 1930–1956*, p. 79.
32   Bates, Robin, 'Audiences on the Verge of a Fascist Breakdown: Male Anxieties and Late 1930s French Film', *Cinema Journal* (36:3, 1997), pp. 25–55, p. 43.
33   Claude Gauteur and Ginette Vincendeau provide an excellent analysis of Gabin's status as icon of troubled masculinity in *Jean Gabin: anatomie d'un mythe.*
34   Bates: 'Audiences on the Verge of a Fascist Breakdown: Male Anxieties and Late 1930s French Film', p. 50.
35   Jeancolas, Jean-Pierre, *Quinze ans d'années trente* (Paris: Stock, 1983), p. 277.
36   Ibid., p. 278.
37   Ibid., p. 279.
38   Ibid., p. 280.
39   Crisp, Colin, *The Classic French Cinema, 1930–1960* (Bloomington/Indianapolis: Indiana University Press, 1993), p. 182.
40   Crisp, Colin, *Genre, Myth, and Convention in the French Cinema, 1929–1939* (Bloomington/Indianapolis: Indiana University Press, 2003), back cover.
41   Ibid., p. 105.
42   The Guitry and Mirande films referred to are both available for viewing in the Bibliothèque de France in Paris.
43   Crisp, *Genre, Myth, and Convention in the French Cinema, 1929–1939*, p. 348.

102   LA RÈGLE DU JEU

he might appear to espouse, while O'Shaughnessy cuts both with the grain of auteurism – his is a director-centred monograph – and against it – through the critical focus he brings to bear on the concept. What seems clear is that the distinction between the political and the auteurist approach(es) to Renoir cannot be a hard-and-fast one. Any critical discourse 'on Renoir', by definition, bears the trace of an auteurist reading and the auteurist readings we have looked at – most strikingly in the case of Serceau and least perhaps in that of Bessy and Beylie – find themselves addressing the political in its widest sense as they seek to define the coherence of the oeuvre. Scarcely any film exemplifies the inseparability of the social and the aesthetic so well as *La Règle du jeu*.

Notes

1   O'Shaughnessy: *Jean Renoir*, p. 59.
2   Leahy, James, in *Senses of Cinema* (2003) – www.sensesofcinema.com/contents/ directors/03/renoir.html, accessed 6 May 2006.
3   O'Shaughnessy: *Jean Renoir*, p. 33.
4   *Premier Plan: Jean Renoir* (Lyon, 1962), p. 274. (This contribution is not individually signed.)
5   Oms, Marcel, 'Renoir, revu et rectifié', in *Premier Plan: Jean Renoir*, p. 44.
6   Ibid., p. 47.
7   Ibid., pp. 49–50.
8   Ibid., p. 50.
9   Fofi, Goffredo, 'The Cinema of the Popular Front in France (1934–1938)', in *Screen Reader I* (London: Society for Education in Film and Television, 1977), pp. 172–221.
10   *Premier Plan: Jean Renoir*, p. 51.
11   An edited version of this interview is included as a supplement to both the American and the French DVD editions.
12   This tendency is identified as a major one in post-war French culture by Pascal Ory in *L'Anarchisme de droite* (Paris: Grasset, 1985).
13   Sylvia Harvey's *May 68 and Film Culture* (London: British Film Institute, 1978/1980) provides excellent documentation on this important cultural conjuncture.
14   Poulle: *Renoir 1938 ou Jean Renoir pour rien?*, p. 134.
15   Ibid., p. 15.

Christine's melancholy preoccupation with marriage and children to Lisette's 'stress on the games of love, transgressing matrimonial rules',[62] and articulating, once again, La Chesnaye's dilemma in seeking to 'restore a lost unity, passionate love within marital love, within a society whose monogamous ideal can only observe its own inadequacy in the light of dominant sexual practices'.[63] Serceau's view of gender relations is more developed perhaps than in the earlier works but remains grounded within an awareness of class politics, manifested in the masters' increasing resemblance to their servants. 'Like their servants, they give way to their drives, want their rivals to be eliminated, forget their rank'[64] – the 'idea of class superiority' thus goes the same way as that of the happily monogamous couple. The exasperated question of Oscar Wilde's Algernon in *The Importance of Being Earnest* – 'Really, if the lower orders don't set us a good example, what on earth is the use of them?' – might be seen to receive, in *La Règle du jeu*, a prolonged tragicomic illustration.

Bessy and Beylie, for their part, argue strenuously against a 'realist Renoir' and foreground the importance of play and artifice in the oeuvre, embodied above all by the theatre. Theirs, probably more than any other approach, constructs 'a "true" Renoir whose work has always followed essentially the same direction'[65] – a disarming or disingenuous approach according to taste – and, in keeping with the centrality of the theatrical, emphasizes Renoir's 'peculiarly homogeneous direction of actors, which does not run away from the risks of casting against type (Dalio) or uses an actor's clumsiness to throw a character into sharper relief (Gaston Modot)'.[66]

Deleuze's approach, often alluded to in my analysis of the film, might also be regarded as an auteurist one for, throughout the two volumes of *Cinéma*, the director is treated as the unquestioned author of the films s/he signs. Deleuze, however, inserts his auteurism into a much broader historical context which aims at nothing less than a narrative of the evolution of cinema from the 'movement-image' to the 'time-image' and, furthermore, explicitly claims that *La Règle du jeu* 'does not give us the key' to Renoir's other films 'because it is pessimistic, and proceeds through violence' – a violence done in the first place 'to Renoir's complete idea'.[67] Deleuze could thus be described as, in a fairly precise sense, deconstructing the auteurism

opposite pole to the over-expansive Jurieux – is figured in his choice of cloak for Lisette:

> Repressive practices themselves are invested with a certain amount of pleasure and take the place of the initial goal. When he gives Lisette a cloth cape, Schumacher derives satisfaction from the saving he has made. He would like a happy life at home, with his wife, but between the money this would cost and his attachment to saving he chooses the second, even if he cannot be happy without the first. He is aware that he is all the time sacrificing himself for a goal which he does not realize is illusory considering his own behaviour.[58]

The final sentence of that paragraph would act, for Serceau, as a virtual epigraph for the entire film, driven as it is by a dialectic of illusion and repression that culminates, for the upper classes, in 'the total destruction of their values and of their images of themselves and everything else'.[59] If this disaster is at least temporarily averted at the end, it is thanks, precisely, to the repressed and repressive Schumacher, whom Serceau describes in Bourdieusian terms as 'ensuring the ideological conditions of the reproduction of the upper bourgeoisie as dominant social class'[60] through his killing of Jurieux and the consequent avoidance of scandal. The final sentence of Serceau's account – 'The shadows file past on the wall'[61] – thus applies not only to the film's final shot but also to its verdict on the French society of its time.

Serceau's auteurism is thus of a highly political kind – indeed, one criticism that might be levelled at his account is that, unusually for an auteurist and utterly unlike Sesonske, he says very little about the film's visual organization. The stress on the conflict between desire and order, epitomized most strikingly by Jurieux and Schumacher respectively, is redolent of the dominant French theoretical discourses of the time – Lyotard, as already mentioned, but also Freudianism in its Lacanian avatar and the post-Bergsonian vitalism characteristic of Deleuze and Guattari's *The Anti-Oedipus*.

Serceau's 1985 monograph on *La Règle du jeu* develops a similar approach to *Jean Renoir, l'insurgé*, though with a less developed theoretical apparatus. He also devotes a 1999 essay, 'La Pomme et la marguerite: la question sexuelle', to gender relations in *La Règle du jeu*, contrasting

THE FILM'S RECEPTION SINCE ITS RE-RELEASE 99

milieu whose weakness undermines his formal authority'[53] and, moreover, a master married to an Austrian woman, may throw into relief, though Sesonske does not spell this out, that the crisis of society staged in the film would, if he had 'really' existed, have posed the most direct of threats not only to La Chesnaye's well-being but to his very life. Octave's precursors, along with his namesake from *Les Caprices de Marianne*, are deemed to include Figaro – who might also claim Marceau as a descendant – Legrand from *La Chienne* and Monsieur Lange – both 'would-be artists' – and, more contestably, 'a touch of Batala'.[54] The combination of affection and detailed scholarship that informs Sesonske's writing ensures that his book, for all its lack of methodological sophistication, remains a major contribution to Renoir studies.

Daniel Serceau's two books on Renoir bear the titles *Jean Renoir, l'insurgé* (1981) and *Jean Renoir: la sagesse du plaisir* (1985), as though to emphasize the break in his oeuvre between the socially aware pre-War work and the more serene films of his later career. The earlier monograph, in which *La Règle du jeu* is analysed, has alas long been unobtainable, doubtless because it was published by the now vanished publishing house Le Sycomore. O'Shaughnessy points out that it treats Renoir's 1930s work 'as a block'[55] rather than dividing it into a pre-political and a political or even, one might add, post-political phase – an eminently auteurist approach – but Serceau still reveals an acute socio-political awareness in viewing the film as the manifestation of the contradictions afflicting the French aristocracy of its time, ending with 'the recapture of power by the bourgeoisie which thereby ensures that its domination will be perpetuated'.[56] The rules of the game are broken in the first instance by Jurieux, who does precisely what a chivalrous hero should not do in demanding – on air – amorous recognition from a woman already pledged to another. Image is more important than reality in a world where 'the ideal, the inaccessible, the immaterial alone have value'[57] – a world that cleaves to chivalrous ideals which, as both Jurieux and La Chesnaye in different ways show, are no longer viable. Serceau's approach bears traces of the work of Lyotard, for whom the connection between the economic and the libidinal, as the title of his major work *Économie libidinale* suggests, is fundamental. Thus, the repression characteristic of Schumacher – at the

her own world'.[48] La Chesnaye is abetted in his perhaps self-defeating task by Octave, who 'has taken openness too far, into placidity and nonentity' – a further suggestion of the de-virilized quality we have often seen attributed to him – and, interestingly, by the major-domo Corneille whose role in attempting to keep order in the château 'helps expand the theme of theatrical control of recalcitrant reality'.[49] Theatricality, a key trope for Braudy as for other auteurist writers on the film, spreads beyond the domain of the aesthetic to which it can never be entirely confined and into the 'recalcitrant reality' of the film's broader socio-historical context. The world of Jean Renoir's films can never, in the last resort, be a unified or self-contained one.

Sesonske's *Jean Renoir: The French Films, 1924–1939* (1980) enthusiastically endorsed by the director, is the best-known Anglophone auteurist study of Renoir's earlier work. Sesonske's approach is an unreconstructed one, utterly unaffected by the *Cahiers/Screen* theoretical discourse that was very influential at the time and emphasizing, above all, the theatrical dimension to Renoir's work. His remark that, for the haute bourgeoisie at the time of *La Règle du jeu*, 'life was more performed than lived'[50] epitomizes this, with its echo of Camilla (Anna Magnani)'s melancholy inability in *Le Carrosse d'or* (1952) to decide where theatre ends and life begins. Yet it also reads nowadays like a kind of pre-echo of more recent work, most notably that of Judith Butler in the domain of gender studies, on the indissociability of identity from performance – a concern clearly fundamental to *La Règle du jeu*. Sesonske reads the film as a *mise en scène* of archetypes – Octave as court jester, what he calls 'Pre-established Harmony' 'transformed to Fate'[51] at the moment of André's shooting, and Berthelin, whose significance Sesonske was among the first commentators to highlight, as Death directing 'the infernal machine'.[52] Sesonske's auteurist approach leads him to pay particularly rewarding attention to La Chesnaye, whom he places in Renoir's line of 'civilized men whose ability to act has been curtailed' – a company that includes Lestingois from *Boudu*, Louis XVI in *La Marseillaise*, The Baron, played by Louis Jouvet, in *Les Bas-Fonds* and Boieldieu and Rosenthal, the latter of course also played by Dalio, from *La Grande Illusion*. That 'the marquis['s] closest affinity may be to Louis XVI, another master in a decadent

in a context very different from the ideological or auteurist views that inform the bulk of writing on it.

Auteurist approaches

The most substantial auteurist approaches to Renoir's work are to be found in monographs by, in chronological order, Raymond Durgnat, Leo Braudy, Alexander Sesonske, Daniel Serceau and Maurice Bessy, and Claude Beylie. Roger Viry-Babel's attractively presented *Jean Renoir: le jeu et la règle* (1986 and 1994), while a very worthwhile companion to Renoir with its detailed filmography and lavish selection of photographs, many from films difficult or impossible to view, is a montage of plot summaries, short histories, extracts from critical articles and interviews with Renoir, rather than a major auteurist analysis.

The British-based but originally Swiss Durgnat adopts an approach described by O'Shaughnessy as 'pragmatic auteurism',[44] articulating the director's personal vision with the specific determinants of each film's history. Many years before gendered criticism became widespread, Durgnat comments on La Chesnaye's 'apparent effeminacy'[45] and suggests that 'Renoir is indicating that the emergence of these people's political selves from their personal selves will unleash the chaos which kills Jurieux'[46] – a view in keeping with the feminist-inspired notion, still comparatively new at the time Durgnat was writing, that 'the personal is political'. His conclusion, with gloomy facetiousness, contrasts the nineteenth-century French poet Rimbaud's '"Je est un autre"' ('"I is another"') with Renoir's '"Je sommes n'importe qui"' ('"I are anybody and everybody"')[47] – the return of the political repressed triggering a disorder which, though Durgnat does not spell this out, is cognate with the rise of fascism.

Braudy's approach, in his *Jean Renoir: The World of his Films* (1977), situates itself within, as the title suggests, a clear-cut auteurist problematic while, to a degree, undermining this drive towards homogenization by its view that 'what La Chesnaye tries to preserve as a society of harmonious aesthetic style is in fact a congeries of isolated individuals, each in his or

cinema is Colin Crisp, whose judgment in *The Classic French Cinema, 1930–1960* that *La Règle du jeu* is marked by a 'fundamental apoliticism'[39] may give rise to question. The film's political pessimism, we have seen, does not – especially with the benefit of hindsight – blunt the acuity with which it dissects class and gender relationships. Crisp's *Genre, Myth, and Convention in the French Cinema, 1929–1939* adopts, as its title suggests, a more textually rather than contextually based approach to its (considerably smaller) corpus, though I am considering it here rather than with auteur- or individual film-based studies because of the breadth of its purview. Crisp draws an analogy between Renoir's film and boulevard comedies such as Guitry's *Désiré* and Mirande's *Sept hommes . . . une femme* (1936) – a step characteristic of his cultural historian's approach which, in a decidedly anti-auteurist move, treats French films of the 1930s as 'a single global textual system'.[40] This leads him to view the 'extraordinary series of curious complicities . . . between characters at opposite poles of the diagram' – Christine and Lisette, Jurieux and Marceau, La Chesnaye and Jurieux, even *in extremis* Marceau and Schumacher – as 'merely an adaptation of generic norms'.[41] The 'merely' seems to me nothing if not coat-trailing but Crisp's analysis is valuable in resituating *La Règle du jeu* within a generic context which, if only because it has long been difficult to view many of the films that make it up, has tended to be neglected by Anglophone commentators in particular.[42] The 'ways in which this film draws on the thirties macrotext' are listed as: 'the exchange of clothing leading to a tragic case of mistaken identity' – as we have seen, a trope going back, if not always in tragic form, to 18th- and nineteenth-century theatre; the sense of 'the working out of a predestined pattern';[43] La Chesnaye's ironic glossing over of the final tragedy as 'a deplorable accident' – identified as a pre-echo of Grémillon's underappreciated *Lumière d'été* (1942), in which the disposal of an unwanted wife is disguised as a hunting accident; and the film's move from comedy to tragedy in its final scenes, identified as characteristic of the *comédie dramatique* genre that was to become popular at the box office only in the 1940s and 1950s – a suggestion that generically, as well as in other ways, the film was some way ahead of its time. Some of these comparisons may convince more than others but, taken as a whole, they are of immense value in placing the film

THE FILM'S RECEPTION SINCE ITS RE-RELEASE   95

Hitler, Franco and Mussolini – thus, of a perceived political crisis of virility. In support of this, he cites the claim made by Lucien Rebatet, a close associate of Bardèche and Brasillach, that 'the men in the film are so weak as to be indistinguishable'[32] – on one level this is manifestly absurd but it does have a certain polemical value when we think of how difficult it would be to imagine any of the characters played by France's major male star of the period, Jean Gabin, in the context of *La Règle du jeu*.[33] The character who, for Bates, acts as a 'symbol of the masculine stance'[34] is Schumacher, whom Renoir nevertheless succeeds in humanizing through the tears that are, in large measure, provoked by what might be described (the term here is mine, not Bates's) as Lisette's castratory behaviour towards him. Gendered readings of *La Règle du jeu* are quite as pessimistic as class-based ones.

Historical and industrial approaches

The 1980s saw a burgeoning of historically based approaches to film, in some degree a reaction against what came to be perceived as the excessive formalism of 1970s *Cahiers* in particular. Jean-Pierre Jeancolas's *Quinze ans d'années trente*, an extremely influential history of French cinema between the beginning of the sound era and the Liberation, describes *La Règle du jeu* as 'perhaps the finest film in 80 years of French cinema'[35] and sees it as a comedy that turns into a tragedy 'from which the gods (destiny) are derisorily absent'.[36] Jeancolas's view is a socio-historical one but of a non-deterministic kind; thus, he takes mild issue with those who see the massacre of rabbits as a prefiguration of the War – 'This is not inaccurate, but it smacks of a mechanistic approach to the work in contradiction with what Renoir is doing.'[37] His assertion that *La Règle du jeu* 'is first and foremost the work of a film-maker, which almost as a bonus takes on itself the anguish of the spring of 1939'[38] would situate him, in O'Shaughnessy's taxonomy, at the intersection of the political and the auteurist approach, though the stress he places on the film's production history adds an institutional dimension not readily subsumable under either heading.

Pre-eminent among Anglophone institutional historians of the French

94   LA RÈGLE DU JEU

period, however, is that of Noël Burch, an American living in France, and Geneviève Sellier, whose *La Drôle de guerre des sexes du cinéma français, 1930–1956* (1996) deals illuminatingly with *La Règle du jeu* among a host of other films. The film, for Burch and Sellier, stages 'a brutal confrontation between a masculine and a feminine world'[28] that is exemplified in the opening sequence, though it is worth remembering how far Jurieux's masculinity, like that of the other main characters, is to be undercut by events. Among the 'several types of sick masculinity' that figure in the film, La Chesnaye's and Octave's are seen as polar opposites – Robert 'forbidding poaching on his own land while poaching on that of others while Octave's "well-padded" appearance and good-natured, childlike behaviour' emphasizes his 'comparative lack of sexual differentiation'.[29] Women, for their part, fare scarcely any better, with the absence of bonding between them – always excepting Christine and Lisette –symptomatic at once of their isolation and, paradoxically, of their power over the men who desire them. Burch and Sellier's reading owes much to Nick Browne's 1982 article on the film, itself influenced by Freud's *Civilization and its discontents*, which views it as a conflict between Eros and Thanatos – a conflict from which, unsurprisingly, the castratory death-drive emerges victorious. Browne's view that '[i]t is as though within the void left by social disorder, Death appears unexpectedly and involuntarily from some other scene, as if from outside what is recognized as society'[30] has clear echoes of Freud's 'other scene' which is that of the unconscious and the world of dreams and of Lacan's use of Holbein's *The Ambassadors*, with its anamorphically embedded death's head on the cover of *Les Quatre concepts fondamentaux de la psychanalyse*. The death here – that perhaps of a civilization, though not necessarily of its discontents – is assimilated by Burch and Sellier, as in a different way by Serceau, to that of a certain order of gender relationships. The film's 'political acuteness' lies in, among other things, its demonstration that 'relations between the sexes are pervaded throughout by the contradictions of society'.[31]

This view is shared, as the title indicates, by Robin Bates in his 1997 article 'Audiences on the Verge of a Fascist Breakdown: Male Anxieties and Late 1930s French Film'. Bates sees the film as symptomatic of France's anxiety about its lack of leadership in what appeared to be the Europe of

inextricably linked with its politics, suggesting, as it does, 'the interrogation of an ideological mode of perception'[26] – an approach very similar to the politics of the image developed by *Cahiers* and practised by film-makers such as Godard in the 1970s. *La Règle du jeu*'s pessimism is perhaps where its politics are most profoundly manifested, in a rejection of the humanist closure of *La Grande Illusion* or the regressive fatalism of *La Bête humaine*. The auteur, for Faulkner, is subject to as well as subject of ideology, as evidenced by his conclusion that the film's 'bleak finality . . . as a judgement on the disintegration of French society in 1939 and the moral/political role of the artist-intellectual makes Renoir's self-exile almost inevitable.'[27] The Popular Front is no more – and, for Faulkner, as even more markedly for Fofi, probably prevaricated so much as to make its failure inevitable – and *La Règle du jeu* is, among a wealth of other things, the final epitaph for the hopes its strategy represented. If the Althusserian Marxism on which Faulkner's approach is grounded is no longer a widespread paradigm within film and cultural studies, that is certainly in part because the very multilayered comprehensiveness of its analyses can appear deterministic, leaving little or no scope for purposive intervention. That said, the strength of *La Règle du jeu*'s impact is, in large measure, due to the unblinking pessimism of its ending, with its amalgam of entropy and corrosiveness. The sometimes cumbersome framework Faulkner deploys to underpin his analysis may slow it down periodically but it emphatically does not invalidate its conclusion.

Gendered readings

Gendered readings of Renoir's work have arguably, in more recent years, become the most significant type of political approach. The work of Daniel Serceau – to be considered later – notwithstanding, gendered views of French films tend, notoriously, to be the province of non-French critics. Significant exceptions include the work of the UK-based academic Ginette Vincendeau and that of Françoise Audé, whose *Ciné-modèles, cinéma d'elles* and *Ciné-modèles 1981–2001* provide thorough and sensitive readings of films made between 1956 and 2001. The only gender-based synoptic view of the pre-war

not have access to this edition at the time of writing – was written at a far less politically eventful time, though the following year's election of François Mitterrand to the presidency was to represent a resurgence for the left. Gauteur is concerned to re-inscribe the Renoir of the 1930s as a committed figure not only as a film-maker but also as a journalist, through his contributions to various left-wing periodicals at the end of the decade. Gauteur presents a useful summary of criticisms of and responses to the film on its release, emphasizing how radical both its form and its subject matter were and averring that 'the *cinematic* execution of the film in 1939 really concealed a *political* execution.'[23] Those critics hostile to the film, such as Jean Fayard, James de Coquet and Georges Champeaux, are described as 'consummate hypocrites and guard-dogs' and it would be difficult to imagine a more full-bloodedly political verdict than Gauteur's: 'The class-struggle can be read here with the naked eye.'[24]

Cahiers du cinéma, in the wake of 1968, became the vehicle for a strongly political approach to the analysis of film grounded in the structuralist Marxism of Louis Althusser and the rereading of Freud by Jacques Lacan. This conspicuous change from the journal's earlier auteurist and often ideologically equivocal stance was marked by an intense, sometimes sectarian, commitment to the politics of form and the image and a concomitant turning-away from any notion of cinema-as-art, viewed as a bourgeois heresy. It is significant that the only extended consideration *Cahiers* gave to Renoir during this extremely important period of its life was an extended, and collectively signed, analysis of *La Vie est à nous* as a militant film, which appeared in March 1970. It was left to an English-language critic, the Canadian Christopher Faulkner, to produce something like a '*Cahiers*-based' analysis of Renoir's major films. *The Social Cinema of Jean Renoir* published in 1986 – by which time such analyses had somewhat gone off the boil – argues that the working class, the Popular Front (while it lasted) and the history of France in and before the 1930s are as important for the films of that period as Renoir-the-auteur. *La Règle du jeu* is doubly significant here, through its 'generic uneasiness (as the film is now a comedy, now a slapstick farce, now a tragedy)'[25] and the intensity with which it denounces the corrupt society of 1939 France. The film's formalistic innovation, in other words, is

ment, seems to subscribe to a kind of biographical determinism that would invalidate the commitment of Prévert, Brecht, Sartre, Godard and countless others besides. Poulle rates Renoir's pre-war films more highly than the later work – a common not to say canonical view, supported here by political as much as artistic considerations. From this perspective, 'La Règle du jeu is the end of an evolution'.[15] Poulle's reading of the film hinges on the omnipresence of trickery if not treachery in its intrigues and characters. '[T]he real conflict is not so much between those who form part of society and those who are marginal to it as between those who do and those who do not cheat'.[16] The latter category, unsurprisingly, is a small one, composed of Jackie – for Poulle the only truly sincere character, even if 'her passion is on a par with her mediocrity'[17] – and Octave, whose conciliatory geniality – 'the bear with a heavy body and a heart of gold'[18] – is equated with that of Renoir the director, like his actorly alter ego, 'betting on a certain goodness in the world'[19] that events bitterly deny. Thenceforth, living for most of the time in the USA and thus out of regular touch with French society, 'he ceases to be a citizen and a witness to become a "wise man"'.[20] Octave's disillusioned departure from the château and Renoir's American exile are implicitly paralleled so that La Règle du jeu, for Poulle, can be read as at least in some sense an autobiographical text – the closure of a narrative of commitment whose inevitable failure does not undercut its significance.

Noël Simsolo's article in La Revue du cinéma, published the year after Poulle's book, describes La Règle du jeu as 'a great political film' but goes on to assert that, for Renoir, 'moral character determines social character'[21] and, like Poulle, identifies Octave as a key character in this regard. Octave's déclassement is at the heart of his significance, making of him 'the only revolutionary – because he is outside the layers of society . . . not even an artist but a failure, the one who precisely through being unable or unwilling to play is closest to reality'.[22] The humanism of this verdict puts it out of kilter with what was becoming the dominant critical discourse of the time. The very politicization of French writing on cinema in the wake of 1968 would appear to have marginalized political analyses of Renoir's film. Claude Gauteur's Jean Renoir: la double méprise (1980) – it has since been republished with some additional material as D'un Renoir l'autre, though I did

90   LA RÈGLE DU JEU

strategy of class collaboration which leads him to brand Renoir a Pétainist whose standing among 'Fifth Republic film-makers' – including those of the New Wave, associated with *Positif*'s arch-rival *Cahiers* – is but the logical extension of 'the Stalinist he once was and the mystifications of the Popular Front'.[10]

The intemperance of Oms's rhetoric and its somewhat dated political context should not mask the fact that he has a point, albeit a grossly exaggerated one. Renoir, thanks largely to his unchallenged status as auteur and jovial 'Father Christmas' persona, sometimes appears almost beyond the reach of hostile criticism, at least of the all-embracing kind proffered by Oms – though he does, in all fairness, praise Renoir's work for its painterly qualities. Yet the flagship film-maker of the Popular Front was also the man who, in the same year as *La Règle du jeu*, was willing to film in Mussolini's Italy and to express the view that Jewish film-makers should be treated as foreigners, as well as to proclaim, in his 1966 interview with Jacques Rivette, that 'I used to believe in progress, but now I have no faith in it at all'.[11] Ideologically charged criticism such as Oms's is far more likely to take 'this' Renoir, whose genially expressed scepticism may sometimes smack of right-wing anarchism,[12] into account than the sometimes hagiographic approach of auteurists.

François Poulle, in *Renoir 1938 ou Jean Renoir pour rien: enquête sur un cinéaste* (1969), takes a more nuanced view, one which might be said to bring together the political and the auteurist approach. Poulle was writing in the immediate aftermath of the May 1968 events, which had involved the cinema world from the outset and inspired a great deal of reflection on what forms revolutionary artistic practice and cultural politics might take. Poulle's approach is, however, very different from the revolutionary formalism that was to characterize *Cahiers du cinéma* from about this time.[13] It is less textually anchored, more individualistic and biographical to the extent of seeing Renoir as condemned by his membership of the artistic bourgeoisie to a purely individualistic and idealistic identification with working-class politics. Renoir shared the goals of such politics 'affectively and instinctively, not through reasoned argument, without harsh personal necessity'[14] – a view that, while it undoubtedly rings true in respect of Renoir's personal involve-

– to the narrative conventions and star system hitherto prevalent in cinema (including often Renoir's own). This, schematically, is how most politically committed readings treat the film, which, as the jewel in its director's crown, poses far fewer problems for auteurists.

In the France of the 1960s, it was *Positif* – rather than the better-known, for Anglophone audiences, *Cahiers du cinéma* – that was most closely identified with a politically committed approach to the reading of film. *Positif*'s anti-colonialist and anti-clerical stance, influenced by a heterodox amalgam of anarchism, Marxism and surrealism, stood in strong contrast to the Catholic existentialism and political ambivalence that characterized *Cahiers* in the period before 1968. *Positif*'s founder Bernard Chardère was also closely involved with the Lyon-based *Premier Plan*, a journal which devoted each of its issues to a different director. The number on Renoir, published in 1962, describes *La Règle du jeu* as 'a very great Renoir', while opining a touch regretfully that Renoir 'is not the Buñuel of *L'Age d'or*'[4] – a comparison doubtless suggested by the presence of Modot in both films, but also evocative of the *Positif* admiration for Buñuel. Marcel Oms, founder of the Institut Jean Vigo in Perpignan and writing as a clearly unwilling conscript in Algeria, is particularly vitriolic about 'the same old reactionary Renoir'[5] whose supposed political commitment is irredeemably tainted with nationalism. 'For Renoir, a Frenchman remains a Frenchman wherever he may be'[6] – a view which, we have seen, is called into question and undercut throughout *La Règle du jeu*. Oms asserts dyspeptically that in *La Règle du jeu* 'to whatever social class they belong, men run after love and nothing else matters',[7] as though that disqualified any claim the film might have to be taken seriously in a political perspective, demonstrating thereby a blindness to the politics of gender that it would be difficult to justify nowadays. Elsewhere in his short chapter, as O'Shaughnessy points out, Oms is trenchantly critical of Renoir's polarization of women into the frivolous and the broody; yet, even here, he over-simplifies, classing 'woman' in *La Règle du jeu* as 'frivolous'[8] in the teeth of Christine's fervent desire for motherhood and distress about Robert's infidelity, to say nothing of the evident suffering of Geneviève or Jackie. Like Goffredo Fofi in his essay on French Popular Front cinema,[9] Oms takes a far-leftist view of the Popular Front and its

88   LA RÈGLE DU JEU

exhaustive nor a rigid one – it is perfectly possible to be, like Bazin or Daniel
Serceau, an auteurist and of the left, or conversely, as the pre-auteurist work
of Bardèche and Brasillach demonstrates, to be neither of those things.
Auteurist approaches may be thought to lend themselves more readily to
celebration, since auteurs, by definition, are deemed to be major figures,
and more political ones may seem better suited to hard-nosed analysis of
the kind once practised by *Cahiers du cinéma* in France or *Screen* in the UK;
but that too will turn out to be a less hard-and-fast distinction than it may
at first appear. O'Shaughnessy's opposition nevertheless has the advantage
of focusing the principal debates on Renoir's work and situating them within
the major debates in film studies over the past half century or so, which is
why I shall be taking it as my starting point in what follows. James Leahy
is scathing about this approach, deeming it humourless and desensualizing
and asking in a Gablesque flourish, 'Frankly, who gives a damn?'[2] Yet an
oeuvre as rich and multiform as Renoir's will inevitably spawn a variety of
critical approaches of which the serious student will need to take at least
some account and whose very existence casts light on developments in the
fast-changing field of film studies over the past 70 years – excellent reasons
it seems to me for giving not one damn but several.

Politically inspired approaches

Auteurism is, in many ways, the quintessentially humanist approach to
cinema, viewing films as the product of a single unifying consciousness – one
reason why, in the politically committed 1960s and 1970s, it fell from grace.
Yet it has its reductionist dangers no less surely than more overtly ideological readings, as in its tendency with Renoir 'to rewrite the pre-war politically
committed films to make them fit better into a model of a unified authorial
consciousness'.[3] *La Règle du jeu* demonstrates, we have seen, an at times
terrifyingly acute political awareness, despite which its historical context alone
would make it difficult to regard it as a 'committed film' in the same way as
La Vie est à nous or *Le Crime de Monsieur Lange*. Its politics operate on the
level of diagnosis – of the corruption of French society – and formal challenge

4 The film's reception since its re-release

Types of critical response and discourse

Renoir is among the most written-about French film-makers – the author catalogue in the Bibliothèque de France has 169 entries for him, compared with 248 for Truffaut and 182 for Godard. Within his output, *La Règle du jeu* is the most written-about film, thanks to its chequered history and the fact that it is, by general consent, regarded as his masterpiece – no one film fills that place for Godard or Truffaut in quite the same way. A further contributory reason is that, in 1999, it became the first film to appear on the syllabus for the *baccalauréat* examination, yielding a crop of short monographs and study guides. To give a full account of this plethora of texts would be a self-defeating task so I propose here to review what seem to me the most significant, be they articles, book chapters or monographs. Biographies, such as the major works by Célia Bertin – *Jean Renoir* (1986 and 1994) – and Claude-Jean Philippe – *Jean Renoir, une vie en oeuvres* (2005) – are clearly important but do not, on the whole, seek to contribute to detailed analysis or non-biographical contextualization of the films of the kind that I shall be looking at here.

I shall be following in the first instance – sometimes the better to depart from it – the schema devised by Martin O'Shaughnessy for whom 'Renoir criticism has been dominated by auteurists and critics of the left and t he quarrel between the two'.[1] O'Shaughnessy's dichotomy is neither an

SEQUENCE-BY-SEQUENCE ANALYSIS AND COMMENTARY

38 Ibid.

39 Ibid.

40 Reader, Keith, 'Chaos, Contradiction and Order in Jean Renoir's *La Règle du jeu*', *Australian Journal of French Studies* (xxxvi:1, January–April 1999), pp. 26–38, p. 37.

41 Curchod: *La Règle du jeu*, p. 178.

42 Mast, Gerald, *The Comic Mind: Comedy and the Movies* (Chicago/London: University of Chicago Press, 1972/1979), p. 236.

43 Godier: *L'Automate et le cinéma*, p. 40.

44 Nancy: 'La Règle du jeu dans *La Règle du jeu*', p. 161.

45 Godier: *L'Automate et le cinéma*, p. 48.

46 Vanoye, Francis, *La Règle du jeu: Jean Renoir* (Paris: Nathan, 1989/1995), p. 70.

47 Joly, Jacques (trans. Randall Conrad), 'Between Theatre and Life: Jean Renoir and *The Rules of the Game*', *Film Quarterly* (21:2, winter 1967–8), pp. 2–9, p. 4.

48 Curchod: *La Règle du jeu*, p. 202.

49 Reader: 'Chaos, contradiction and order in Renoir's *La Règle du jeu*', pp. 30–1.

50 O'Shaughnessy: *Jean Renoir*, p. 149.

51 Guislain: *La Règle du jeu*, p. 47.

52 Quoted in Nancy: 'La Règle du jeu dans *La Règle du jeu*', p. 158.

53 Lacan, Jacques, *Le Séminaire VIII: Le Transfert* (Paris: Seuil, 1991/2001), p. 164. (Those wishing to explore the *objet a* and Lacan's work in general further may find it helpful to consult Malcolm Bowie's *Lacan* (London: Fontana, 1991) or Chapter Two of Keith Reader's *The Abject Object* (Amsterdam/New York: Rodopi, 2006).

54 Nancy: 'La Règle du jeu dans *La Règle du jeu*', p. 158.

55 Bordwell, David and Kristin Thompson, *Film Art: An Introduction* (New York: McGraw-Hill, 1993), p. 210.

56 Nancy: 'La Règle du jeu dans *La Règle du jeu*', p. 148.

57 Cauliez, Armand-Jean, *Jean Renoir* (Paris: Éditions Universitaires, 1962), pp. 92–3.

58 Ibid., p. 84.

59 Wollen, Peter, 'La Règle du jeu and modernity', *Film Studies* (no. 1, spring 1999), pp. 5–13.

60 Joly: 'Between Theatre and Life: Jean Renoir and *The Rules of the Game*', p. 2.

61 Damour, Jean-Pierre, *Renoir*: La Règle du jeu (Paris, Ellipses, 1993), p. 59.

84   LA RÈGLE DU JEU

Hauntology, Spectres and Phantoms', *French Studies* (lix:3, July 2005), pp. 373–79, p. 373.

21   Simsolo, Noël, '*La Règle du jeu*', *Revue du cinéma*, (November 1970), pp. 117–25, p. 123.

22   Sesonske: *Jean Renoir: The French Films*, p. 398.

23   This line is reprised by Nathalie Baye/Joëlle in Truffaut's 1973 film *La Nuit américaine/Day for Night*.

24   Quoted in Gauteur, Claude, '*La Règle du jeu* et la critique en 1939', *Image et son* (282, March 1974), pp. 49–73, p. 68.

25   Vanoye, François, *La Règle du jeu: Jean Renoir* (Paris: Nathan, 1989 and 1995), p. 67.

26   Vincendeau, Ginette, 'Daddy's Girls: Oedipal Narratives in 1930s French Films', *Iris* 8, Cinéma et Narration 2 (5:1, January 1989); and Burch and Sellier in *La Drôle de guerre des sexes du cinéma français*. Both analyse the prevalence in French cinema, during this period, of quasi-Oedipal relationships, in which symbolic fathers figure a wider crisis of masculinity in French society. The rarity or absence of biological children serves, in this context, the better to concentrate attention on these symbolically Oedipal relationships. We shall see that while there is no bad father figure in *La Règle du jeu* analogous to Jules Berry/Batala in *Le Crime de Monsieur Lange* the film nevertheless, partly through the childlessness of its major characters, articulates a pervasive crisis of masculinity.

27   The French word 'chasse' does duty for both.

28   Deleuze, Gilles (trans. Hugh Tomlinson and Robert Galeta), *Cinema 2: The Time-Image* (London: Athlone, 1989), p. 85.

29   Guislain et al.: La Règle du jeu: *profil d'une oeuvre*, p. 167.

30   This painting is reproduced on the cover of the original French edition of Lacan's *The Four Fundamental Concepts of Psychoanalysis*, in which text it serves as a figure of the inescapable death-drive. Rose-Marie Godier invokes the Holbein painting in her discussion of the importance of automata in *La Règle du jeu*.

31   Nancy: 'La Règle du jeu dans *La Règle du jeu*', p. 155.

32   The French 'jeu' carries both these meanings.

33   Burch and Sellier: *La Drôle de guerre des sexes du cinéma français*, p. 75.

34   Liselotte, *Le Guide des convenances* (Paris: 1915, 10th edition, no publisher given), p. 287.

35   Forbes, Jill, '*La Règle du jeu*', in Jill Forbes and Sarah Street (eds), *European Cinema: An Introduction* (Basingstoke/New York: 2000, Palgrave), pp. 80–92, p. 85.

36   Curchod: *La Règle du jeu*, p. 173.

37   Deleuze: *Cinema 2: The Time-Image*, p. 85.

SEQUENCE-BY-SEQUENCE ANALYSIS AND COMMENTARY

grim seriousness underpinning Renoir's 'merry drama' is nowhere more apparent than in this final sequence.

Notes

1 Bazin: *Jean Renoir*, pp. 82–3.

2 This latter point is made in Burch, Noël and Geneviève Sellier, *La Drôle de guerre des sexes du cinéma français, 1930-1956* (Paris: Nathan, 1996), p. 74.

3 Curchod, Olivier (ed.), *Jean Renoir: La Règle du jeu* (Paris: Livre de Poche, 1999), p. 36.

4 Sesonske, Alexander, *Jean Renoir: the French Films* (Cambridge, Massachusetts and London: Harvard University Press, 1980), p. 428.

5 O'Shaughnessy: *Jean Renoir*, p. 146.

6 Bazin: *Jean Renoir*, p. 78.

7 Bron, Jean-Albert, *Jean Renoir: La Règle du jeu* (Paris: Ellipses/Résonances, 1998), p. 120.

8 Godier, Rose-Marie, *L'Automate et le cinéma* (Paris: L'Harmattan, 2005), p. 82.

9 Serceau, Daniel, *Jean Renoir l'insurgé* (Paris: Sycomore, 1981), p. 129.

10 Esnault, Philippe, *L'Avant-scène du cinéma* (lii:1, 1 October 1965), p. 11.

11 Bardèche and Brasillach: *Histoire du cinéma*, vol. 2, p. 69.

12 Guislain, Pierre et al., *La Règle du jeu: profil d'une œuvre* (Paris: Hatier, 1998), p. 152.

13 Godier : *L'Automate et le cinéma*, p. 65.

14 Curchod, Olivier, *Jean Renoir:* La Règle du jeu (Paris: Livre de Poche, 1998), p. 277.

15 Faulkner, Christopher, *The Social Cinema of Jean Renoir* (Princeton: Princeton University Press, 1986), p. 117.

16 The reference here is to Edmond Rostand's 1897 romantic drama, filmed by Jean-Paul Rappeneau in 1990 with a memorable performance from Gérard Depardieu in the title role.

17 Sesonske: *Jean Renoir: The French Films*, p. 413.

18 Bron, Jean-Albert and Daniel Serceau, *Contre bande:* La Règle du jeu *de Jean Renoir* (Paris: Université de Paris I – Panthéon – Sorbonne, 1999), p. 47.

19 Sartre, Jean-Paul, *Réflexions sur la question juive* (Paris: Gallimard, 1954), pp. 100–101.

20 This term, coined by Jacques Derrida in *Spectres de Marx* (1993), is used to refer to a mode of reading attentive to 'the presence of the ghost as that which is neither present nor absent, neither dead nor alive' (Colin Davis: '*État présent:*

82 LA RÈGLE DU JEU

on whose behalf Schumacher is unwittingly acting is, of course, Robert, whose final speech recognizes this in claiming that Schumacher was acting within his rights. Having been dismissed from the Marquis's employment, in fact, Schumacher was doing no such thing. His deed – in this respect, the very reverse of Lange's – is an act of personal vengeance retroactively disguised as a legitimate defence of the existing order. The complicity between Schumacher and Robert implicit in this final speech is reinforced by the fact that both will shortly cease to be regarded as French – the former presumably to be redefined as German by the occupying forces who will condemn the latter to exile or worse. Of course, Renoir could not have 'known' that at the time *La Règle du jeu* was made but the film, we have seen, 'knows' a great deal about the France, indeed the Europe, of its time and its reception would surely not have been so tempestuous had that 'knowledge' not been manifest to the 1939 audience too. With the departure of Marceau, Robert too lacks a double. If that role seems to be filled by Schumacher at the end, it is for reasons of structural rather than personal affinity. Robert and Schumacher re-enter the château as master and servant once more but that relationship, as Hegel well knew, is a notoriously reversible one, never more so than in the ethnic and historical context of this film. Schumacher's 11th-hour discovery of a double – if that is what it is – may appear to repair what Deleuze has called the cracked crystal of the film, but the crystal of the society it depicts is thereby damaged beyond repair.

The contrast between the music that accompanied the credits and that which we hear at the end – the only two instances of non-diegetic music in the entire film – suggests this damage by a further and final mirroring, with the buoyancy of Mozart's 'German Dance no. 1 in C major' contrasting with the crepuscular tones of the intermezzo by Pierre-Alexandre Monsigny that are the last sounds we hear. That intermezzo occurs between the first and second act of a 1769 opera by this now forgotten composer, which bears the title *Le Déserteur*. The ironies of that title are multiple, echoing as it does the emotional inconstancy of so many of the film's characters and, on a larger scale, the impending fall of France. The shadows on the wall are like spectres returning to the feast, to resume dancing on a volcano. The

SEQUENCE-BY-SEQUENCE ANALYSIS AND COMMENTARY   81

château, their shadows loom large and ghostly on the wall, in a final shot whose resonance goes well beyond the intrigues we have just witnessed.

Mirrorings and doublings – structure and history

Working on this analysis of La Règle du jeu, I have been repeatedly struck by the manner in which the film at once eludes and elicits structural analysis. The openness of the filming, the use of deep focus so admired by Bazin, the apparent naturalism of the transition between one scene and the next all give the impression of a seamless whole, yet close attention to the film reveals a host of formal and structural parallels and echoes that clearly knit the text together in all its contradictions. Pre-eminent among these seems to be the topos of the mirror – literal (as when Octave's glance at himself confirms the cruel accuracy of Lisette's verdict), metonymic (the spyglass mirroring the specularity of the cinematic medium) or metaphorical (as in the complex array of doublings-up and reflections between the characters). Deleuze's assertion that Schumacher is 'the only character not to have a double or a reflection' is true as far as it goes but perhaps misleading in that it appears to suggest that each character, whether above or below stairs, retains the same doppelgänger throughout the film. This is true of Christine and Lisette, and perhaps too of The General and Saint-Aubin, but more contentious elsewhere. Robert's affinity with Marceau constructs the two men as doubles for much of the film, but Marceau's expulsion from the château at the end situates him, we have seen, as the alter ego of Octave. That place has, so to speak, become free with the killing of André, hitherto identifiable as Octave's double because of their long-standing friendship and the very different ways in which both are ill-adapted to the world of high society, signalled by Lisette's perception that neither would prove a suitable partner for Christine.

It would be possible to go beyond Deleuze and see the film's denouement as providing Schumacher too with the double he alone among the major dramatis personae has lacked. Marceau says when admitting that Schumacher fired the fatal shot, 'I went along with him', but the character

conducting and his own earlier presentation of the *limonaire* inside the château. La Chesnaye tells his guests and servants:

> Gentlemen, what has happened was nothing more than a deplorable accident. My gamekeeper Schumacher thought he saw a poacher, and fired as he had every right to do. Fate meant that André Jurieux was the victim of this error . . . Gentlemen, tomorrow we shall leave the château weeping for this exquisite friend, this excellent companion who was so good at making us forget that he was a famous man.

The final sentence was not included in the 1939 print.

This shot, like the two it echoes, is among the film's many great moments of performance. The difference with the two earlier shots is, of course, that their performances have shown their protagonists at their most sincere, whereas here Robert is telling the kind of omnipresent lie humorously denounced by Octave. His speech can be seen as an ironic echo of Lange's shooting of Batala at the end of *Le Crime de Monsieur Lange* – another action carried out by an individual in order to preserve the cohesion of a menaced social group. The distance between the qualified, and far from total, optimism of *Lange*'s denouement and the monstrous cynicism at the end of *La Règle du jeu* measures how the situation in France had changed within the space of three years. The sacrifice of one scapegoat – Jurieux – and the expulsion of two others – Marceau and Octave – are the price to be paid for the reassertion of a status quo which has saved La Chesnaye's marriage and restored the gamekeeper-turned-poacher-turned-gamekeeper as guardian of the order he has all but fatally disrupted.

Saint-Aubin sceptically observes, 'That's a new definition of the word "accident"!' but it is The General – the most fatuous representative of the old order – who appropriately has the film's final word, 'La Chesnaye's not short of class, and that's becoming rare, my dear Saint-Aubin, believe me . . . That's becoming rare!' The irony is twofold. La Chesnaye here receives the consecration of his aristocratic status from one who is all too likely, at least on the quiet, to regard him as an interloper; and that final acceptance, for a contemporary audience, is inevitably overshadowed by the exclusion that would have followed it on the fall of France. As the guests re-enter the

SEQUENCE-BY-SEQUENCE ANALYSIS AND COMMENTARY   79

Jackie return there from the greenhouse. Lisette reminds Jackie, close to collapse, of the obligations conferred by her social standing – 'A young woman like you, well brought-up and educated, has to be brave!' – and Christine more soberly informs her erstwhile rival in love – 'Jackie, people are looking at you.' Jackie's tragedy has consisted in her marginalization, a helplessly lovelorn figure all but disregarded by André whose most intimate words have been to tell her that he does not love her. Jean-Pierre Damour's description of her as 'incarnating . . . an idealism vanquished and imprisoned within the codes of high society'[61] is never truer than now, when, for the most fleeting of moments, she is the focus of an attention she has assuredly not wanted.

The codes of high society absorb her and her grief along with all the hurly-burly of the evening, for all the hint of gentle supportiveness in Christine's 'I'll take care of this young lady'. The film's penultimate shot reasserts those codes by way of a bravura piece of collective hypocrisy, in which La Chesnaye delivers a short speech from the steps ironically echoing at once Octave's miming, from the same spot, of Christine's father

78   LA RÈGLE DU JEU

pessimism – 'Lisette, you should have let me go. What's going to become of me now?' – to which Lisette, ever faithful to her mistress, replies, 'Leave me, Monsieur Octave, Madame needs me.' Octave bids her adieu, she responds, 'Goodbye, Monsieur Octave, I was very fond of you' – the past tense doing more to underline Octave's definitive exclusion from the world of the château than her use of 'au revoir' rather than 'adieu' does to counteract it – and pays a more flirtatious farewell to Marceau, who is entitled to a kiss and to the intimate 'tu' form, we may suspect, not on grounds of social class alone. Octave and Marceau, never more clearly signalled than now as the film's two most déclassé characters, have their first and last tête-à-tête, with Marceau proposing to 'cobble together bits and pieces' in the nearby woods while Octave says that he will return to Paris ('I'll try to get by'). The verb Octave uses here, 'me débrouiller', is similar in meaning to Marceau's 'bricoler', reinforcing the sense that the two men are now like mirror images of each other. They gloomily leave the château while, in the next shot, Christine, Lisette, Schumacher and

implausible. The crisis in Christine's marriage, we recall, has been provoked by Robert's embracing Geneviève like the lover he has been but will be no longer. To the feigned re-enactment of a dying passion corresponds the genuine – albeit, as we shall see, fleeting – acknowledgement of one long repressed, on Christine's side at least. 'Whom does Christine really love?' is, by this stage, a virtually unanswerable question and one that circumstances will soon combine to render cruelly irrelevant.

Schumacher, seconded by Marceau, goes to get his rifle while, within the château, Robert and André, for the moment unknowingly marginal players in the drama, agree that Octave is 'a really, really good fellow' – two ironically asymmetrical moments of male bonding. Robert sententiously opines, 'I don't believe in anything much, you know, but I get the feeling that I'm going to begin believing in friendship.' Octave asks Lisette to fetch her mistress's coat, to her obvious displeasure. Clothing, as an indicator of what Bourdieu would call 'distinction', looms large in these scenes. Octave's irritation at discovering that his already battered hat has vanished is suggestive of the straitened circumstances that cause Lisette to disapprove of the projected elopement on grounds not only of age – 'I believe the young should stay with the young and the old with the old!' (a harsh verdict considering that only seven years separated Renoir and Nora Gregor) – but of money – 'A woman like Madame needs a great many things, and if you've no money what will you do?' We see Octave, in reflection, finding his hat, dusting it down and catching a view of his own image the while which, in a poignant mirror-phase moment, brings it home to him that Lisette is right. André enters, asking where Christine is, and Octave, in a noble gesture of self-renunciation that will directly precipitate the final tragedy, tells him that she is waiting for him in the greenhouse.

André gratefully embraces his friend and runs out towards his beloved, only to be gunned down by Schumacher. This – the only human death in the film – we see in long-shot, as André rolls over when the bullet hits him like the rabbits in the hunt sequence. This comparison is made explicit by the horrified Marceau when he rushes back to the château, breaking the news to Jackie and Octave who, on hearing the shot, have already feared the worst. Octave's response is one of narcissistic

76   LA RÈGLE DU JEU

have gone before, is conspicuous by its absence. There is, on the other hand, irony in the fact that Christine has donned her servant's cloak to protect her from the cold – the very reason why Schumacher, stereotypically putting practicality before style, chose it for his unenthusiastic wife.

Christine vows that she will never return to the château and retreats to the greenhouse with Octave. We see them in long shot while, in the foreground, Schumacher curses the fact that he has no bullets in his revolver, saying to Marceau, 'I fired them all at you!' The tenderness Christine displays towards Octave is of a complex kind, rendered all the more ambiguous by Nora Gregor's inexpressive acting. Octave has earlier compared Christine to his sister, yet here her feelings for him seem more maternal – 'All you need is somebody to look after you. I'm going to look after you.' This tenderly incestuous combination of emotions leads to a mutual avowal of feeling and Christine's asking Octave to kiss her 'on the mouth, like a lover' in yet another of the symmetries in which the film abounds. This, according to Faulkner, was cut after the film's premiere, probably because the less sympathetic presentation of Octave in the shorter 1939 version made it somewhat

SEQUENCE-BY-SEQUENCE ANALYSIS AND COMMENTARY   75

poacher-turned-gamekeeper but the next best thing to it, while Schumacher
bids fair to travel in the opposite direction.

Octave, meanwhile, in another sequence absent from the 1939 print,
unburdens his sense of failure to Christine, describing himself as 'a parasite'
– in material terms conceivably an accurate judgement – and regretting the
'contact with the audience' he would have had if he had succeeded in becoming a conductor. This is a discreet but acute reflection on Renoir's double
role in the film, perhaps achieving, as an actor, the contact with a live audience that the director, of necessity, cannot have. (Renoir was, of course, to
achieve this at the film's first screenings, albeit in an unwanted manner). A
gently flirtatious warmth pervades their conversation as they are spied on
by Marceau and Schumacher who mistake Christine for Lisette whose cloak
she is wearing. Imbroglios based on mistaken identity, often connected with
the adoption of disguise and sometimes with cross-dressing, are a common
device in comic theatre (*Twelfth Night* and *Le Mariage de Figaro* are among
the best-known examples), but here the comic, in contrast to the scenes that

74   LA RÈGLE DU JEU

The anxious Lisette joins her mistress, telling her that Robert's affair with Geneviève pre-dated their marriage. Christine is devastated that, for three years, her life has been based on a lie, to which Octave retorts, in another of the film's memorable formulations absent from the 1939 version, 'We live in a period where everybody lies: pharmaceutical prospectuses, governments, the radio, the cinema, the newspapers! So why do you expect mere private individuals not to lie as well?' The reliability of media in general and the cinema in particular is here called into question by the film's director, reflecting at once on the veracity of the camera (as in the spyglass episode) and on the political and ideological conjuncture of the years immediately before the Second War. Joly's remark that, in this film, 'individual duplicity . . . symbolizes the elevation of the lie to the status of an institution'[60] is distilled in Octave's words. Christine, cleaving to her childhood friend and playmate as the only man she can trust, suggests to Octave that they go for a walk in the park. Lisette fears that she will catch cold and, in a gesture of kindness that helps to precipitate the tragic denouement, lends her mistress her cloak – the one proudly presented to her by Schumacher a few scenes earlier, whose practical qualities – 'It's warm and guaranteed waterproof' – she has dismissed with a curt, 'Yes, but it's not very becoming!' Imbroglios grounded in disguise were fundamental to the early modern theatre, with Beaumarchais's *Le Mariage de Figaro* and Mozart's opera making extensive use of them. It is unlikely that Christine would, in any normal circumstances, wear a garment so dowdily functional as that of which Lisette is the unwilling owner, so that her 'disguise' – not deliberately adopted as such – will prove to be a lethally effective one.

Marceau and Schumacher run into each other on the way out of the château and a gloomy moment of two-shot male bonding – not in the original version – occurs when both realize that Lisette is lost to them and Marceau comments, 'She's not married to you, she's married to "Madame"!' Marceau sparkily outlines future plans which involve getting a game-dealer's licence to legitimize his activities while the crestfallen Schumacher, never more titanically abject than here, can only sob that he will stay in the area 'because of my wife, you understand? I'll get her back from them'. The potential role-reversal here is a piquant one – Marceau is not quite a

SEQUENCE-BY-SEQUENCE ANALYSIS AND COMMENTARY   73

send Schumacher packing and leave Marceau in the château with his wife. Marceau's lachrymose response – 'The Marquis wanted to raise my station by making me a servant: I'll never forget that!' – is, perhaps, not to be taken entirely at face value. Armand-Jean Cauliez's remark that 'Marceau, sympathetic though he is, is in fact the most *reactionary* character in the film'[57] is, in part, undercut by his earlier observation that Figaro – Beaumarchais's harbinger of revolution – 'speaks through several voices at once: Octave's, Marceau's and La Chesnaye's'.[58] We may also be reminded here of the ironic resignation speech of the eponymous valet (played by the director himself) in Guitry's *Désiré* who, having come close to having a love affair with his mistress, gravely informs her as he departs, 'To serve, madam, is a wonderful thing.' Marceau's evident incapacity to adapt to the stringently regulated world of château life certainly suggests that he is not cut out for the world of service and that the catch in his voice can be read ambiguously as a resigned expression of regret or as an extension of the badinage he has engaged in with his employer.

André and Robert, shocked back into the world of convention, converse affably, with Robert reflecting that their fisticuffs have reminded him of stories he has occasionally read in the papers about 'an Italian navvy who tried to make off with the wife of a Polish labourer, which led to a knife fight' – a distant echo perhaps of Renoir's *Toni*, about internecine love rivalries between Italian, French and Spanish workers in Provence. The veneer of civilized living is hastily re-established in Robert's declaration that he is happy for Christine to go off with André but anxious about the aviator's precarious living – 'You might have an accident!', a remark whose ironic force will shortly become clear. Cut to Octave and Christine on the terrace, where Octave is reflecting that André may be triumphant in the air but, on the ground, he is 'defenceless and clumsy'. Peter Wollen has commented on the widespread construction of the aviator as modern hero in the 1930s, citing figures as disparate as Saint-Exupéry and Cary Grant in Hawks's 1939 *Only Angels Have Wings*.[59] In this context, Octave's remark – proffered by the Renoir who had been invalided out of the First War after a flying accident – acquires great elegiac force, even before we realize how tragically literal it will turn out to be.

72   LA RÈGLE DU JEU

Corneille to 'put a stop to this comedy' to which the major-domo, in one of
the film's greatest lines, fully worthy of his theatrically glorious name,
responds, 'Which one, monsieur le marquis?' As Schumacher advances,
Marceau hides behind the ample Charlotte, while the guests, realizing that
this is no concert-party turn, freeze in terror with their hands up – a gesture
often read as a prefiguration of France's collapse in 1940 and particularly
suggestive in the light of Schumacher's Alsatian origins. Berthelin decides to
turn off the *limonaire* – by now, in an incongruous piece of *viennoiserie*,
playing a Strauss waltz – but, in keeping with his quietly sinister role, he
succeeds only in disrupting it so that it emits hideously inharmonious sounds.
As 'mood music', this is by now all too appropriate. Schumacher cries as he
is apprehended by two servants, 'Let go of me! It's me, Schumacher!', in an
ironic reassertion of an order and an identity on which he has all but lost
his grip. Marceau effusively thanks Charlotte for the cover she has unwittingly
provided – farce at its most basic mutating into verbal comedy – while Robert
unavailingly tries to give a double dose of sleeping pills to the by now thoroughly hysterical Geneviève, whom he picks up bodily and takes to her room.
This is to be the last we see of her. It is significant that, during this episode,
Jackie is fainting into André's arms and also being taken to her room by the
man she vainly loves – yet another mirroring, this time synchronic rather
than diachronic, and an implicit rapprochement of two women who do not
address a word to each other in the course of the film but are, in a sense,
united by the frustration of their passion.

The 'B-players' Berthelin and The General retire to bed, for the time
being at least, along with Charlotte who blithely accepts Robert's apology
for the conduct of his staff – 'Those people have to enjoy themselves like
the rest of us!' – ambiguously a crass misreading of the deadly serious issues
at stake or a recognition that passion forms a part of as well as a challenge
to the rules of the game. The La Bruyères follow suit, clearing the stage for
a denouement which will concern only the major characters. Robert tells
the mortified Schumacher that he will have to leave his employment without, it would seem, Lisette who tartly refuses to follow him into the Alsatian
unknown – 'If Madame still wants me, I'm staying in her service!' Marceau
is likewise laid off, on the grounds that it would be immoral for Robert to

SEQUENCE-BY-SEQUENCE ANALYSIS AND COMMENTARY 71

evocation of a bygone world of cultured harmony analogous to that wistfully recalled by Boieldieu and Rauffenstein in *La Grande Illusion*. Yet it is also profoundly and multiply ironic for Octave, as he finishes his mime, is bitterly aware of his own failure as a musician and that failure is, so to speak, redeemed by Renoir's role on the other side of the camera, orchestrating and conducting the all-too-organized chaos we have been witnessing. Like, in their different ways, the opening sequence at Le Bourget and the spyglass episode, this scene is self-reflective, the film operating a *mise en abyme* not of its own technologies as in the previous examples but of the very process of its directing. Octave's staging of his own failure is also Renoir's staging of his own triumph.

Schumacher meanwhile is running amok in the salon, the guests initially unconcerned since, like The General, they take Schumacher's rampage for 'another comic turn' following on the earlier theatricals. The General goes on to remark disapprovingly, 'I can't stand shooting!' Following on from his role in the hunt sequence, this is rich indeed but we scarcely have time to appreciate it, caught up as we are in the rhythm of the chase. Robert orders

70   LA RÈGLE DU JEU

The following scene sees Schumacher, in the ultimate breach of the rules for a gamekeeper, reach for his revolver, shooting out a lamp beside the still brawling Robert and André. Stendhal, in *Le Rouge et le noir*, famously compared politics in a work of art to a pistol-shot in the middle of a concert – an all but literal description of what we have just heard – but has one of his characters retort, in substance, that the political cannot plausibly be evicted from the novel for all that. Something very similar is true of *La Règle du jeu*, where Schumacher's pistol-shot at once disrupts and comes as the logical continuation of the increasingly discordant social concert we have been witnessing. Robert, already arguably feminized at and by the moment of his collector's triumph, responds hysterically (the word is in the screenplay) to the shot and to André's assertion that Christine has disappeared, waving his arms and gesticulating. Geneviève, finally scenting her moment, declares that Christine has gone off with Octave, before asking Robert, first calmly then in an explosive shriek, 'When are we leaving?' It is as if Schumacher's loss of control were affecting the characters around him too.

There follows a second scene (absent from the version originally shown), a reflection and counterpart to that between Robert and Marceau earlier, which affords a moment of peace, like an adagio interlude amid the frenzied presto of the violence erupting all around. The musical comparison is appropriate, for Octave is relating to Christine his recollection of watching her father (and his former teacher) conduct. The first shot of this scene is of the French windows leading out on to the terrace; only, after a few seconds, much as in the car-crash scene involving André and Octave, do the two characters walk into view. They move outside on to the terrace, where the remainder of the short scene is filmed largely in long shot, something of a relief from the unrelenting close-ups and medium shots of the previous episodes, and relies as much on movement and body language as on verbal narration. Renoir-as-Octave walks across the terrace in imitation of the performance he is describing – 'He crossed the stage without seeing a thing!' – and mimes Christine's father conducting before slumping depressively down on the steps. The tranquil power of this scene resides partly in the gentle tenderness between Octave and Christine and partly in its

SEQUENCE-BY-SEQUENCE ANALYSIS AND COMMENTARY 69

about to be explosively brushed aside by the irruption of a naked truth that will significantly, if inadvertently, take Robert's *limonaire* for one of its targets.

It is Schumacher – the guardian of order, a tense superego from beneath which an uncontrollable id is about to burst forth – who is the agent of that irruption, as Deleuze's analysis demonstrates. Marceau and Lisette are flirting in the kitchen when Schumacher appears down the stairs, causing the former poacher to hide. The spouses have a thunderous face-to-face in the kitchen, the gamekeeper proposing to take her back to Alsace where the likes of Marceau are 'shot down at dead of night in the forest'. Marceau, seen first in shadow and then attempting to slink out in the background – a reversal of the earlier kitchen scene where Schumacher has appeared in the background to surprise the flirtatious couple – is understandably spooked by this threat and noisily knocks over a tray. With all restraint now dissipated, Schumacher charges into the salon in pursuit of the other two, flagrantly disregarding Robert's shouted instructions and even knocking his master to one side.

In the next few scenes, the action proceeds with such breakneck speed, and on so many planes at once, that anything like a full account would slow this analysis down absurdly; there is really no substitute for a viewing or, indeed, repeated viewings here. Robert, doubtless profiting by the example of one of his servants as he has done earlier with Marceau, punches André in the face, sending him flying on to a sofa. David Bordwell and Kristin Thompson refer to this as an example of 'the use of a sixth zone – the offscreen space behind and near the camera'[55] – and, thus, a further instance of the extraordinary creativity with which Renoir uses off-screen space. The horrified Christine confides in Octave that she has proclaimed her love to André and that she is grievously disappointed that he has been so insistent on abiding by formalities – the very ones that are exploding all around her as she speaks. Octave's reply – 'There's one thing you quite forget; he's a hero!' – is less dismissive than it may seem, implying as it does that the apparently high-tech André is really a hero from the age of chivalry, anachronistically attached to bygone courtesies – 'the quotation of a hero in a world where heroes are out of date'.[56]

68 LA RÈGLE DU JEU

Limonaire was the name of a well-known French make of fairground organ, which ceased production in 1932 but, for nearly a century before that, had specialized in the largest and most glittering instruments of their kind. La Chesnaye, shown initially in a crane shot the better to heighten the theatrical suspense, presents to his guests what he describes as 'the culmination of my career as a "collector"' – a majestic *limonaire*, whose dimensions and éclat are likely to blind a contemporary audience to its comparative vulgarity and low value compared, for instance, to some of Robert's eighteenth-century dolls. Perhaps, for the beleaguered husband, size is everything – something certainly suggested by Jacques Lacan's comment on the shot in which the camera focuses on Robert's 'derisory and disturbing rictus of ecstasy'.[52] This shot occurs after the camera has tracked across the *limonaire*'s moving figures before coming to rest on its owner, shown wiping his mouth with a handkerchief. Lacan invokes the shot fleetingly during a discussion of Plato's *Symposium*, a text which proffers a strikingly pre-modern *mise en scène* of desire and the motility of its object(s). Desire, for Lacan, is always at least potentially castratory and systemically doomed to fix itself on this or that object rather than achieving a totality necessarily out of reach. Robert, at this point in the narrative, is grappling with a threat to his masculine dominance of a somewhat more circumscribed, but no less menacing, kind than that articulated by Lacan, so that the fetishistic pride he evinces in the *limonaire* is all too understandable. For Lacan the *limonaire* is the '*objet a* of his fantasy' – the '*objet a*' in Lacanian discourse being any part-object on which desire focuses – and his libidinal investment in it is manifested in the 'womanly blush with which he steps back after directing his phenomenon'.[53] Robert's 'rictus' – a term often associated with a death's head – is thus that at once of an ecstatic collector and a derisory prospective cuckold, which no doubt accounts for its disturbing quality for Lacan. Renoir himself regarded this shot as one of the very best he had ever filmed and, for Nancy, the intensity of its effect is closely connected with the 'emphatic emotion' Robert displays. 'Truth is indecent when it is no more than what it appears';[54] Nancy's remark, reminiscent of the classical adage that Truth is to be found at the bottom of a well and of Oscar Wilde's 'The truth is seldom plain and never simple', distils the rules of the game in Renoir's film, rules that are

SEQUENCE-BY-SEQUENCE ANALYSIS AND COMMENTARY

this time to denote homosexuality. Such a reading, which I have developed at more length elsewhere,[49] is certainly lent credence by the presence of the homosexual Dick among the singers.

For O'Shaughnessy, the singers' wigs and costumes 'suggest they are Orthodox Jews',[50] a reading that might imply a not entirely courteous satirization of their host's ethnicity, in keeping with the undercurrents of anti-Semitism elsewhere in the film. They could equally well be seen (the two views are not incompatible) as burlesque representatives of the petite bourgeoisie otherwise absent from the film, like the bank clerk and 'Sunday painter' played by Michel Simon in *La Chienne* eight years before, who comes to grief through his extra-marital affair with Janie Marèze's femme fatale. The film's two songs, as potently if not so obviously as 'Danse macabre', thus comment acerbically on the world we are watching. Entertainment in *La Règle du jeu* is, as the hunt scene has also shown, always in deadly earnest.

'Nous avons l'vé le pied' is followed by what for Pierre Guislain is the epiphanic moment of the entire film, what Renoir called 'the *limonaire* shot'.[51]

66   LA RÈGLE DU JEU

is the modern-day one of technology and the media, contemptuously refuses, declaring that, if Saint-Aubin's witnesses turn up the following morning, he will throw them out. Saint-Aubin furiously replies that he will have André disgraced; the verb he uses is the rare and archaic 'carencer' which, to quote Curchod, is 'quite in the style of the ridiculous oaf he is'.[48] The decline of the old aristocracy had been matter for regret in *La Grande Illusion*, set nearly a quarter of a century before. By the time of *La Règle du jeu*, that class's manners and conventions have become a risible and etiolated shadow of their former selves, so that Saint-Aubin's cleaving to them merely shows up his fundamental coarseness.

André may not duel but he is no pacifist either, as he shows when kicking Saint-Aubin up the backside in a profoundly un-aristocratic gesture by any standards. Saint-Aubin punches him twice and, for the first time in a film where violence has long simmered beneath the surface but become apparent only in the hunt scene, a fight breaks out, in the course of which the pugilists fall through a door and are then seen from the other side literally brawling their way up the stairs. The mobilization of the (studio-set) decor here is extraordinary yet, at the same time, unobtrusive. Jackie collapses on witnessing what is going on, while the imperturbable Corneille has Saint-Aubin helped up. André now confronts Christine with her failure to meet him at Le Bourget; she admits her love for him and wants them to run away together at once. André's response is that he must speak to La Chesnaye first because 'there are rules' – the closest the film ever comes to the words of its title.

Cut from the bemused Christine to a song that presents more difficulty to the audience than any of the others in the film because of its exceptionally quick-fire delivery. La Bruyère, Berthelin, Cava and Dick, wearing bowler hats and false beards, sing 'Nous avons l'vé le pied' by the early impresario and alleged inventor of payola Francis Salabert. The song's chorus recounts how its singers, married though they are, have 'cleared off' (which 'levé le pied' translates as) – a light comic version of the conjugal dissatisfaction that suffuses the film at this point and conceivably one with gay overtones, for the term 'pédale' was just coming into use as a not always pejorative term for a homosexual. The singers also have crazy ideas in their heads or 'des idées folles en tête', and 'folles' was likewise coming into use at about

SEQUENCE-BY-SEQUENCE ANALYSIS AND COMMENTARY   65

defenceless, you can do whatever you like with her.' – and asks why the marquis does not do the same. Robert's reply – 'You have to have the gift for that!' – is greeted by Marceau with the disingenuously modest, 'Of course.' It is tempting to read this conversation as an overleaping of the barriers so marked in the film, a man-to-man heart-to-heart rendering social class irrelevant, but such a view would be a dangerously partial one, for considerations of class are right at the centre of the stage here. Robert's material wealth and Marceau's agile wit – what Bourdieu might have called 'economic capital' and 'cultural capital' – are each ineffectual without the other, the aristocrat incapable of parlaying his way out of a tight corner and the rustic proletarian bereft of the wherewithal to turn his seductive drollery to the advantage he might like. Jacques Joly contrasts *La Règle du jeu* to its theatrical antecedents by pointing out that:

> whereas Marivaux, Beaumarchais and Musset present their plays basically as a 'geography of the heart' and a poetics of sentiment, Renoir's point of departure is on the contrary a reflection on the notion of class, so that the film in a way 'historicizes' the conventional scheme of these comedies.[47]

It is Renoir's 'reflection on the nature of class' that gives this scene seemingly so dominated by the 'poetics of sentiment' its distinctively ironic flavour – an irony reinforced when Marceau enlists Robert as his 'servant' by asking him to keep an eye out for Schumacher while he makes good his escape.

In yet another of the mirrorings that permeate this film, the gamekeeper is now to turn poacher – albeit in defence of what is 'rightfully' his – much as his rival the poacher has turned manservant. Schumacher is stopped by Robert as he stalks through the hall and curtly told to go back to the corridors – 'Tonight, I've allowed you access to the corridors and that's all. Why not use my bathroom while you're about it?' A farcical triangular argument follows between the jealous André, Saint-Aubin and Christine, who refuses to justify her behaviour. Saint-Aubin challenges André to a duel – a supposedly aristocratic way of settling accounts, but one that was well and truly in decline by the time the film was made, not least because killing one's opponent was punishable by life imprisonment. André, whose 'aristocracy'

64   LA RÈGLE DU JEU

idiot Saint-Aubin!' – and demands unavailingly that Robert should leave with her.

The following scene is one of two to mark a moment of relative tranquillity amid the hubbub – action briefly giving way to reflection and 'alternating movement and calm establishing a rhythm'.[46] Marceau, hiding from Schumacher, pulls Robert behind a pillar – as we have seen, it is not the first time pillars have assumed an important role in the film's *mise en scène*. He asks his master not to give him away – the first time the marquis has realized the imbroglio among his servants – and the two alter egos have a wistfully cynical two-shot exchange about what Robert calls 'the notorious question of relations between men and women'. The Muslim harem, for him, would be the best way of avoiding the painful choice he has always been reluctant to make, and he displays a degree of bedraggled self-knowledge in admitting, 'I don't want to hurt anybody – especially not women! That's the drama of my life.' Marceau's remark that one needs money to have a harem finds a rueful echo when he has explained to Robert that the important thing is to make women laugh – 'When a woman laughs, she is

phically as in Holbein's painting but in a manner that abolishes the 'fourth wall' of theatrical representation as the spectres, filmed in extremely deep focus and flickeringly lit, descend into and mingle with – even touch – the audience. At one point, the camera even goes behind the dancers, reinforcing the sequence's powerful dramatization of the hauntological.

The guests squeal and cower in mock – or is it entirely mock? – terror in the darkness, where Lisette and Marceau embrace under the scrutiny of Berthelin disguised as Death. In the background, echoing his earlier appearance in the kitchen scene but this time in tragic rather than comic mode, Schumacher – described by Godier as Berthelin's 'long-standing ally' – makes the entry which is to 'precipitate the comedy towards its funereal conclusion'.[45] The transgressive couple, alerted by Robert's driver, hastily separate and pretend to be entirely caught up in the entertainment. We see Christine, dizzy with drink, hesitating between André and the lewder attentions of Saint-Aubin while Schumacher pulls Lisette back and sets off in pursuit of Marceau. The characters here, in the progressive inexorability with which they lose control, are exemplars of what Deleuze and Guattari in *The Anti-Oedipus* call 'desiring machines', cyborgs of passion the rules of whose games bring them ever more into tragic as well as comic conflict with the rules of their society.

Upstairs and downstairs, in a blatant violation of the regulation of social space, are now playing out their amorous rivalries on the same level. Robert asks André whether he knows where Christine is; André replies that he too is looking for her; Christine – seen at one point ducking out of sight in the background – is meanwhile the recipient of Saint-Aubin's attentions; and Octave, who through his very *déclassement* bridges more than any other character the world of the masters and that of the servants, is still the prisoner of his bearskin, which nobody has the time to help him remove. Schumacher meanwhile utters a zombie-like 'No' to André's question whether he has seen Christine. It is Geneviève who finally stops to help Octave out of his disguise, as though to emphasize that she is now marginal to the emotional currents swirling all around her. In a final desperate attempt to reassert control over Robert, she denounces Christine – 'But she doesn't love you any more! . . . If she did, she wouldn't be off with that

62   LA RÈGLE DU JEU

to make it an anthem for supporters of the putschist manqué General Boulanger, who had been on the verge of carrying out a coup d'état in 1888. In the light of the humiliating defeat the French army was to experience less than a year after the film's release, the blithe self-confidence of the lyrics – 'Cheerful and contented, we marched unhesitatingly and triumphantly towards Longchamp, our hearts at ease' – rings distinctly ironic. As the curtain descends, a series of manic pursuits begins – Geneviève hot on Robert's tail, Robert like André in search of Christine, Octave looking for anybody who will help him out of his bearskin disguise. Berthelin pleads that he has no time to help and, uttering the ominous 'Let's talk about serious matters!', puts on a death mask. He and three fellow revellers disguised as ghosts then perform a dance to the strains of Saint-Saëns's 'Danse macabre' – uncanny because of the absence of words or, indeed, of any visible human source for the music. Charlotte, who has enthusiastically accompanied the earlier song on the piano, stares in wonderment as a piano roll – the first technical device making it possible to hear music on demand, predating even the wax cylinder – causes Saint-Saëns's tune to be heard and the keys to move seemingly of their own accord. The hitherto carefree stage is transformed into 'the place from which death shows itself'[44] – not anamor-

SEQUENCE-BY-SEQUENCE ANALYSIS AND COMMENTARY 61

It is worth noting, before we begin a detailed analysis of this 'final act', that this is where the differences between the 81-minute version originally screened and the current 106-minute version are most marked. Christopher Faulkner has provided an admirable analysis of these on one of the Criterion DVDs, pointing out that the additional footage presents Octave in a far more sympathetic light than the truncated version would have done and thus renders the film as a whole less harsh and condemnatory. Key moments of divergence between the two versions will be indicated below.

The evening's amateur theatricals, as we see them, begin with the end of a sketch in which the principal characters are all dressed in Tyrolean costume. There follows a song – 'En r'venant d'la revue'/'On our way back from the review', a popular music-hall *chanson* from the late nineteenth century – performed by Dick, Berthelin, La Bruyère and the Italian guest Cava. According to the celebrated photographer Cartier-Bresson, who worked as an assistant to Renoir on the film and has a minor role as an English manservant, this was added at the last minute by way of a joke. If so, it is an extremely telling one. The song's daredevil militarism had helped

60   LA RÈGLE DU JEU

and around the chaotic (in a strong sense) transformation of Schumacher from superego to id',[40] from enforcer to destroyer of society's order.

This may seem an excessively apocalyptic approach to the farcical scene analyzed here, but the violence with which Schumacher grabs hold of the flirtatious Marceau, shaking him until his teeth rattle, sits disquietingly with the demands of his role. He has already flouted these, as Corneille tartly reminds him, by straying into the kitchens; meanwhile, the guests are waiting for the shoes Marceau should by now have cleaned. Corneille's remark, 'It's a real revolution in the château!', will turn out to be less of an exaggeration than it may appear. Schumacher, mortified, leaves the kitchens, Lisette taunting him by echoing Corneille's reproach that he is 'getting in the way of our work'.

From fancy dress to tragedy in less than an hour

The next sequence is separated from what precedes it by a gap of about ten hours – the final interruption in the temporal continuity of the film. What Curchod describes as 'the mad *soirée* and the tragic night at La Colinière'[41] thus, in fact, lasts no more than 44 minutes though any sense of chronometric time is likely to evaporate given the rapidity with which events unfold. The average shot length in this final section is actually very similar to that of the film as a whole – 24 seconds compared to 21; it is the rapid movements of the characters, and of the camera between and around them, rather than quick-fire cutting that give the sense of a headlong pile-up of events. Tracking shots and depth of focus combine throughout this part of the film to delirious effect. Gerald Mast's view that '[t]he premise of *The Rules of the Game* is to reduce human beings to the same kind of clockwork puppets as the Marquis' birds and music boxes'[42] seems to me exactly the reverse of the truth here for, as Godier points out, the Bergsonian definition of comedy as 'the mechanical overlaying the living' is inverted in these scenes.[43] The smoothly functioning mechanisms of society, represented metonymically by Robert's collection of toys, are to malfunction ever more catastrophically as the film nears its end.

a mechanical doll seen in close-up next to Marceau the better to underline the similarities between Marceau and Robert already hinted at. Lisette, Eve-like, munches an apple and inadvertently treads on Marceau's hand; while she is tenderly nursing him, we see Schumacher, in one of the great comic deep-focus shots, enter in the background, a disruptive force appearing, as he is to do more than once hereafter, at the most inconvenient moment possible. This scene bears the imprint of farce rather than the sophisticated verbal comedy we more readily associate with this film, yet the two coexist quite happily for much of its length – one reason why it has sometimes been called 'Shakespearean' in contrast to the more stratified and segregated French theatrical tradition.

Schumacher has hitherto presented himself as the champion of law and order, directing operations during the hunt and denouncing Marceau's depredations, but this scene is the first suggestion that there is more to him than that. Deleuze uses the metaphor of the crystal to render the symmetries by which *La Règle du jeu* is structured, particularly through the use of deep focus which engenders:

> a coexistence of the actual image of men and the virtual image of beasts, the actual image of living beings and the virtual image of automata, the actual image of characters and their virtual image of their roles during the party, the actual image of the masters and their virtual image in the servants, the actual image of the servants and their virtual image in the masters.[37]

The symmetry between Christine and Lisette, André and Octave, Robert and Marceau certainly bears this argument out. But – and this is the strength of Deleuze's analysis – this crystalline equilibrium is not a closed, homeostatic formal system, for 'depth of field always arranges a background in the circuit through which something can flee: the crystal is cracked'.[38] That cracking – of a crystal but also of a human being – is strikingly portended when Schumacher appears in the background in this scene. Schumacher, indeed, is, for Deleuze, the exception to the film's symmetrical rule, for as 'the only character who does not have a double or reflection . . . he is the one who breaks the circuit, who shatters the cracked crystal with rifle shots and causes its contents to escape'.[39] Thus it is possible to claim that 'the film's narrative is ordered by

58   LA RÈGLE DU JEU

Tyrolean but at one point dresses as a skeleton. Other French films of this period laid great stress on disguise, either as part of a popular theatrical tradition – Carné's *Les Enfants du paradis* in which Jean-Louis Barrault's Baptiste is based on the real-life mime Debureau, who introduced elements of the *commedia dell'arte* into nineteenth-century French boulevard theatre – or in the more moneyed context of a masked ball – Jean Grémillon's *Lumière d'été* (1943) whose ball sequence clearly owes much to *La Règle du jeu*. Renoir's film, however, is surely second to none in the unspectacular richness and suggestiveness with which its disguises are deployed.

Before they can be donned, however, the guests' shoes have to be cleaned – a task with which we see Marceau busying himself in the kitchen, quoting the while from Corneille and Hugo. Implausible though this may seem from a poacher (albeit reformed), Olivier Curchod suggests that it stems from 'a culture probably inherited from the Third Republic's village schools'[36] and it unquestionably adds to his powers of seduction with Lisette, who steals up on him while he is declaiming. There follows a comic but unmistakably erotically charged game of catch between them, accompanied by music from

SEQUENCE-BY-SEQUENCE ANALYSIS AND COMMENTARY 57

suggests, such costumes worn by some of the other French guests may serve rather as a sharp reminder of the *Anschluss*. Less allegorically, it appears, from a 1915 manual of etiquette, that the Tyrolean hat with its 'fantasy cockerel-feathers'[34] was commonly worn by women who went hunting.

Octave, for his part, decides to go as a bear, reverting we may think to type as Christine will do. Jill Forbes's view that '[p]erhaps these costumes are intended to reveal "true" identity rather than to disguise'[35] is a convincing one, echoing as it does the *commedia dell'arte* tradition in which masks served to identify characters rather than to hide them – and in which we may remember the *innamorati* or central loving couple alone went unmasked, as though the purity of their passion would admit of no dissembling. André, first an *innamorato* and then a sacrifice, adopts less disguise than any of the others, pretending to be the tamer of Octave's bear by way of scarves draped over his head and shoulders but with his evening dress still on display. Robert is a Tyrolean male, as though subordinating himself to Christine redux, while the ineffectually lecherous Saint-Aubin dresses as a goatherd and Berthelin, in a striking figuration of the film's political subtext, is also a preterite one, dependent upon an optical illusion. (Might we imagine the Godard of 1969's *Vent d'est* peering out from behind Berthelin's spectacles and seeking to console Christine with the notorious bon mot – 'Ce n'est pas une image juste, c'est juste une image'?) Nancy admirably condenses the interplay of truth and illusion in saying:

> Thus, she [Geneviève] will believe or play at believing, for as long as a kiss lasts, in the love whose end is sealed by that feigned or forced kiss, while unknown to her she will be seen by the wife who will take this double illusion – of the kiss and of the pretence of believing in it – for the truth of an adultery of which she was unaware, and which is genuinely revealed to her just as it is coming to an end. Two truths answer each other in the guise of two illusions.[31]

The convolutedness of the play or game[32] of truth and illusion stands in inverse proportion to the comparative simplicity of the *mise en scène* at this point – a chamber drama of passion, largely in close-up, in contrast to the open vistas and frenetic activity that have gone before.

Back in the château

We return to the château and what at first appears to be a stand-off between Christine and Geneviève evolves into a curious alliance between them. For Burch and Sellier this demonstrates Christine's 'misunderstanding of the rules of the war of the sexes French-style, founded on division between women'[33] though it could equally well be read as a moment, however fleeting, of female solidarity in a male-dominated world. They share a worldly complicity, expressed largely through two-shots, in condemning Robert's venial personal habits, such as smoking in bed – something more surprising in Christine than in her rival. It is almost as if Christine were learning from Geneviève's example, dismissing André as too sincere 'and sincere people are tiresome!', and taking her ostensibly more worldly-wise rival in hand to help her choose a costume – in the event, a gypsy one – for the fancy-dress soirée. Christine elects to dress as a Tyrolean, which may suggest a nostalgia for the comforting certainties of her homeland though, as O'Shaughnessy

SEQUENCE-BY-SEQUENCE ANALYSIS AND COMMENTARY   55

The spyglass also, of course, represents the film camera – that camera which it was widely believed, in those pre-special-effects days, could not lie. Berthelin boasts that the spyglass enables the watcher to 'share in the most intimate life' of the squirrel but its range turns out to be significantly greater. During this episode, Geneviève and Robert are at some distance from the others, embroiled in an at once sophisticated and heartbroken exchange in which Robert declares that he no longer loves her and, after threatening to tell Christine of their affair, she acknowledges, 'One can fight against hatred, but against boredom there's nothing to be done.' Might Cocteau have had this scene in mind when he wrote the dialogue for Bresson's 1944 *Les Dames du bois de Boulogne*, in which Jean (Paul Bernard) tells his mistress Hélène (Maria Casarès), 'My heart is detaching itself from you'? Renoir's scene is the double of the earlier one between the two lovers in Geneviève's apartment and, here again, body language is to belie the characters' true feelings as well as expressing them. The intensity of feeling beneath the coolly civilized surface was sardonically thrown into relief in the Paris scene by the couple's standing next to two Buddha statues; here, it is a simulacrum of passion rather than of indifference that is acted out as Geneviève asks Robert to feign love for her one last time. She is seen in sombre close-up with Robert behind her as she makes this final request, 'I'd like you to take me in your arms as you used to do. I'll close my eyes, and just for a moment I'll believe everything I want to.' Robert embarrassedly makes to call her by a pet name – 'My little . . .' (what we shall never know) – before, as befits his good nature, complying in a gesture that is to prove the determining moment of the film's intrigue.

Christine meanwhile takes her turn with the spyglass, just as Robert and Geneviève are locked in their farewell embrace. Octave/Renoir observes, 'What you can see over there seems damn interesting', to which Christine, in Nora Gregor's finest acting hour – there is, admittedly, little competition – replies in a shocked voice and seemingly pale-faced, 'Very interesting.' The ironies here are multiple: the director playing a character excluded from the spectacle within the film – he has asked Christine in vain to pass him the spyglass; a passion acted that is taken by the spectator – Christine – to be a passion lived; the 'truth' revealed by the camera's surrogate – a partial and

54 LA RÈGLE DU JEU

The group spot a squirrel cavorting in the branches of a tree, causing Saint-Aubin to regret having handed back his gun. It is Berthelin, a minor character but one whose importance is often underrated, who offers the use of his new spyglass, which he vaunts in a primitive version of advertising parlance that echoes that of the aircraft engineer in the opening sequence – 'A spyglass is an indispensable companion, and as this one is so small you can always carry it with you.' It seems curious to assert, as Guislain and his co-authors do, that so stilted and passionless a character 'represents . . . desire and death'[29] yet his gesture here is to set in motion a chain of events that will lead to the shooting of André, he dresses as Death for the *danse macabre* during the fancy-dress soirée and his attempt at extracting Schumacher's bullet from Robert's fairground organ causes it to malfunction completely. The very cadaverousness of the character – played by Tony Corteggiani, Renoir's adviser on the firearms used in the film – may tempt us to read him as a kind of death's head, peering out from the world of polite society like that depicted anamorphically in Holbein's *The Ambassadors*.[30]

SEQUENCE-BY-SEQUENCE ANALYSIS AND COMMENTARY   53

For much of this sequence, particularly the later part in which the quarry is rabbits rather than pheasants, there is no conversation – simply the noise of hunting horns, guns and beaters hitting the trees and occasionally shouting directions. During this unusually long interlude in such a talkative film, passions are clearly running high, for La Bruyère and Saint-Aubin, so elaborately civil a few minutes back, now engage in a shouting match over a disputed pheasant, while Christine, perhaps repelled by the slaughter she has just witnessed, tells Jackie, 'I think I've gone off hunting.' The film's negotiation of the borderline between the tragic and the comic is distilled in the anecdote The General tells about somebody who, the previous year, inadvertently shot himself in the thigh and was dead within 20 minutes – a 'punchline' delivered with a guffaw that is shared not only by the equally insensitive Saint-Aubin but by Octave. Any sensitivity on display in this sequence, it would seem, is the prerogative of the women – Christine, in the remark just quoted but also Jackie who commiserates glumly with André, saying, 'You're in pain, and so am I.'

52 LA RÈGLE DU JEU

SEQUENCE-BY-SEQUENCE ANALYSIS AND COMMENTARY 51

film are extraordinary – a virtuoso exercise less widely acclaimed than it deserves to be because it is too often overshadowed by what follows it.

The hunt sequence

Even the hostile Vinneuil praised the hunt sequence. Its position at the chronological and narrative heart of the film corresponds to the metaphor of the hunt or chase[27] and is recognized by virtually all commentators as central to *La Règle du jeu*. Venus, we may remember, was the goddess of the hunt as well as of love and was, therefore, the source of many plays on words in Shakespeare and elsewhere. The hunt in this film is, of course, more than a metaphor, pursued, as it is, in deadly earnest first in the open air and then, towards the end of the film, through the corridors of the château. This repetition exemplifies Deleuze's comment, that the film is made up of 'mirror-images, distributed in depth',[28] is nowhere truer than in the hunt sequence, where beaters and hunters, on the one hand, and their quarry, on the other, correspond precisely to his description. The sequence – the first to be shot – lasts for $\frac{1}{25}$ of the film yet it contains a quarter of its total shots, thus standing in sharp contrast to the kitchen sequence that has not long preceded it. It is characterized by a mobility of the camera that is extraordinary even for this film, running the gamut from close-up to tracking shot but with no sense of self-conscious virtuoso display. The sequence opens with an almost parodic exchange of courtesies between La Bruyère and Saint-Aubin, each apologising profusely for attempting to shoot the other's pheasant. The rapidity with which this courtesy is to degenerate acts as a metonym for the precariousness of the 'rules of the game' – asserted *in extremis* at the end of the film but, by then, all but mortally wounded. Octave foreshadows the denouement by warning André against going to a spot where 'they'll think we're rabbits' and tries to console his friend who is furious at Christine's seeming rapprochement with her husband. Octave tells André that he will know he is cured of his passion when he notices that his concierge's daughter had wonderful eyes – a reassurance that is undercut by Octave's exhortation, 'Trust my long experience', bearing in mind that, as we have seen, his experience would not appear to have been a particularly fruitful one.

individuals in positions of authority whose national identity is, in different ways, regarded as suspect.

This is the longest shot in the entire film, lasting nearly two minutes, though, as Curchod points out, the speed and fluidity of the camera movements work against any impression of length. It concludes as Marceau arrives, shot against a background of chefs and sous-chefs going about their business in the deepest focus to be found in the interior scenes at least – a suggestion of the complexities of the world he is about to enter. His arrival transplants into the château the rivalry we have already witnessed in the grounds and hints at the new turn that events will take when he makes eyes at Lisette, biting voraciously into a sausage the while. Back upstairs, the guests engage in different conversations, with Madame La Bruyère asking Jackie spectacularly inane questions about her study of American art before the arrival of Columbus. This she initially takes to refer to blacks ('Negroes') and, when told that America at the time was peopled by Indians, makes a laughing allusion to Buffalo Bill. Like the concierge Beznard in *Le Crime de Monsieur Lange*, Madame La Bruyère – who represents, we may remember, the industrial class that was becoming increasingly powerful at the time – is a lethally comic denunciation of the colonialist mentality. Mock hunting and duelling in a crane shot with a 150-degree pan precede the guests retiring to bed. Robert elaborately thanks his wife for the panache with which she has dealt with a delicate situation. Christine turns melancholically to Lisette and asks whether she would like to have children. Lisette's response is that of the cosmopolitan socialite – 'Yes . . . but they take up a lot of time! You have to be around them all the time, or else it's not worth having any!' – while Christine's reaction is that of the wistful would-be mother – 'That's what's lovely – you don't think of anything else!' Francis Vanoye points out that no character in the film, so far as we know, has a child[25] – implausible perhaps in the real world but less so in the cinematic context of the time.[26]

The men, meanwhile, bid one another goodnight, with The General praising Christine's class as he is to do for Robert at the end of the film and André and Octave reinforcing their bonding by sharing a room. The expository wealth and destiny of this first section of the La Colinière part of the

SEQUENCE-BY-SEQUENCE ANALYSIS AND COMMENTARY 49

supper and commenting on their masters' antics almost like a Greek chorus. The chef peremptorily dismisses Madame de la Bruyère's dietary sensitivities – 'I accept diets, but not fads'[23] – before the conversation turns to La Chesnaye's Jewishness. Below stairs is the only place, we may infer, that so delicate an issue can be broached. Such, at least, was the view of the extreme right-winger François Vinneuil, who wrote in *L'Action française* on the film's release, 'Only the common people remember the marquis's origins and judge them pitilessly. The salons, vain and distracted, have forgotten all about them.'[24] The views expressed by the servants are, in fact, somewhat more equivocal than Vinneuil suggests, particularly in the chef's speech, when he declares that his previous masters did not entertain Jews but nevertheless 'ate like pigs', whereas La Chesnaye, 'half-caste though he is', had recently complained about the poor preparation of a potato salad. The sound of a piano can, meanwhile, be heard coming from upstairs, evocative perhaps of a certain closeness between the world of the servants and that of the masters. Frenchness and nobility here would seem to be cultural as much as ethnic, as evidenced when the chef proclaims his master to be 'a man of the world' – a remark echoed by The General in the final line of the film. The answer to the question 'Who is French?', posed in this scene more explicitly than anywhere else in the film, emphatically does not exclude La Chesnaye, for all the racist remarks of which he is the target.

It is worth noting too Schumacher's arrival just after the chauffeur has alluded to the fact that La Chesnaye's mother was called Rosenthal (like the character Dalio plays in *La Grande Illusion*). Asked for his view, Schumacher, seen coming down the stairs in the background, can only reply, 'I don't know what you're talking about. I've only just got here' – indicative maybe of a certain slowness on the uptake, but surely also to be understood in the context of the Alsatian origins which mean that he will have held French nationality for only about 20 years. His partial exclusion from the conversation may thus figure a calling into question of his Frenchness arguably at work in Simsolo's reference to his 'fascistic' qualities too. The strained relationship between Robert and Schumacher, thrown into relief by the former's warmth towards Marceau, is, among other things, one between

48 LA RÈGLE DU JEU

partly because of Nora Gregor's profoundly unerotic performance but also because André in his other-worldliness and his commitment to performing daring deeds for his lady is constructed as a hero of chivalry, which is to say that his love must remain a chaste one. From this perspective, it can be argued that it is for attempting to break this implicit vow of chastity that he meets his death at the end.

When Christine delivers a composed, if unconvincing, speech about the hours she has spent with André 'under the all too rare sign of friendship', Robert and Octave, visible behind her, react with a mixture of tension and would-be light amusement. Robert's suggestion for an evening's entertainment – 'We'll play a comedy, we'll disguise ourselves!' – can be seen as an ironic comment. Robert's body language, nervous not to say twitchy beneath its veneer of poise, is revelatory at this point and, indeed, throughout the film, suggesting as it does his precarious command of the various situations that unravel. A few hours have doubtless passed before we find ourselves, once again, in the kitchens, where the servants are having their

SEQUENCE-BY-SEQUENCE ANALYSIS AND COMMENTARY 47

unmistakable. The camera tracks from the steps outside the château into the entrance hall (a studio reconstruction), with the slightly edgy aplomb it is to display throughout the film's interior sequences, reaching a climax, of course, with the final pursuit.

A brief scene below stairs, in the kitchens, precedes the arrival of André, accompanied by Octave. Here, the camera, at one point, goes behind a pillar, almost as though it were spying on the guests from a hiding place – one instance of the way in which it can be seen as functioning as a character in the film. Overlapping dialogues and agile camera movements suggest the multiple layers of emotional revelation and courtly concealment at work, with the perfidious Saint-Aubin opining that 'they're keeping it all in the family' while The General displays his disapproval, or quite possibly his ingenuousness, by asking, 'What does that mean?' The probably homosexual Dick asks his accomplice Charlotte, 'Well, have they or haven't they?' Charlotte – herself perhaps signalled as gay since she has a companion, Juliette, who appears but does not speak – gives the arch response, 'They have.' We, on the other hand, may well get the impression that they have not – partly because of Christine's evident attachment to conjugal fidelity,

46 LA RÈGLE DU JEU

la lettre.[20] Noël Simsolo hints at the possible political connotations of the rivalry between Schumacher and Marceau when he says, 'Marceau's amusing anarchist comes into conflict with the fascistic gamekeeper, reminiscent of a Mirbeau character.'[21] Such a character might be the child killer and fascist sympathizer Joseph in Octave Mirbeau's 1900 novel *Le Journal d'une femme de chambre/Diary of a Chambermaid*, twice adapted for the cinema – by Buñuel in 1964 but, before that, by Renoir in 1946. Robert, to Schumacher's disgust, offers Marceau a job putting down rabbits and their complicity is reinforced when Marceau shows him another snare he has set. Marceau says that he would prefer a job in the château, partly to avoid Schumacher's attentions but also because he has always wanted to be a servant – 'Wearing a suit – that's my dream.' Sesonske contrasts Marceau to Renoir's earlier great force of nature Boudu in asserting that 'Boudu suspects that Lestingois had rescued him because he wants a servant; being rescued, Marceau confesses that a servant is what he has always wanted to be',[22] but Carette's pawky delivery and the sardonic persona he carries with him from other roles – notably in *La Grande Illusion* – make it difficult, for this writer at least, to take his craving for respectability altogether seriously. Certainly his behaviour, once in the world of the château, will demonstrate scant regard for social order. Like Robert, in a curious sense his alter ego – an affinity perhaps reinforced by a certain physical resemblance between the two actors – Marceau has little time for barriers and walls.

In the following shot, reprised by Robert Altman at the opening of *Gosford Park*, the guests arrive at La Colinière amid torrential rain. It is in this sequence that we make the acquaintance of a number of characters who might be classed as 'minor' but who, nevertheless, play important roles at different points. The General, whose name we never learn, displays throughout a tediously irrepressible bonhomie which, as more than one critic has commented, may veil distinctly Pétainist sentiments – nowhere more so than in the film's final line. The La Chesnayes' niece Jackie, who nurses a hopeless infatuation with Jurieux, Charlotte de la Plante (played by the mountainous Odette Talazac) and the fatuous La Bruyères, a couple of industrialists, also make their appearances. However, they are upstaged for the moment by Geneviève whose delight at Jurieux's impending arrival is

poacher Marceau, observed in silence extracting a rabbit from the noose he has set for it. (Incidentally, he shares his name with that of a leading general in the Revolutionary armies). Caught red-handed, Marceau feigns childlike innocence – 'Hello, Schumacher! Do you want my rabbit?' – but is welcomed by Robert, who orders him to be instantly released. We see Schumacher and his entourage, the hapless Marceau in tow, in deep focus with Robert in the foreground – visual space, as so often in this film, suggesting its social equivalent. The sympathy between Robert and Marceau – reinforced perhaps by a distant physical resemblance – is to be one of the most subversive relationships in the film, leading to further disruption rather than protective reinforcement of the existing order. Schumacher's furious assertion – 'During the war, I shot at fellows who'd done less than he has' – is ironically ominous considering that he would have been fighting on the German side and that the scenes of *La Grande Illusion*, ostensibly set in Germany, had had to be filmed in Alsace because of the tense political situation. The spectre of the coming global conflict haunts *La Règle du jeu* as it were just off-screen, making the film in this respect an exemplar of the hauntological text *avant*

SEQUENCE-BY-SEQUENCE ANALYSIS AND COMMENTARY 43

son or grandson, is capable of true ownership. To own a hovel in a village, it is not enough to have bought it cash down; you have to know all the neighbours, their parents and grandparents, the neighbouring farms, the beeches and oaks of the forest, you need to know how to plough, to fish, to hunt, to have carved notches in the trees as a child and find them grown bigger with age. We can rest assured that the Jew does not fulfil these conditions.[19]

Robert, as witnessed by his rapid connivance with Marceau and the evident care and affection he bestows on La Colinière, might be thought to come close to fulfilling them; but the racist remarks made about him – by the servants, in particular – suggest a prevalent suspicion that is to be finally dispelled only by The General – not unlikely to harbour anti-Semitic feelings himself – in the film's final line: 'La Chesnaye's not short of class, and that's becoming rare, my dear Saint-Aubin, believe me . . . That's becoming rare!' We shall also find these sentiments echoed by the cook at La Colinière. Robert and Christine, at all events, show themselves *châtelains* to the manner born in the arrival scene, inquiring solicitously about domestic arrangements but also about the well-being of their servants. Prominent among them is, of course, Schumacher, whom we meet for the first time. However, his anxiety about the enforced separation from his wife gets short shrift from Robert – 'If your wife wants to stay with you and leave Madame's service, that's her business, not mine!' – a remark that is all the crueller since we already know Lisette's feelings on the matter. Robert's debonair style, as befits an aristocrat, is not incompatible with a certain authoritarianism, for all his professed phobia of barriers and walls.

More concerned with joining her mistress, Lisette responds unenthusiastically to Schumacher's delighted greeting, making it quite clear that nothing short of dismissal will make her abandon Madame's service.

The next scene, probably taking place the following morning, shows Robert and Schumacher in the woods near La Colinière, anxious about the destructive antics of the local rabbits. Schumacher's suggestion of building a fence to protect the domain is rejected by Robert. 'I don't want a fence, but I don't want any rabbits either!' – an echo of his professed opposition to barriers and walls in conversation with Octave. That opposition will be redefined and complicated by the introduction into the château of the

42   LA RÈGLE DU JEU

convenient since it is only about an hour and a half from Paris. The château still exists and can be visited, though you will look in vain, on the spot or on its website, for the slightest reference to *La Règle du jeu*; the current owner apparently takes no interest in cinema and is more concerned with making money from the tourist trade by way of a model railway and children's zoo in the grounds.

Part, at least, of the anti-Semitic resentment of which La Chesnaye is the target is undoubtedly due to his acquisition of a property that would have been perceived by many, including some who benefit from his hospitality, as the rightful possession of the 'traditional' – in other words, non-Jewish – French aristocracy. Sartre's *Réflexions sur la question juive*, published four years after the release of *La Règle du jeu*, includes a remarkable passage anatomizing anti-Semitic discourse on ownership, which could almost have been inspired by Renoir's film:

> He [sc. The Jew] can acquire all the property he wants, land and châteaux if he can afford them: but when he becomes the lawful owner, that property subtly changes its meaning. Only a Frenchman, the son of a Frenchman, a countryman's

generally display great sympathy for his characters, this is by no means universal – the counter-examples he gives from *La Règle du jeu* are Saint-Aubin and the industrialist couple the La Bruyères – and that Octave's remark could indeed be read in a directly contrary sense, referring to 'the triumph of an unbridled egotism, the social community breaking up into a myriad of individuals who recognize only their subjective interests to the exclusion of others'.[18] He does, after all, say that 'there is one terrible thing' and the collapse into anarchy towards the end of the film is admirably encapsulated by Serceau's observation. Robert decides to invite Jurieux, proclaiming himself to be 'against barriers, against walls' while choosing a cylinder record to play on his vintage phonograph. 78-rpm records would, by this time, have been the norm so that Robert's 'music-centre', like his other mechanical toys, will be a collector's piece. To the strains of a fin-de-siècle comic song about a well-oiled fishing excursion to the suburb of Meudon – a nod to *Partie de campagne*? – Robert tells Octave that he is 'a poet – a dangerous poet' in an all but direct echo of Octave's earlier description of Christine as a dangerous angel. The echoes and rhymes here are not only verbal but visual, produced largely by the use of deep focus and repetition, as with Robert's ceaseless manipulation of his mechanical toys in a form of nervous displacement activity. A sense of increasing complexity and entanglement is engendered as the Parisian section of the film – its 'first act' in theatrical terms – comes to an end.

From Paris to the countryside

The next scene takes us to La Colinière where, in a long tracking shot, we see the hosts and their retinue arriving for the shooting party, watched over by the major-domo Corneille, whose sharing of a name with one of France's leading dramatists is assuredly not innocent. The building we see is in fact the seventeenth-century Château de La Ferté Saint-Aubin, in the marshy countryside of Sologne, near Orléans, though most of the interior scenes were filmed in the studio. This is rich hunting country, favoured by, among others, former French President Valéry Giscard d'Estaing and particularly

40   LA RÈGLE DU JEU

him – 'This is the first time I've known Monsieur Octave without an appetite!' The answer, of course, is André or at least Octave's undertaking to him, which is, as we might suspect, not an easy one. He suggests that André should be invited to a forthcoming weekend party at La Colinière. Christine, at first, finds this 'indecent' and only when he mockingly threatens never to see her again, feigning to leave and replacing his initial 'au revoir' with 'adieu', does she relent, not wishing to be 'the woman who reduced the "hero of the day" to despair' and proclaiming, with unwittingly prescient irony, that she 'cannot stand martyrs'. Octave describes her as 'a dangerous angel' and demands of Lisette eggs, bacon and white wine – more serious, even perhaps more virile, fare than the 'Continental breakfast' he was unable to face a moment ago.

The pace of this scene, a seemingly light-hearted negotiation of an extremely delicate, and ultimately of course tragic, situation, is structured by its interplay of the theatrical and the cinematic. On the one hand, the quick-fire dialogue and proverbial interpolations – Octave, for example, says, 'On ne peut pas être au four et au moulin', the nearest English equivalent to which is 'You can only be in one place at a time' – call to mind *La Règle du jeu*'s theatrical pre-texts. On the other, the use of deep focus, notably in the visual rhyme between Octave and Christine in conversation and their reflection in a mirror placed above Christine's bed – thereby designated as a potential site of conflict – acts as a visual and cinematic reinforcement of and commentary on the seriocomic social and emotional drama it frames.

Robert confides in Octave his anxiety over the relationship with Geneviève and Octave undertakes to do what he can to help in exchange for an invitation for André. He attempts to allay Robert's misgivings by assuring him that nothing has happened between André and Christine – almost certainly a correct assessment given Christine's evident attachment to the institution if not the emotional reality of her marriage – and admits his own ethical bafflement in what has become the most famous line in the film: 'In this world, there is one terrible thing, which is that everybody has their reasons.' This is often read as betokening a diffuse global goodwill towards the characters perhaps belied by Renoir's own remark that none of them was worth saving.[17] Daniel Serceau observes that, while Renoir does

site sides. The impact of this sudden opening of the film's space, after the particularly claustrophobic scene in Geneviève's apartment, is immense, not least because those who already know how the film is to end may see in André's romantic heedlessness a foreshadowing of his death. Octave upbraids him benevolently – an expostulation that is also an exposition, during which we learn that he had studied with Christine's father and that she is for him 'like a sister'. How erotic Octave's feelings are for Christine – and, indeed, for Lisette – is a difficult question to answer. For Serceau, he is the film's most sexually alienated character, while Faulkner goes further in assimilating him to a pander or sexual go-between and in asserting, 'Like the traditional pander, he is impotent.'[15] (Today's audiences may be more likely to compare his lumberingly cuddly quality to a panda but that animal, we may remember, is not distinguished by its sexual fervour.) Yet it will be difficult to see the tenderness between him and Christine towards the end as purely platonic. Particularly given Renoir's role as author of the script, it is not implausible to see Octave as a latter-day Cyrano de Bergerac,[16] the subject of a passion that, for most of the film, he does not dare to speak but masochistically lives out through his efforts on the part of a rival. For the moment, however, he is less concerned with his own feelings for Christine than with André's and the ridicule to which they expose him. The scene concludes with Octave reminding André that her world has 'very rigorous rules' before pandering to his desire by undertaking to bring about another meeting between them.

The following scene returns us to the La Chesnayes' town house, in which Octave arrives to make good his promise to André. Robert tells Lisette that Schumacher is missing her badly and would like her to join him at the La Chesnayes' country home, La Colinière, to which Lisette responds that she would rather divorce. The significance in this brief discussion is that Christine ironically pronounces Schumacher's name as if it were German in response to Robert's speaking of him as 'Chumachère' – a phonetic transcription into French – as if to remind us that he is from Alsace, a province annexed by Germany between 1871 and 1918 and imminently to be claimed again as the rightful property of the Third Reich. Octave refuses Lisette's offer of coffee, bread and jam, causing her to wonder what is troubling

now and his somewhat fluttery response – 'Everything . . . everything!' – is
a striking echo of Batala (Jules Berry) likewise laying down his terms just
before the denouement of *Le Crime de Monsieur Lange*. Robert's sheepish-
ness is matched by Geneviève's vulnerability. She says, 'If you left me, I'd be
very unhappy! And I don't want to be unhappy.' – a remark that is echoed,
just before the end of this so often symmetrical film, when Robert says to
Octave, 'I'm suffering, dear boy . . . And I can't stand that!' As the couple
speak, they take up positions beside two Buddha statuettes, at once a metonym for their affluent collector's way of life and an ironic reference to an
impossibly distant world of serenity. Nirvana is to have no place in the world
of *La Règle du jeu*, as Geneviève shows when she closes their exchange by
declaring, 'I don't know if it's because of our emotional preoccupations, but
I'm starving today!'

   Cut to a scene in which André is driving back to Paris so fast and care-
lessly that the car, with Octave squirming in terror in the front passenger
seat, veers off the road. We see the top of an embankment and the sky and
hear André's and Octave's voices off before they come into view from oppo-

the assembled company that she is a great devotee of Chamfort's maxim that '[l]ove, in our society, is the exchange of two fantasies and the contact of two epidermises'. This, like Lisette's less culturally dignified deployment of proverbial wisdom earlier, suggests a confident distance from the hurly-burly of amorous relationships – less true, we shall find, for Geneviève than it appears – but also serves to place Geneviève in a milieu rich in what Bourdieu would call cultural as well as financial capital. Chamfort was also, we may remember, both an active participant in and a victim of the French Revolution (he was put to death in 1794), as though to remind us of the wider socio-political context against which the film is set.

The first interruption in the film's temporal continuity occurs now, with a cut from evening to daytime. Geneviève is once more at home, this time in the company of Robert who proclaims that it is time for their affair (which predates his marriage) to come to an end. This decision she accurately imputes to the disturbance caused by Jurieux's outburst. Their dialogue is poised and nervous at once; Geneviève asks Robert what is likely to change

36 LA RÈGLE DU JEU

La Chesnaye's disparaging account of André's supposed feelings is indeed an attempt at asserting the reversibility of his potentially menaced situation – a reversibility figured too by the anachronistic dolls with their evocation of a period in which the aristocracy's domination was uncontested.

Thus far, at least, that attempt seems to be working but it is soon called into question when we meet Robert's long-term mistress Geneviève de Maras – seen for the first time, like her lover, in a back view. She is at home in an apartment overlooking the Palais de Chaillot and thus in an extremely chic area of Paris. The radio broadcast continues, giving the impression of temporal continuity but also emphasizing how wide the audience for Jurieux's interview must have been. Christine's guests include Saint-Aubin, who is to play a clumsily lascivious role in the denouement of the film and is tartly described by Curchod as 'not a man of the world',[14] and the camply effeminate Dick, who responds archly to Saint-Aubin's evocation of Christine's plight, 'She didn't have to get married! I'm not married, am I?' We learn here too that Christine's father was a celebrated orchestral conductor in Austria, a detail later to acquire great significance. Geneviève announces to

the heart of the film, whose very title suggests the subordination of the natural to the structured and regulated against which in different ways all the characters, at one time or another, fight – desire against the machine – but which is nevertheless to triumph in the end.

Bardèche and Brasillach take it as given that 'the gamekeeper's wife sleeps with the guests'[11] but nothing in the film as it stands is clear evidence of that – all the more so, as Christine uses the term 'amoureux' whose connotations, unlike those of 'amant', are not necessarily sexual. Lisette's responses to her mistress's questions are flirtatiously evasive, culminating in the assertion that 'the more you give them [sc. men], the more they want' and dismissing the possibility of friendship with a man – doubtless how Christine at this stage would describe her relationship with André Jurieux – as 'talking about the moon in the middle of the day'. This is one of a number of exchanges in this film to conclude with a proverb or aphorism, the sedimented wisdom of social convention maybe providing the least contentious closure to the almost insurmountable problems it raises.

Our first sight of Robert, rhyming with that of Christine earlier, is a back view in a mirror of him telephoning his long-term mistress Geneviève de Maras. After this conversation has finished, Christine appears, whereupon Robert turns off the airport broadcast and proudly presents the newest addition to his collection of mechanical toys – a small 'romantic Negress' (so described by him) – of which Christine ironically says, 'I prefer it to the radio.' That radio, the instrument of Christine's current discomfiture, is described by Pierre Guislain and his collaborators as a 'new social mechanism',[12] wide-ranging and unpredictable in its effects compared to the predictability of the mechanical doll. Robert's suave depreciation of André's outburst – 'And he thought it was love! . . . Men are so naive!' – is accompanied by his placing the 'romantic Negress' next to a small wind-up soldier, as if to suggest his domination of the potentially threatening couple of Christine and André. For Rose-Marie Godier, Robert resembles a golem – the clay model brought to life in Jewish folklore – or a sorcerer's apprentice and his automata represent an attempt to block the film's narrative flow or at least to assert an ultimately doomed control over it. 'To the fixed and repetitive time of the automaton, Renoir opposes the linear flow of fate.'[13]

34   LA RÈGLE DU JEU

by the fact that she is an object of desire at various times for four men –
Jurieux, Octave, Saint-Aubin and, even if only to maintain the facade of
their marriage, her husband. Lisette's demeanour towards her is also
distinctly flirtatious, causing Marceau to suggest to the distressed Schumacher
near the end of the film that 'she's not married to you, she's married to
Madame!'. Philippe Esnault, writing long before the time of queer textual
readings, describes her as 'devouring Christine with her eyes',[10] scarcely an
exaggerated account. Lisette consistently refuses to join Schumacher full-
time on the country estate, preferring, it would seem, the company of her
mistress and perhaps also the bright lights of Paris to the dogged devotion
of a spouse whom it is difficult to imagine inspiring much passion in her
or, indeed, anybody. When Christine asks whether she is happy, her response
is to describe her husband as 'not much of a nuisance' and she does not
give a direct answer to the question of whether she has any lovers. She is
coquettishly reluctant to hand Christine the lipstick she wants, proclaiming
it to be too violet and hence not natural looking, to which Christine
responds, 'What is natural nowadays?' This is one of the great questions at

SEQUENCE-BY-SEQUENCE ANALYSIS AND COMMENTARY   33

neer from Caudron, the company who manufactured André's aeroplane. This company really existed and, indeed, Roland Toutain was well known for his aerial stunts in their planes – a further example of the almost documentary realism that often characterizes the film. Octave berates André for 'behaving just like a kid' and the crestfallen ace frets that he will never dare to appear before Christine again. Back in the Paris apartment, we see Christine in a long two-shot with her maid Lisette who, we discover, has been married to the gamekeeper Schumacher for two years. Initially Christine is heard in voice-off while we see only her reflection in the mirror – one example among many of the use of mirrors in these Parisian scenes to emphasize the preoccupation of the characters and, more generally, of high society with appearance as, it sometimes seems, the only guarantor of reality. If there is a major implausibility in this film, it surely resides in the apparent lack of chemistry in the La Chesnaye and Schumacher couples. Daniel Serceau points out that, throughout the film, 'Robert and Christine will never show the least sexual tenderness towards each other'[9] and the unquestionably wooden performance of Nora Gregor, at least in part the result of her shaky grasp of French, may leave today's audience perplexed more or less everywhere. Moreover, he is played by the film's director for whom he is something of a surrogate – or even a doppelgänger, bearing in mind that term's association with death – on the other side of the camera. Michel Simon, who had worked with Renoir four times before – on *Tire-au-flanc* (1928), *On purge bébé* (1931), *La Chienne* and *Boudu sauvé des eaux* – was originally considered for this role, which might have yielded a fine performance but would have amputated a whole dimension from the part. Diegetically and extra-diegetically, Octave/Renoir is the film's wild card. Octave brings together disparate characters and milieux much as Renoir does differing filmic genres – something figured by his presence, surrounded by the apparatuses of representation, in this opening sequence.

Machines of all kinds occupy an important place in *La Règle du jeu* and nowhere more so than in this opening sequence, where the mechanisms of broadcasting – Élina's unfeasibly large microphone and the cable we see being unwound right at the beginning – are foregrounded. Rose-Marie Godier provides the most extensive treatment of the topos of the machine in the film, dwelling in particular on La Chesnaye's collection of mechanical toys but going beyond this to draw attention to how 'all the *philistines* of *La Règle du jeu* . . . speak a mechanical language that gradually empties humanity of its substance'.[8] The Radio-Cité interviewer can be seen as the first of these – a modern-day answer to the conventions and clichés of the moribund aristocratic society in which the bulk of the film's action is to be set. The tension between this repressive apparatus and the desiring spontaneity of Jurieux, announced in this sequence, is only part of the story, for Jurieux's desire is itself a mechanism in which he is caught up – something which is true in different ways for the other desires, socially sanctioned or not, that are to erupt throughout the film. Gilles Deleuze, whose analysis of *La Règle du jeu* will be particularly important when we come to consider the role of Schumacher, popularized the notion of the 'desiring machine' in his 1972 text, written with Félix Guattari, *L'Anti-Oedipe/The Anti-Oedipus*. That term, and the interplay of the mechanical and the supposedly organic it figures, could be considered a leitmotif of the film.

We then cut to a reaction shot of Christine in the La Chesnayes' Paris home, listening to the radio reporter announcing an interview with an engi-

SEQUENCE-BY-SEQUENCE ANALYSIS AND COMMENTARY   31

which is clearly true for the characters on one side of the camera is no less so for the audience on the other, in keeping with Bazin's assertion that *La Règle du jeu* is 'the classic example of a film which demands considerable participation from its viewers'.[6]

The drama takes shape

The opening scene plunges us into a world that now appears comically *vieux jeu* but, for a contemporary audience, would have represented the acme of media sophistication. André Jurieux has just landed at Le Bourget Airport, after his record-breaking flight, and is greeted not only by an excited crowd but also by a reporter from Radio-Cité. This role is taken (though she is not credited) by Lise Élina, a real-life reporter for the station playing herself in a clear invitation to read the film as some kind of contemporary document. The opening shot, focusing on Élina and her frenetic presentation of 'the great aviator', lasts something like 30 seconds – a striking prefiguration of the atypical length of the film's shots which, according to Jean-Albert Bron, last on average 21 seconds as compared to the ten or so more usual at the time. Élina is swept out of view by the excited surge of spectators running towards Jurieux who is greeted by Octave, bearing the unwelcome news that Christine has not felt able to come to meet him. Jurieux's on-air cry of pain and indignation – 'If she's listening, I tell her publicly that she is disloyal!' – already reveals him as out of step with the conventions of polite society, the flouting of which is to prove fatal to him. Octave's presence amid the airport melee, motivated by his long friendship with André, also suggests that, unlike the other characters– most obviously the absent Christine – he 'alone is entitled to move through all the spaces of the film'.[7] For this, there is a twofold reason. On the one hand, Octave is an impecunious bohemian whose down-at-heel dress and evident financial difficulties mark him out from the other guests at the château. If he is the only one on the hunt not to carry a gun, it is, in all likelihood, because he cannot afford one. It is his very *déclassement*, however, that permits him to circulate with such freedom; belonging nowhere fully, he is, until the end at least, at home

of their version to the memory of André Bazin. The director and shooting personnel are then listed, to the accompaniment of one of Mozart's 'German Dances', before the cast – the filmic taking implied precedence over the pro-filmic or, indeed, the cinematic over the theatrical. Bazin's privileging of the former over the latter element can lead him to underestimate the pivotal importance of the theatrical in the film, as when he asserts that Renoir 'has succeeded in dispensing entirely with dramatic structures'.[1] This is belied first by the title's description of the film as a 'dramatic fantasy' and then by the credit sequence, which lists the female actors before the men, in a foreshadowing of the importance that the 'battle of the sexes' is to have in the unfolding of the film.[2] The spelling of certain names here, and in many secondary sources, differs from that used in Renoir's original shooting script, reprised in Curchod's screenplay. The Renoir/Curchod spellings will be used here.

There follows a disclaimer making the evidently disingenuous assertion, 'This *divertissement*, whose action takes place on the eve of war in 1939, makes no claim to be a study of its time. Its characters are purely imaginary.' Curchod points out that the reference to 1939 was in fact added by Gaborit and Durand, 'doubtless unintentionally encouraging the usual socio-political interpretation of *La Règle du jeu*'.[3] There follows an epigraph from Beaumarchais's *Le Mariage de Figaro*, asking the clearly rhetorical question, 'If Cupid has wings, is it not to fly?' – an evident allusion to Jurieux's profession and thereby hinting at a dramatic structure which many critics, notably Gerald Mast and Christopher Faulkner, have seen as informing the film – that of the five-act French comedy. Alexander Sesonske, however, demurs to the extent of perceiving rather 'a three-part structure, imposed by both the power and form of the hunt, which separates itself from the surrounding scenes',[4] while Martin O'Shaughnessy might almost seem to align himself with Bazin in proclaiming theatrically based analyses to be 'of dubious value'.[5] The point is clearly not to produce a diagram, laying bare in a formalist frenzy the 'real' underlying dramatic structure of the film but to recognize, in these overlapping and conflicting perceptions, the manner in which *La Règle du jeu* at once elicits and eludes such analysis, hinting at a kind of order whose reassurance remains perpetually out of reach. That

3 Sequence-by-sequence analysis and commentary

Breaking a film down into its component parts or sequences is inevitably something of an arbitrary exercise, especially with a work as fluid in its structure as *La Règle du jeu*. With no English-language screenplay in print, I shall base my analysis here on the Livre de Poche edition prepared by Olivier Curchod and published in 1999. There is a much more comprehensive edition of the original script and its variants, prepared by Olivier Curchod and Christopher Faulkner, published by Nathan in the same year, but this is likely to prove of interest primarily to specialists. The film is issued on DVD in the UK (by the British Film Institute) and the USA (in the Criterion Collection), in substantially similar versions, though the Criterion is a 'double album' with much extra material. There is also a French double DVD, issued by Éditions Montparnasse, which offers subtitles in French and may – especially considering the film's linguistic complexity-therefore be useful for those working with students of French. Dialogue, except when otherwise stated, is taken from the Livre de Poche screenplay. The translations are my own.

Credits

The credits begin with an acknowledgement of the role played by Gaborit and Durand in the reconstruction of the film, along with Renoir's dedication

14 For this and much other information in this section, I am particularly indebted to Curchod, Olivier and Christopher Faulkner, *La Règle du jeu: scénario original de Jean Renoir* (Paris: Nathan, 1999), pp. 19–21.

15 Curchod and Faulkner, *La Règle du jeu*, p. 23.

16 According to Guislain. Pierre (ed.), *La Règle du jeu, 1939, Jean Renoir* (Paris: Hatier, 1998), p. 11. A helpful website bringing a number of critical responses (in French) together is http://www.ac.nancy–metz.fr/enseign/Lettres/ressourc/Nancy/Renoir/Virybab/vbcritique.htm (accessed 23/6/06).

17 Snyder, John, 'Film and Classical Genre: Rules for Interpreting *The Rules of the Game*', *Literature and Film Quarterly* (10:3, July 1982), pp. 162–79, p. 162.

18 Quoted in Serceau, Daniel, *La Règle du jeu* (Limonest: L'Interdisciplinaire, 1989), p. 108.

19 Faulkner, Christopher, 'Un cocktail surprenant: la projection et la réception de *La Règle du jeu* dans l'après-guerre en France', in Frank Curot (ed.), *Renoir en France* (Montpellier: Université Paul Valéry, 1999), p. 99.

20 Chabrol, Claude, 'Renoir, "La Règle du jeu" et moi', *Positif* (no. 537, November 2005), p. 100.

21 Faulkner: 'Un cocktail surprenant , . .' p. 101.

22 Ibid., pp. 120–1.

23 Powrie, Phil and Keith Reader, *French Cinema: A Student's Guide* (London: Arnold, 2002), p. 58.

24 Ibid., p. 59.

25 Bazin: *Jean Renoir*, p. 74.

26 Ibid., p. 77.

27 Ibid., p. 78.

28 Ibid., p. 81.

29 Ibid., p. 83.

30 Astruc, Alexandre, 'Naissance d'une nouvelle avant-garde: la caméra-stylo', *L'Écran français* (30 March 1948, no page number).

31 Bazin: *Jean Renoir*, p. 87.

32 Ibid., p. 90.

33 Bardèche, Maurice and Robert Brasillach, *Histoire du cinéma* (vol. 2) (Paris: André Martel, 1954), p. 162.

34 Bardèche and Brasillach: *Histoire du cinéma*, p. 163.

a far more sophisticated grasp of *La Règle du jeu* than the majority of critics
of their time, as is illustrated by their description of the film as 'close to a
masterpiece'.[34] This, I would contend, is true even of the passage quoted
above, which suggests that its authors knew all too well how acutely the film
asks 'Who is French?' and how relevant to the France of the time of its
making that question was. Bardèche and Brasillach's comments represent
what, for certain French milieux of their time, was the intellectually respectable face of the uproar with which *La Règle du jeu*'s early screenings had
been greeted. This, in the face of their loathsomeness, is why I have chosen
to consider them here.

Notes

1 Nancy, Jean-Luc, 'La Règle du jeu dans *La Règle du jeu*', in Antoine de Baecque and Christian Delage (eds), *De l'histoire au cinéma* (Paris: Éditions Complexe, 1998), p. 145.
2 Ibid, p. 162.
3 Renoir: *My Life and My Films*, p. 169.
4 *Entretiens et propos*, special issue of *Cahiers du cinéma* (1979), p. 124.
5 Renoir: *The Rules of the Game*, pp. 37–8.
6 Browne, Nick, 'Deflections of Desire in *The Rules of the Game*: Reflections on the Theatre of History', *Quarterly Review of Film Studies* (vii:3, summer 1982), pp. 251–61, p. 252.
7 Brassel, Domenica and Joël Magny, *Jean Renoir*: La Règle du jeu: *lecture accompagnée* (Paris: Gallimard, 1998), p. 7.
8 I owe this information to the programme of the exhibition organized by the Bibliothèque du Film in Paris, in 1999, to celebrate the film's 60th anniversary.
9 Passek, Jean-Loup (ed.), *Dictionnaire du cinéma français* (Paris: Larousse, 1987), p. 99.
10 Bessy, Maurice and Claude Beylie, *Jean Renoir* (Paris: Pygmalion, 1989), p. 179.
11 Quoted in Dalio, Marcel, *Mes années folles* (Paris: J-C. Lattès, 1976), p. 132. (The original French had 'israélite', a term with distinctly pejorative connotations; thus, Léon Blum was habitually referred to in many right-wing circles as 'Blum l'Israélite'.)
12 According to Grelier, Robert, 'Dialogue avec une salle', *Cinéma 68* (124), p. 22.
13 For this, see Reader, Keith, *Robert Bresson* (Manchester/New York: Manchester University Press, 2000), p. 4.

26 LA RÈGLE DU JEU

piece to be considered here, by Bardèche and Brasillach, can be the subject of no such claim, for its distinctiveness resides in its unconcealed anti-Semitism. Bardèche and his brother-in-law Brasillach were the leading Fascist intellectuals in 1930s and 1940s France, always excepting the novelist Louis-Ferdinand Céline. Graduates of the École Normale Supérieure, an institution more generally associated with the Left, they wrote prolifically on French literature and were among the first Parisian intellectual figures to take a serious interest in the cinema, which is evidenced by the publication of the first edition of their *Histoire du cinéma* in 1935. They were to become more notorious through their actively collaborationist activities under the Occupation for the journal *Je suis partout*, whose baleful title was matched by its ferocious anti-Semitism. Brasillach, the journal's editor, was tried and shot at the Liberation, while Bardèche continued his militant Fascist activities until his death in 1998.

Histoire du cinéma, written when its authors were in their mid 20s, remains a landmark in French writing on film – the first comprehensive survey of the cinema produced in French and the first Western text to give serious attention to the work of Japanese film-makers such as Ozu Yasujir and Mizoguchi Kenji. The work, first published in 1935 and updated for the sound era in 1943, pays significant attention to *La Règle du jeu*, described as Renoir's greatest film, but its 1954 edition is notorious above all for the repulsive rhetoric directed at Marcel Dalio as the Jewish nobleman La Chesnaye. The passage below, originally published in *L'Action française*, has been expunged from subsequent editions of the work:

> A surprising Dalio, more Jewish than ever, at once attractive and sordid, dominates all this like a hunchbacked ibis in the midst of the marshes: he is a man from another planet, not only strange but a foreigner to these rules of the game which are in truth not his. Another odour wells up in him from the depths of the ages, another race which does not go hunting, which has no château, for which the province of Sologne is nothing and which simply *looks*. The *foreignness* of the Jew had perhaps never been so strongly and brutally shown.[33]

The reference to the 'race . . . which has no château' is a clear allusion to Dalio's role in *La Grande Illusion* – that of a (comparatively) nouveau riche who claims that his forefathers had no land. Bardèche and Brasillach display

'[t]he spectator wants to believe in the story that the actor brings to life', s/he is likely to be disappointed in a director for whom '[w]hat counts . . . is not verisimilitude but accuracy of detail',[28] for whom logical development of character and adherence to dramatic are set at naught by the 'tangle of reminders, allusions, and correspondences'[29] that makes *La Règle du jeu* Renoir's masterpiece. Bazin's comparison of the film to a painting or a symphony throws into relief the inadequacy of many earlier criticisms of the film, resting as they did on assumptions about its modus operandi which now – in large measure thanks to Bazin – appear quite inappropriate. Thus, Jurieux's death at the end is, by conventional dramatic standards, an extraordinary coincidence which Renoir succeeds in making inevitable thanks to what has gone before – the literary pre-texts (*Le Mariage de Figaro*, *Les Caprices de Marianne*) but also the hunting metaphor that has pervaded the entire film.

Bazin attaches particular importance to what might be described as the eye of the camera – an avatar of what Alexandre Astruc, in an article that was to prove immensely influential on the New Wave, had, a few years before, called the 'caméra-stylo'.[30] His comparison of the camera in the final part of the film to 'an invisible guest, wandering about the salon and the corridors with a certain curiosity, but without any more advantage than its invisibility' – oddly prefigurative, for this critic at least, of the opening sequence of Resnais's *L'Année dernière à Marienbad* (1961) – evokes the disconcerting fluidity of the shooting and the manner in which '[t]he significance of what the camera discloses is relative to what it leaves hidden'.[31] Yet Bazin's analysis is anything but chilly and formalistic, for he places equal stress on the sensual quality of Renoir's filming. 'In Renoir's films acquaintances are made through love, and love passes through the epidermis of the world';[32] Bazin's final paragraph is haptic, even caressive, in no way diminishing the savagery of the knowledge the film puts into play but tempering it with a tenderness whose very sensuality guards against the risks of a naive or sugary humanism.

In its reading of *La Règle du jeu* as summit of its director's oeuvre as in the careful attention it pays to the film's inescapable but distinctly unorthodox realism, Bazin's essay has exercised a major influence over later critics – even if, as Faulkner argues, a sometimes conservative one. The other

24   LA RÈGLE DU JEU

in which Bazin had been an important early figure. Yet Bazin placed an all but equal stress on cinema's linguistic dimension, the codes and structures by which it is inescapably pervaded, so that it is not surprising that *La Règle du jeu* – a film in which 'the tension between . . . realist plenitude and signifying system'[24] is paramount – should have been the object of one of his most influential essays. He was the first major critic to focus on the way in which the seeming realism of the film constantly undercuts itself so that '[s]lip-ups in detail and even casting "errors" abound in the films of this renowned "realist"'.[25] For Bazin, only Gaston Modot and Paulette Dubost in *La Règle du jeu* are clearly cast according to type – something unlikely to be obvious to a modern-day audience. We have already seen how unlike a Sologne poacher Julien Carette is and how Jurieux's fatal maladroitness is out of kilter with Roland Toutain's screen persona. Renoir's benign gruffness as Octave – exemplified when he dresses up in a bearskin for the fancy-dress party – is obviously at odds with the more sophisticated demeanour of the other 'upstairs' characters, which serves to foreground at once his less well-heeled status and his dual position as director of the film and actor in it.

The fact that Renoir's actors 'do not face the camera but each other, as if acting for their personal pleasure',[26] is linked by Bazin to the absence of major stars, which inscribes the sense of connivance and complicity – not always for the best – that pervades the film and, in so doing, draws the audience into its web. The lack of fit between 'the scene in the script and the one he ends up making' is the gap, the margin, from which will emerge 'a sudden revelation of truth when we are no longer expecting it'[27] – Jurieux's keeling-over like a shot rabbit, one of the emotional climaxes of the film, is the example Bazin chooses. Theoretical writing on cinema has dwelt extensively on the interplay between on- and off-screen space (Noël Burch's *Theory of Film Practice* and André Gardies's *L'Espace au cinéma* are two major examples). Bazin ranks among the first major writers on film to see how important this interplay is to *La Règle du jeu* in particular but also to cinema in general.

The question of plausibility is a difficult one for most contemporary viewers of *La Règle du jeu*, given how unfamiliar the film's milieu is. For Bazin, Renoir's greatness, like the problems he often experienced with audiences, resides precisely in his flouting of conventional norms of the plausible. If

reasons why the film was so influential on the New Wave directors inspired by Bazin and, more generally, on a French cinematic culture in which he was and remains a towering figure. They also suggest the acuity with which the film poses what I shall argue to be one of its key questions – 'Who is French?' – and the viciousness of the responses it was capable, almost by way of a tribute *a contrario*, of unleashing.

Bazin's 1952 article 'Jean Renoir français', reprinted as part of his book *Jean Renoir*, was the first time *La Règle du jeu* had been dealt with as an integral part of the director's oeuvre, rather than as the puzzling aberration many 1939 critics had perceived it to be. Christopher Faulkner has commented that this approach tended 'to situate the film in such a way as actually to contain its impact and produce a much more conservative role for it both within Renoir studies and French film history',[22] disregarding as it did the richness of its intertextuality and the complexity of its historical inscription. Bazin's tragically early death undoubtedly if unconsciously favoured a hagiographization of his work that may well have had excessively conservative effects, at least for a time. However, it seems legitimate to point out that both the film's intertextuality and its historical inscription have, inevitably, grown in the 50 years since Bazin's death to proportions he could scarcely have suspected and that the auteurism Bazin unapologetically embraces was a less conservative stance than it is often – some might say far too often – perceived as being now. The forced relocation of Renoir's post-1939 career posed particular problems for his status as auteur (to which Serceau's eulogy of the later work conceivably constitutes a reaction), so that Bazin's situation of *La Règle du jeu* was more radical in 1952 than it appears now.

Bazin's work was and remains distinctive through its 'championing of a cinema that respected the spectator's freedom as opposed to what he saw as the coerciveness of montage'.[23] This stance led him to favour realist filmmakers such as Rossellini or Renoir as against the more overtly manipulative work of Eisenstein or the German Expressionists. It was an ethical as much as an aesthetic position, rooted in Bazin's Catholic existentialism and social-democratic variant of leftist politics, and significantly nourished by the *ciné-club* culture, with its stress on open discussion of the films screened,

22   LA RÈGLE DU JEU

in 1992 and came only tenth in the corresponding poll in 2002. In December 1952, Renoir saw his film for the first time since 1939 at a New York film society screening, which was very well received.

The true renaissance of *La Règle du jeu*, however, had to wait until 1958. In the summer of that year, Jean Gaborit and Jacques Maréchal searched through the 224 boxes of film they had discovered in the GTC film laboratories outside Paris. Over that summer, with the help of editor Jacques Durand, they assembled a 105-minute version which was to become the standard one. There was one scene – a conversation between André and Octave – for which only the soundtrack had survived and which has, therefore, never been restored. The 'new' version came second, after Murnau's silent classic *Sunrise*, in a *Cahiers du cinéma* critics' poll in December of that year. Renoir was given a private showing in the summer of 1959 and shed tears of joy at the restoration of his masterwork; on 31 August, it was shown, at a screening dedicated at the director's request to the memory of André Bazin, who had died aged only 40 the previous year, at the Venice Film Festival. Curiously it was to receive its commercial premiere in New York in January 1961, before being issued in France in April 1965. The restored print won instant and unanimous acclaim and, with the publication of a shot-by-shot breakdown of the film in *L'Avant-Scène du cinéma* (no. 52) in October of that year, *La Règle du jeu* had finally achieved the canonical status it was never to lose, while retaining the power to shock through the intensity of its social satire and the generic fluidity and hybridity that had so scandalized many of its earliest spectators.

Two key early critical views of the film

Chapter 4 will give a broad overview of discourses on *La Règle du jeu* between the time of its banning and the present day. I should, however, like to preface and contextualize the sequence-by-sequence analysis of Chapter 3 by here dealing with probably the most famous and certainly the most notorious early criticisms of the film by, respectively, André Bazin and the overtly Fascist writers Maurice Bardèche and Robert Brasillach. These illustrate the

radical *Le Matin* (10 July), which concludes that Renoir 'treated the characters he wanted to demolish with a certain indulgence'.

La Règle du jeu was reissued, in an 86-minute version, on 26 September 1945 and was shown four times a day at two different cinemas for a fortnight – as Christopher Faulkner points out a good run for a re-release in those days.[19] The film was advertised as having been banned by the Germans (though no mention was made of its banning by Vichy) and, perhaps because of this, screenings attracted some disturbances from right-wing groups. It was also shown at the Ciné-Club de Paris on 26 November – an important date since it was through these voluntary organizations, which not only screened films for their members but also provided time and space for discussion of them afterwards, that the film was to acquire much of its status over the next 13 years. Claude Chabrol first saw it at a university ciné-club and went to see it again several times – 'an additional adventure', as he describes it, since the same version was never shown twice.[20] Truffaut, by 1950, had seen it 12 times, while Resnais's overwhelmed response has been cited in the Introduction. *La Règle du jeu*'s influence on the New Wave generation was a rapid and powerful one.

Reviews on the film's re-release were more or less evenly divided and characterized, like their pre-war counterparts, by what Faulkner describes as 'distress at the film's generic instability and tonal shifts'.[21] It began to have a presence outside France in 1947, when it was shown at the Venice Biennale. In 1949, it had its UK premiere at the London Film Club and, in 1950, a badly mutilated version was shown in New York, to public and critical incomprehension – Howard Thompson described it in the *New York Times*, 10 April 1950, as dealing with 'addle-headed lounge-lizards tangling up their amours on a weekend house party in the country' with a finale that 'would shame the Keystone Cops'. Not until 1952, when the great critic André Bazin published an article on it in *Cahiers du cinéma*, did the film begin to receive the acclamation that was its due. In the same year, the UK journal *Sight and Sound* organized the first of its international critics' polls, in which *La Règle du jeu* occupied tenth place. These polls have been repeated every ten years since then and *La Règle du jeu* has consistently occupied second or third place, though curiously it did not figure at all in the directors' poll organized

lavishly in *Regards* (20 July), drawing attention to its absence of stars and use of a troupe of actors, while, for Marcel Lapierre in *Le Peuple* (15 July), it was remarkable for its 'combination of genres that hitherto have remained separate' – observations that show a sensitivity to the film's innovative qualities. So too, in his own way, did Émile Vuillermoz (*Le Temps*, 16 July), who compared the film unfavourably to *La Grande illusion* and *La Bête humaine* and asked plaintively, 'Are we in Shakespeare's world or at the circus?' before concluding, 'Everything in this film defies common sense.' The film's melange of genres proved its most troublesome feature for critics at the time of its release, amply supporting John Snyder's claim that '[n]o film is more liable to distorted interpretation because of inadequate generic conceptions or incomplete application of traditional genre'.[17] Such 'inadequate generic conceptions' were most clearly demonstrated by explicitly right-wing critics, who unsurprisingly – with one highly significant exception to be dealt with at the end of this chapter – were generally hostile. Thus, François Vinneuil in *L'Action française* (7 July), while praising Renoir's 'wish to achieve a new register, as well as to react against the clichés of Marcel Carné's style of populism', is critical of the party scene in the château, in which the director supposedly 'loses his footing through trying to mix too many situations, intentions and genres'. James de Coquet, in *Le Figaro* (12 July), similarly apprehends the film's most distinctive quality in a negative manner when he finds himself unable to attribute a genre to it: 'A comedy of manners? Whose manners, since these characters belong to no known social species? A drama? The plot is so puerile that this is not a satisfactory hypothesis.'

The Communist critic Georges Sadoul, previewing the film in *Regards* (11 May), predicted conversely that it would at least equal if not surpass *La Grande Illusion*, while Marcel Lapierre (*Bordeaux-Ciné*, 28 July) demonstrated similar foresight in describing it as important not only for its director but for the whole history of French cinema. Lapierre's remark about the film's stormy initial reception is particularly noteworthy: 'If the "elegant" audience at the Colisée "reacted", it was to situations and dialogues which are a delectable satire of the social world.'[18] The interplay of stylishness and venom that characterizes the film is well encapsulated in Lapierre's observation and also in a curiously ambivalent review by Gilbert Bernard, in the

collaborationist Marcel Déat and banned at the Liberation), which ran a non-illustrated serialisation between 6 and 14 July. This was signed by Raymond Varinot, who was to author an illustrated adaptation for the publishers Tallandier in 1940 and had published a similar version of Renoir's Gorky adaptation *Les Bas-Fonds* in 1937. All these novelizations – available in the Bibliothèque de France – are likely to strike a contemporary reader as bizarre, interleaving, as they do, dialogue lifted verbatim from the film with often laboured and sugary narrative paraphrasing. Thus, the final sentence of Varinot's *L'Oeuvre* adaptation says of Christine, 'In the monotony of the existence she accepted with her husband, she was to keep the radiant memory of André Jurieux's love wretchedly mown down by a blind destiny, one clear October night, stretching his arm powerlessly out towards a goal he was never to reach . . '. It is, however, interesting to note that the longer Varinot version features an epilogue detailing what happened to the characters four years after the ending of the film. Christine and Robert, having learnt their respective lessons, live a tranquil life together, while Jackie and Geneviève make appropriately upwardly mobile marriages (to her research supervisor and a count respectively). Lisette, on Christine's advice, goes to live with Schumacher in Alsace and Robert asserts his fundamental benevolence by seeking out Octave and ordering that Marceau be left in peace to poach. All of this is perfectly plausible – or would have been were it not for the war and the fall of France. The storm clouds that *La Règle du jeu* all too clearly discerns on the horizon seem, for whatever reason, to have escaped its novelistic adaptors.

La Règle du jeu was finally banned by Vichy in February 1942, the same year that Allied aviation destroyed the laboratories that housed the original negative. Not until after the end of the war was the film to be re-released, in a variety of versions all lasting 80 minutes or slightly more, so that, as Curchod and Faulkner say, 'post-war audiences never saw the same *La Règle du jeu* twice'.[15]

Critical responses to the film on its release were varied, tending unsurprisingly to polarize between Left and Right. Of 37 contemporary reviews, 14 were hostile, six ambivalent, six favourable with reservations and five almost wholly favourable.[16] The Communist Georges Sadoul praised it

The reception of the film between its release and the restored version of 1959

La Règle du jeu was given a gala première on Friday 7 July 1939 in two large Champs-Élysées cinemas, the Aubert-Palace and the Colisée. The film's reception was tumultuous, marked by jeering, damage to seats and even, allegedly, a spectator using a copy of the right-wing nationalist journal *L'Action française* in an attempt to start a fire. The first public screenings took place on the following day, ironically preceded by a documentary, *L'Empire français*, glorifying the civilizing mission of the French Empire. The screenings sold out and sharply divided the audience, whose raucous response, notably to Nora Gregor's accent, led the cinema managers to demand cuts. The precise nature of these is open to question but what seems certain is that they reduced the film's running time to only about 80 minutes, thereby making it extremely difficult to follow.[14] Even so, it was to play for a total of 11 weeks at the two Paris cinemas, making it the third longest-running film of what was admittedly an atypical year. Most cinemas closed once war was declared on 3 September and, shortly afterwards, films deemed to be 'depressing, morbid, immoral or disturbing to the young' were banned. In a series of paradoxes somehow typical of its career, *La Règle du jeu* did not (contrary to many assertions) appear on this list but was, nevertheless, 'unbanned' in March 1940, only to be unequivocally banned by the German censors on 10 October. However, Vichy did not follow suit, enabling the film to be shown for a fortnight in Lyon at the end of the year. La Nouvelle Édition française, meanwhile, had gone into liquidation the previous January.

In 1939 and 1940, *La Règle du jeu* was the subject of three novelistic adaptations of a kind that was common at a time when other means of publicising films were less widespread. The magazine *Le Film complet du samedi* featured a film each week, complete with illustrations, including Carné's *Le Jour se lève*, and ran an adaptation of *La Règle du jeu*, signed by Lucien Ray, on 30 September 1939. They were, however, beaten to the punch by the then socialist daily *L'Oeuvre* (subsequently to be taken over by the

and quick-wittedness – not to say low cunning – make him a precursor of Quinquina, the small-scale black marketeer played by Carette in Carné's last cooperation with Jacques Prévert, *Les Portes de la nuit* (1946). In the woods and marshes of the province of Sologne, he might have appeared an urban fish out of water.

Audiences of the time would, in all probability, have viewed these performances as ironic commentaries on the actors' screen personas, just as they might well have perceived Schumacher's frenzy at the film's climax as a prolongation of his surreal intensity in *L'Age d'or* (another film, we may remember, which provoked the riotous indignation of the French far Right). *La Règle du jeu* is about the rules of acting – another sense of the word 'jeu' – as well as about those of the multiple games it encompasses. It is fascinating, in this perspective, to learn that Renoir asked his actors to read their text as if were a telephone directory,[12] a mode of direction that might almost prefigure Robert Bresson's instructions to his 'modèles'[13] and suggests that the naturalistic bonhomie of the film's acting style is not the whole story.

Two of the film's female 'stars' – the quotes suggest my reservations about the appropriateness of the term for this film – are still alive at the time of writing. Mila Parély (Geneviève) was to go on to appear in Bresson's first feature *Les Anges du péché* (1943) and in Cocteau's *La Belle et la bête* (1946). Her last recorded screen appearance was in 1989, whereas Paulette Dubost (Lisette) appeared in Jérôme Bonnell's *Les Yeux clairs* (2005), at the age of 94. She also had roles in Truffaut's *Le Dernier Métro* (1980) and Malle's *Lacombe Lucien* (1974), both set at two other key moments of recent French history – under the Occupation and during the events of May 1968 respectively.

The filming of the outdoor scenes of *La Règle du jeu* was initially marred by rainy weather, which gave the cast and crew the opportunity for good-humoured bonding sessions in various Sologne restaurants. Carette's wife disapproved of his drinking so he secreted a bottle of pastis in the lavatory and used stomach ache as a pretext to pay it regular visits. Modot accompanied singsongs on the accordion, and the proceedings generally seem to have taken place in an atmosphere of bonhomie that contrasts with the tensions and rivalries that permeate the film. Was the spirit of *Lange*'s courtyard and the Popular Front still alive on a smaller scale in Renoir's cinematic community?

16   LA RÈGLE DU JEU

Duvivier – *Pépé le Moko* (1937). Unsurprisingly, given this and his strong Popular Front sympathies, he worked with Renoir more than any other actor, appearing in *La Vie est à nous*, *La Grande Illusion* and *La Marseillaise* and, after the war, in *French Cancan*, *Eléna et les hommes* and *Le Testament du Docteur Cordelier* (1959).

Renoir also cast Marcel Dalio, who plays the wealthy Jewish officer Rosenthal in *La Grande Illusion*, as the Marquis de la Chesnaye. The Larousse *Dictionnaire du cinéma français* refers to Dalio's earlier roles, notably as the informer in *Pépé la Moko* and in Pierre Chenal's *La Maison du Maltais* (1938), as 'marked by the behaviour of a typical "Oriental bastard" required by xenophobic imagery'.[9] *La Règle du jeu*, even more than *La Grande Illusion*, represented a move upmarket for his persona, which is why Bessy and Beylie refer to it as 'casting against type'.[10] It is also one reason why his role aroused more controversy at the time of the film's release than any other, in keeping with the anti-Semitic tendencies particularly marked in the France of the time. Thus, a pseudonymous critic wrote in *Les Annales* (25 July 1939) that 'to interpret a landed nobleman, they [sc. Renoir] went and cast the little Jewish officer from *La Grande Illusion*!'[11] Dalio was to make a career in Hollywood during the war years, notably in Michael Curtiz's *Casablanca* (1942), which includes a sequence in which 'La Marseillaise' is sung in defiance of German troops – perhaps an intertextual homage to Dalio's first Renoir film.

The only other member of the cast to have acted for Renoir before – if we except Renoir himself, whose gruff geniality had been on display as the innkeeper in *Partie de campagne* and the poacher Cabuche in *La Bête humaine* – was Julien Carette, who played the music-hall actor in *La Grande Illusion* and the railway fireman Pecqueux in *La Bête humaine*. Carette's performance as the poacher Marceau should alert us that the seemingly naturalistic bonhomie of the film's acting style is not the whole story. Just as not only Dalio but Roland Toutain, renowned as a deft and agile romantic lead as well as for his comic roles, is, to some extent, cast against type as the idealistic but ultimately, and fatally, maladroit André Jurieux, so Carette's broad Parisian faubourg accent renders him realistically implausible as a poacher from the countryside near Orléans. Marceau's flexible principles

PREHISTORIES, FILMING AND EARLY RECEPTION **15**

of salt Renoir's assertion that he was seeking merely to make 'a merry drama – my life's ambition'.[7] Its merriment is, we shall see, that of those who do not know, or choose not to see, that they are 'dancing on a volcano'.

Filming

For all the controversy the film was to arouse on its release, the actual process of filming seems to have been a good-humoured and affable one. *La Règle du jeu* was the first production of La Nouvelle Édition française, a company set up by Renoir, his brother Claude, his assistant André Zwobada and the singer Camille François (who collaborated on the dialogues) with a view to becoming as influential in France as United Artists was in the USA. The dream was a short-lived one – *La Règle du jeu*, the company's first production, was also to be its last. Its hostile reception and the outbreak of war were primarily responsible for that but the fact that it doubled its original shooting budget of 2.5 million francs clearly played a part in its demise.

Work on the script began in October 1938, at the same time as the first approaches were made to actors. Simone Simon and Fernand Ledoux, stars of *La Bête humaine*, were originally destined for the roles of Christine and the gamekeeper. Renoir, however, was to meet, and allegedly become infatuated with, the Austrian Nora Gregor, who had appeared in Dreyer's silent film *Michael* and had fled Austria at the *Anschluss* with her militantly anti-Nazi husband. Nora Gregor was actively looking for filming work in Paris and was soon to replace Simone Simon, who demanded too much money. Simon apparently thought little of Renoir's acting ability in the earlier work and was even to declare in a 1979 interview that she did not regard *La Règle du jeu* as a good film.[8] Ledoux was to be replaced, under the name of Schumacher, by Gaston Modot, a less saturnine and more comically gifted actor who had appeared in Buñuel's *L'Age d'or* (1930). Modot's 52-year career could serve as a veritable who's who of pre-New Wave French film history, including, as it did, work with Becker – notably *Casque d'or* (1952) – Carné – *Les Enfants du paradis* (1945) – Clair – *14 juillet* (1933) – and

Daladier was also a co-signatory of the Munich Agreement in September 1938, which authorized Germany's annexation of the Sudetenland from Czechoslovakia. The French Left at the time was strongly pacifist (though Blum was not) – largely as a result of the bloodshed of the First War – while on the Right many had, for a while, seen Germany as a providential bulwark against the Soviet Union and a possible return to power of the Left. 'Better Hitler than the Popular Front' was a not uncommon sentiment and one that many of the characters in *La Règle du jeu*, such as Saint-Aubin or The General, would have been likely to share. The scene in *La Marseillaise* where the royalist émigrés, exiled in Koblenz, wistfully recall 'their' lost France derives much of its force from its implicit allusion to this political climate.

The anti-Semitism of which La Chesnaye is the periodic target in *La Règle du jeu* was also a feature of the French political landscape at the time (as many would argue it has remained). The 1934 suicide – or murder – of the swindler Stavisky, whose shady dealings reached deep into the heart of the French political establishment, provoked anti-Semitic riots and led to the downfall of Camille Chautemps's Radical government. Resnais directed a feature-film version of Stavisky's career, starring Jean-Paul Belmondo and called simply *Stavisky*, in 1974. The extreme right-wing groups that sprang up in the 1930s, such as the Parti Populaire Français led by the former Communist Jacques Doriot, often overtly embraced anti-Semitism, of which Léon Blum, dubbed 'Blum the Israelite', was an obvious target. Fascism in the strict sense of the term, of course, remained much more marginal in France than in neighbouring countries but elements of its ideology – authoritarianism, racial nationalism, vicious anti-Bolshevism – undoubtedly infected the French body politic and their traces are to be found in the milieu in which *La Règle du jeu* is set.

The aphoristic cynicism that pervades the film, like the atmosphere of gloomy foreboding that shrouds the final sequence in particular, is thus closely linked to the time of its making. *La Grande Illusion* partially redeems its mourning for an era of spontaneity and fraternity in human relationships through the solidarity, however circumstantial and temporary, between Maréchal and Rosenthal at the end. The narrative of *La Règle du jeu* offers no such redemptive possibility, inviting us to take with a substantial pinch

– exported to Peru – figures in *Le Carrosse d'or*. The aphoristic badinage characteristic of much of the dialogue draws upon Corneille (who gives his name to the Marquis de la Chesnaye's major-domo), Hugo and the late eighteenth-century cynic Chamfort, whose adage that 'in society, love is the exchange of two fantasies and the coming together of two epidermises' is archly quoted by La Chesnaye's mistress Geneviève.[5] Other writers whose imprint has been perceived in the film include Chamfort's libertine near-contemporaries Laclos and Sade, Stendhal, a romantic cynic writing in a classical style at a time of immense social upheaval, and Proust, in whose work the role of the artist *manqué*, exemplified by Octave in the film, is extremely important. Nick Browne even draws a comparison, apposite enough in a film whose central couple are Jewish and Viennese, with Freud's *Civilization and its Discontents*, a near-contemporary master text of 'a society that acts out its own destruction'.[6] Direct literary allusions or quotations will be indicated in the detailed analysis of the film that follows but these by no means exhaust *La Règle du jeu*'s extraordinary range of reference.

The historical context

Fundamental to an understanding of Renoir's film is the historical context of the time at and about which it was made. The fraternity and solidarity of the Popular Front lasted just long enough to remain for long afterwards an important part of the French Left's political imaginary; it was no coincidence that two of the first policies enacted by the incoming Socialist government in 1981 were a reduction in the working week and an increase in paid holiday entitlement, direct echoes of Léon Blum's measures 45 years before. Blum finally stepped down in April 1938, the victim of dissatisfaction on the Left with his policy of non-intervention in Spain and, more importantly, of a 'strike of capital' whose effects were accentuated by the government's refusal to devalue the franc. Édouard Daladier became Prime Minister of a government of national unity which adopted a less interventionist economic policy and brutally repressed working-class protests.

impetuous avowal on live radio at the beginning through to the staging of the sublime collective lie that closes its narrative, is closely linked with the stress on theatricality pointed out by numerous commentators on the film and, more generally, with the centrality of performance throughout. It thus comes as no surprise that Renoir claims to have had the original idea after an evening spent listening to French baroque music. Even though such music does not figure in the film for, as Renoir says, 'I based my thought on it only at the beginning',[3] his remark suggests how much *La Règle du jeu* bears the intertextual imprint of a high French culture that may well be quite unfamiliar to many readers of this guide. The film was originally announced as an adaptation of Musset's *Les Caprices de Marianne* (1833), a Romantic drama in which the well-meaning albeit debauched Octave acts as the intermediary for his friend Coelio with Marianne, who is married to Claudio. Marianne in fact loves Octave and tragedy occurs when Coelio is killed by Claudio's hired assassins. The name Octave and the drama of mistaken identity that closes Musset's plot clearly recur in Renoir's film, which also bears the mark of other canonical works of French theatre – Marivaux's *La Double Inconstance* (1723), as its title suggests a comedy hinging on amorous indecision, and even more strikingly Beaumarchais's *Le Mariage de Figaro* (1781), better known nowadays in its operatic guise as Mozart and da Ponte's *The Marriage of Figaro*. Both play and opera draw on the dramatic staples of disguise and mistaken identity to forge a narrative imbued with savage social criticism. Napoleon famously described *Le Mariage de Figaro* as 'the French Revolution in action', a statement to which may be counterposed Renoir's assertion that his characters and the world they inhabit are 'dancing on a volcano'.[4] It is noteworthy that that expression became current in French on the eve of the July Revolution of 1830. The apparent levity and omnipresent humour of both play and film make all the more powerful and corrosive the sense that the societies with which they deal are headed for disaster – one reason for the ferocious reception of *La Règle du jeu* on its release.

A full list of the other literary texts to which La Règle du jeu has been compared would occupy several pages. The fancy-dress ball may recall the Italian *commedia dell'arte* of the sixteenthth and seventeenth centuries that

2   Prehistories, filming and early reception

Pre-texts and intertexts

La Règle du jeu more than virtually any other major French film is steeped in intertextuality, a notion deployed by Julia Kristeva to denote the manner in which any text is always-already inhabited by other texts and may go on to exercise a similar influence in its turn. This will form a major thread in my scene-by-scene reading, which will attempt to make explicit not only influences undergone and reshaped by the film but also echoes of it in later works. Alain Resnais's *Mon oncle d'Amérique* (1980) and Robert Altman's 2002 *Gosford Park* are striking examples of films that unmistakably pay tribute – in the case of the Altman of more than a passing kind – to this Everest of the French cinema. In filmic terms, *La Règle du jeu*'s cinematic posterity is far more significant than its ancestry, which is not to say that it has no cinematic precursors. Its farcical elements may recall the silent comedies of Chaplin, while the periodic bouts of repartee have echoes of Ernst Lubitsch and the overlapping intrigues involving masters and servants call to mind Sacha Guitry's filmic adaptation of his own play *Désiré* (1937).

Yet, unsurprisingly, considering that it was made only ten years after the advent of sound cinema, the pre-texts for *La Règle du jeu* are primarily literary and theatrical. The film is what Jean-Luc Nancy calls 'a *performance* of truth'[1] which does 'not show truth as theatre does – but shows what showing the truth is'.[2] This second degree of revelation, from André's

7   Bazin, André (trans. W. W. Halsey II and William H. Simon), *Jean Renoir* (New York: Simon and Schuster, 1973), p. 45.

8   Renoir, *My Life and My Films*, p. 127.

9   Poulle, François, *Renoir 1938 ou Jean Renoir pour rien?: enquête sur un cinéaste* (Paris: Cerf, 1969), p. 19.

10   In *Pour vous* (1 November 1939); quoted in the collectively written *Jean Renoir: La Règle du jeu* (Paris: Ellipses, 1998), pp. 105–6.

11   *Renoir on Renoir*, p. 208.

12   Poulle, *Renoir 1938 ou Renoir pour rien?*, p. 124.

13   Serceau, Daniel, *Jean Renoir: la sagesse du plaisir* (Paris: Cerf, 1985), p. 9.

8   LA RÈGLE DU JEU

function more than the earlier works as star vehicles – for Anna Magnani, Jean Gabin and Ingrid Bergman respectively.

Considerations such as these lend support to the view, shared by most commentators, that Renoir's protracted if partial exile blunted the force of his wartime and post-war films. He was, by this stage, avowedly sceptical about the idea of progress, despite proclaiming, in a 1966 interview with Jacques Rivette, 'I think that our lives are made not of revolutions but of the desire for constant revolution'[11] – an assertion with possible echoes of Camus's *L'Homme révolté* and one frequently, if ironically, illustrated by *La Règle du jeu*. Thus, François Poulle says of the later work, '[H]e is not one of us any more: he has stopped being a citizen and a witness to become a "wise man".'[12] There are dissenting voices, most eloquently Daniel Serceau who considers Renoir's later work 'the apogee of his career as a filmic auteur'[13] but the broad critical consensus allied to the generally wider availability, in cinemas and on video and DVD, of the pre-war work systemically casts *La Règle du jeu* – as we shall see a profoundly elegiac film in a great many respects – in the role of summation of, if not epitaph for, the most important part of Renoir's career. That career came to an end in 1969 with the series of four sketches entitled *Le Petit théâtre de Jean Renoir*. He died in California, early in 1979, at the age of 84.

Notes

1   Truffaut, François, 'Jean Renoir', in Jean Renoir, *Ma vie et mes films* (Paris: Flammarion, 1974), p. 273. (This essay is not included in the published English translation from which future references to this text will be taken.)

2   Renoir, Jean (trans. Norman Denny), *My Life and My Films* (London: Collins, 1974), p. 11.

3   Renoir, Jean (trans. Carol Volk), *Renoir on Renoir* (Cambridge: Cambridge University Press, 1989), p. 6.

4   Renoir, *My Life and My Films*, p. 12.

5   Guislain, Pierre, La Règle du jeu: *Jean Renoir* (Paris: Hatier, 1990), p. 44.

6   O'Shaughnessy, Martin, *Jean Renoir* (Manchester/New York: Manchester University Press, 2000), p. 5.

JEAN RENOIR   7

First War, its relevance to the time of its making, at a period of growing tension between France and Germany, is nevertheless clear. Theatricality – the film, like *La Règle du jeu*, includes a concert party scene – is an important theme, along with the complex intersection of class, national and gender relationships. *La Grande Illusion* ends, however, on a somewhat more positive note than the later film, with the two escaped officers Maréchal (Jean Gabin) and Rosenthal (Marcel Dalio, La Chesnaye in *La Règle du jeu*) making their way across the Swiss border, invisible in the snow, to safety of however precarious a kind. Even such tentative optimism had become out of the question two years later.

This inevitably brief account of Renoir's pre-war films suggests, I hope, consistencies in preoccupations and *mise en scène* that recur in *La Règle du jeu*. That film marks an inevitable caesura in his output for it was to be the last he was to make as an entirely French-based director. His attempt to shoot an adaptation of Victorien Sardou's play *Tosca*, the inspiration for Puccini's opera, in Italy, at Mussolini's invitation, understandably angered his erstwhile political allies, among them Louis Aragon; but such symbolic hostilities were brought to an abrupt halt by the real thing when war broke out. Renoir's involvement with the Popular Front meant that it would have been extremely unsafe for him to remain in France so, acting on an invitation from the documentary film-maker Robert Flaherty, he left for the United States, of which he subsequently became a citizen.

Renoir was to retain his Montmartre home throughout his life but, from 1940 to his death, his primary residence was to be in Beverly Hills, in a Provençal-style 'farmhouse' as though to bear witness to his nostalgic cleaving to traditional France at a distance. He made six films in the US during and just after the war, of which the best-known is probably *The Southerner* of 1945, before returning to work in France in the early 1950s. Among his work of the post-war period, most evocative of *La Règle du jeu* through their emphasis on theatricality are three costume dramas – *Le Carrosse d'or* (1952), *French Cancan* (1954) and *Eléna et les hommes* (1956) – whose rich Technicolor and absence of evident social or political engagement differentiate them sharply from, for instance, *La Marseillaise*. These films, perhaps because of Renoir's experience of the Hollywood system, also

6   LA RÈGLE DU JEU

within and political events without and France was all but surrounded by dictatorial right-wing regimes.

The ominous climate of the late 1930s, all-pervasive in *La Règle du jeu*, will be explored in more detail in the next section. The period leading up to and dominated by the Popular Front came to be seen as something of a golden age in retrospect – a time when, as Renoir said, 'the French really believed that they could love one another'.[8] The nature of Renoir's political commitment was clearly ethical and affective rather than ideological; as François Poulle puts it, not without irony, 'through the people he met and the drinks he had in cafés, he followed the way the country was going'.[9] The consequences of that were not always positive ones, as can be seen from a 1939 interview in which he offered the view that film producers whose names ended in 'ich' or 'zy' should be employed as if they were foreigners.[10] The goal of this study is not, however, to construct Renoir as an impeccably liberal figure but rather to understand how many of the most distinctive features of *La Règle du jeu*, such as the teamwork characteristic of the filming and the precarious solidarity between often socially as well as personally disparate figures, are to be found in his work of the Popular Front years.

La Règle du jeu also bears traces of the elegiac lyricism that is a hallmark of *Partie de campagne* (1936, though never completed and released only in 1946), a Maupassant adaptation in which an outing to the country triggers, for the two main female characters – a mother and a daughter – romantic interludes which will afterwards be the object of bitter-sweet recollection. It is generally (though not always), as we shall see, the women in *La Règle du jeu* who hark back to an emotionally happier past, and the nostalgia which suffuses both films is inseparable from the time of their making – not long after the collapse of Popular Front solidarity and just before the slide towards war and catastrophe. The personal and the historical, the individual and the social are as so often in Renoir indissolubly linked and this imbues his work, of the pre-war years at least, with political significance even where we might least expect to find it.

La Grande Illusion (1937), which immediately preceded *La Marseillaise*, is, along with *La Règle du jeu*, Renoir's best-known work and has much in common with the later film. Set in a prison camp for officers during the

gentle to the acerbic' and the interplay of the realistic and the theatrical.[6] Thus, *La Chienne*'s largely location-shot evocation of a bilious petit-bourgeois household and a milieu of pimping and fraud are prefaced by a short sequence featuring puppets from the popular Lyonnais Guignol puppet theatre, as though to undercut the realistic status of what we are about to see.

The mid and late 1930s were a period of intense political turbulence in France as in the rest of Europe, by which Renoir's work was deeply affected. *Le Crime de Monsieur Lange* (1935), scripted by Jacques Prévert, was made, appropriately for a film about a workers' cooperative, with the left-wing theatre troupe known as the Groupe Octobre and is perhaps the clearest example, before *La Règle du jeu*, of Renoir's determinedly non-star-struck, anti-hierarchical use of actors. The political radicalism of the film, which depicts the murder of a brutally exploitative capitalist (Batala, played by Jules Berry) as justified, is inseparable from its formal properties, notably the 270-degree pan around the courtyard before Lange shoots Batala. André Bazin accurately observes that this 'synthesizes the whole spatial structure of the film' while, at the same time, it vividly evokes the solidarity that has developed among those who live and work around the courtyard.[7] *Mise en scène* and narrative reinforce each other here as strikingly, if not in so complex a fashion, as they are to do in *La Règle du jeu*.

Le Crime de Monsieur Lange was the first film of what might be called Renoir's committed period, which saw him working closely with the Popular Front alliance of left-wing parties (including the Communists) that was briefly to gain power in 1936. It was for the Popular Front that Renoir made what might be described as one of the first party political broadcasts, *La Vie est à nous* of 1936, financed and distributed through trade-union and party-political channels. He was also one of the moving spirits behind the leftist Ciné-Liberté group, which sought new production and distribution strategies for films outside commercial norms. Ciné-Liberté's showpiece film, *La Marseillaise* (1937), a reconstruction of the French Revolution whose heroes are ordinary men and women rather than such iconic figures as Danton or Robespierre, came, in a sense, too late for, by the time it was released, the Popular Front government had fallen victim to dissensions

to make my films as marketable as possible'[3] and who declared, in the introduction to *Ma vie et mes films*, 'It is arrogance which leads us to believe in the supremacy of the individual.'[4] Pierre Guislain's assertion that '[m]ise en scène in Renoir's cinema, more than in any other, begins with the actor'[5] may appear belied by the comparatively minor importance assumed by star actors in his work. Only *Boudu sauvé des eaux* (1932) can be properly described as a star vehicle, for Michel Simon in the title role, while his use of the other French male megastar of the 1930s, Jean Gabin, is revelatory. Gabin appears in *Les Bas-Fonds* (1936), *La Grande Illusion* (1937), *La Bête humaine* (1938) and *French Cancan* (1954) but, in all these films, he forms part of a group, such as the railwaymen in *La Bête humaine* and the prisoners-of-war in *La Grande Illusion*, rather than being counterposed to a society against which he finds himself in doomed and solitary revolt as in his work for Julien Duvivier – *Pépé le moko* (1935) – or Marcel Carné – *Le Quai des brumes* (1938) and *Le Jour se lève* (1939). The cooperative nature of Renoir's film-making is a major part of its specificity but we should bear in mind that, at the same time, it works to subvert the hallowed authorial status it is impossible to deny him.

Jean Renoir was born in Montmartre in 1894, the son of the Impressionist painter Pierre-Auguste Renoir and Aline Charigot. Wounded first in the cavalry and then in the air force in the First War, he shortly thereafter married one of his father's models, the actress Catherine Hessling, with whom he was to father his only child (Alain) and from whom he separated in 1930. It was in large measure to further Catherine's ambitions that Renoir, helped by the artistic contacts he had made through his father and the money inherited from him, became a film-maker. His silent work ranged over a variety of genres, from literary adaptations, such as *Nana* (1926), based on the Zola novel, through to the quasi-surrealist fantasy of *Sur un air de Charleston* (also 1926). His earliest sound films included *La Chienne* (1931) and *Boudu*, both with Michel Simon, as well as the Marcel Pagnol-produced *Toni* of 1934, whose location filming in Provence and proletarian setting prefigure the Italian neo-realists. These early films bear many of the hallmarks later to characterize *La Règle du jeu*, notably the anatomization of the bourgeoisie in 'a satirical tone that ranges from the

1   Jean Renoir

Jean Renoir (1894–1979) is all but universally regarded as one of the very greatest of French film-makers. François Truffaut, particularly with his 'Antoine Doinel' cycle, running from *Les Quatre Cents Coups* (1959) to *Domicile conjugal* (1970), has almost certainly reached a larger audience; Jean-Luc Godard, in a career spanning nearly 50 years, has probably been more written about and undoubtedly provoked more critical and intellectual controversy; but Renoir stands unchallenged as the dominant French director of the pre-Second War period and as the one whose open and fluid style of shooting has had the greatest influence on later generations of film-makers. According to Truffaut, '*La Règle du jeu* is certainly, along with *Citizen Kane*, the film which has inspired the greatest number of directors' vocations'.[1]

Yet such a hagiographic approach to his work inspires a certain unease, not least because, in important respects, it runs counter to the assumptions that underpin it. Renoir was indisputably a great auteur in the sense in which *Cahiers du cinéma* were to popularize the term – a writer-in-film whose work across different genres (and indeed continents) was to reveal a striking consistency beneath its unevenness and heterogeneity. But Renoir's enthusiastic participation in what he termed 'the war of the film-maker against the industry'[2] should not be taken as endorsing a romantic individualism largely foreign to his oeuvre. It was that same Renoir, after all, who proclaimed that – apropos *La Règle du jeu* at that – 'I try my hardest

2   LA RÈGLE DU JEU

to the efforts of the two French cinephiles Jean Gaborit and Jacques Durand. Since then, the film has consistently been voted the second greatest of all time in the ten-yearly *Sight and Sound* critics' poll, bested only by Orson Welles's *Citizen Kane* (1941), and has generated an almost intimidating volume of critical response and discourse, close attention to which is almost as fascinating as the film itself.

My focus here will thus be on *La Règle du jeu* in context – the context of the time at which it was made but also that of the currents of intertextuality by which it is unendingly traversed. Renoir here looks back to canonical works of French literature – Marivaux's *La Double Inconstance*, Beaumarchais's *Le Mariage de Figaro*, Musset's *Les Caprices de Marianne* and arguably too the novels of Laclos and Proust – as well as forward to the New Wave and more recent films such as Rohmer's *Le Signe du lion* (1959, released 1962) and Altman's *Gosford Park* (2001). To trace such echoes and influences is a necessary part of any attempt at understanding why *La Règle du jeu* remains so central not only to French cinema but to the whole history of French and indeed European culture.

Notes

1   Roud, Richard, *Cinema: a Critical Dictionary* (London: Martin Secker and Warburg, 1980), vol. 2, p. 841.
2   Renoir, Jean (trans. John McGrath and Maureen Teitelbaum), 'Alain Resnais and Jean Renoir' (interview between Resnais and Richard Roud), *The Rules of the Game* (London: Lorrimer, 1970), p. 14.

Introduction

Today's British or American students, confronted with *La Règle du jeu*, are likely to respond with amusement and bewilderment. Amusement at the film's farcical elements – such as the frantic chase sequences through the corridors of the château – and at some of its more verbal comic moments – Marceau's sardonic repartee in particular; bewilderment at its evocation of a world whose effete opulence and supposedly rigorous codes of behaviour seem almost impossibly archaic. What may well escape such an audience is the film's extraordinary subversive charge on the one hand and its dynamic effect on subsequent generations of film-makers on the other. It may seem barely credible that such a period piece should have provoked jeering and violence – including an attempt to set fire to the cinema – at its first screening or that a film with little readily apparent reference to the politically fraught period of its making should have elicited from Richard Roud the extravagant-sounding but entirely justified claim that 'if France were destroyed tomorrow and nothing remained but this film, the whole country and its civilisation could be reconstructed from it'.[1] Scarcely less surprising may be Alain Resnais's claim that his first viewing of *La Règle du jeu* was 'the most overwhelming experience I have had in the cinema in my whole life' and that, on emerging from the cinema he walked the streets of Paris for two hours, feeling that 'everything had been turned upside down, all my ideas about the cinema had been challenged'.[2]

Resnais's enthusiasm is all the more remarkable when we reflect that the print of the film he saw, in 1944, was a severely mutilated one – little more than two-thirds of the 110-minute version we have now. *La Règle du jeu*'s quasi-mythical status has much to do with its having long been a *film maudit*, banned by French censors shortly after its release as well as by the Vichy and Occupation regimes, whose original negative was destroyed by an Allied bombing raid and which was only to be restored in 1959, thanks

Synopis

Aviator André Jurieux arrives at Paris's Le Bourget Airport after a record-breaking Atlantic crossing, only to find that the woman he loves – Austrian-born marchioness Christine de la Chesnaye – is not there to meet him. He denounces her over the radio and all but kills himself and his close friend, bohemian and failed musician Octave, in a car accident.

Octave gets Christine's husband, the Jewish aristocrat Robert de la Chesnaye, to invite Jurieux to a hunting party at his country estate near Orléans. During the preparations for this, Robert engages the poacher Marceau as a domestic, despite the hostility of his Alsatian gamekeeper, Schumacher. It is while the hunt is going on that Christine finds out about her husband's long-standing affair with Geneviève de Maras, ironically while he is in the midst of breaking it off despite her protests. During the fancy-dress party that follows the hunt, Christine shows herself responsive to the advances of Jurieux and of the lecherous Saint-Aubin, who brawl while Marceau is being pursued by Schumacher with a gun because of his attentions to the latter's wife, Lisette.

Octave, long since devoted to Christine, persuades her to run away with him but, at the last minute, defers to Jurieux, seemingly her true love. The furious and recently sacked Schumacher, deceived by Christine's having borrowed Lisette's cloak, pursues her and guns down Jurieux, who dies instantly. Marceau and Octave gloomily leave the château, while the others all resume their places in a reimposed status quo.

For detailed credits, please see Appendix 1 at the back of this book.

Acknowledgements

My thanks go in the first instance to Ginette Vincendeau, who asked me to write this book and was a most patient and encouraging editor. Christopher Faulkner sent me valuable material and answered a number of online queries promptly and comprehensively. The School of Modern European Languages and Cultures at the University of Glasgow funded research trips to Paris and provided considerable moral support. The staff of the British Film Institute Library in London and of the Bibliothèque du film and the Bibliothèque de France in Paris were extremely helpful in assisting me to locate secondary sources and documents. Lucille Cairns, Eleonore Kofman, Martin O'Shaughnessy and Noel Peacock were sources of different types of advice and encouragement at different times. Finally, the students at three universities with whom I have discussed and worked on *La Règle du jeu* over a period of 30 years have contributed substantially to what I hope is still a developing understanding of this extraordinary film.

4	The film's reception since its re-release	87
	Types of critical response and discourse	87
	Politically inspired approaches	88
	Gendered readings	93
	Historical and industrial approaches	95
	Auteurist approaches	97
5	*La Règle du jeu* as filmic pre-text	105
	Alain Resnais's *Mon oncle d'amérique*	107
	Robert Altman's *Gosford Park*	109
	Conclusion	115
	Appendix 1: Credits	117
	Appendix 2: Filmography	119
	Appendix 3: Bibliography	121

Contents

	Acknowledgements	vii
	Synopsis	ix
	Introduction	1
1	Jean Renoir	3
2	Prehistories, filming and early reception	11
	Pre-texts and intertexts	11
	The historical context	13
	Filming	15
	The reception of the film between its release and the restored version of 1959	18
	Two key early critical views of the film	22
3	Sequence-by-sequence analysis and commentary	29
	Credits	29
	The drama takes shape	31
	From Paris to the countryside	41
	The hunt sequence	51
	Back in the château	56
	From fancy dress to tragedy in less than an hour	60
	Mirrorings and doublings – structure and history	81

Published in 2010 by I.B.Tauris & Co. Ltd

6 Salem Road, London W2 4BU

175 Fifth Avenue, New York NY 10010

ibtauris.com

Copyright © Keith Reader, 2010

The right of Keith Reader to be identified as the author of this work has
been asserted by him in accordance with the Copyright, Designs and Patents
Act 1988.

All rights reserved. Except for brief quotations in a review, this book, or any
part thereof, may not be reproduced, stored in or introduced into a retrieval
system, or transmitted, in any form or by any means, electronic, mechanical,
photocopying, recording or otherwise, without the prior written permission of
the publisher.

ISBN: 978 1 84885 054 5
eISBN: 978 0 75569 997 1
ePDF: 978 0 85771 626 2

A full CIP record for this book is available from the British Library

A full CIP record is available from the Library of Congress

Library of Congress Catalog Card Number: available

Typeset in Minion by Ellipsis Books Limited, Glasgow

LA RÈGLE DU JEU
(Jean Renoir, 1939)

Keith Reader

I.B. TAURIS
LONDON · NEW YORK

CINÉ-FILES: The French Film Guides
Series Editor: Ginette Vincendeau

From the pioneering days of the Lumière brothers' Cinématographe in 1895, France has been home to perhaps the most consistently vibrant film culture in the world, producing world-class directors and stars, and a stream of remarkable movies, from popular genre films to cult avant-garde works. Many of these have found a devoted audience outside France, and the arrival of DVD is now enabling a whole new generation to have access to contemporary titles as well as the great classics of the past.

The **Ciné-Files French Film Guides** build on this welcome new access, offering authoritative and entertaining guides to some of the most significant titles, from the silent era to the early twenty-first century. Written by experts in French cinema, the books combine extensive research with the author's distinctive, sometimes provocative perspective on each film. The series will thus build up an essential collection on great French classics, enabling students, teachers and lovers of French cinema both to learn more about their favourite films and make new discoveries in one of the world's richest bodies of cinematic work.

Ginette Vincendeau

Published Ciné-Files:
Alphaville (Jean-Luc Godard, 1965) – Chris Darke
Amelie (Jean-Pierre Jeunet, 2001) – Isabelle Vanderschelden
Casque d'or (Jacques Becker, 1952) – Sarah Leahy
Cléo de 5 à 7 (Agnès Varda, 1962) – Valerie Orpen
La Grande Illusion (Jean Renoir, 1937) – Martin O'Shaughnessy
La Haine (Mathieu Kassovitz, 1995) – Ginette Vincendeau
La Règle du jeu (Jean Renoir, 1939) – Keith Reader
La Reine Margot (Patrice Chereau, 1994) – Julianne Pidduck
Le Corbeau (Henri-Georges Clouzot, 1943) – Judith Mayne
Les Diaboliques (Henri-Georges Clouzot, 1955) – Susan Hayward
Nikita (Luc Besson, 1990) – Susan Hayward
Rififi (Jules Dassin, 1955) – Alastair Phillips
Un chien andalou (Luis Buñuel, 1929) – Elza Adamowicz

LA RÈGLE DU JEU